Going Up?

Generation Y's Elevator to Financial Success

Anna Stanley

Box of Ideas Publishing

Internet addresses and telephone numbers were accurate at press time.

Cover designed by Cheryl Solheid Staples (ssquaredproduction-design@yahoo.com)
Cover/interior art by Caroline D'Arcy (cmdandrews@cox.net; www.geocities.com/caro_darcy)
Editor Joan McColly
Editor/Proofreader Laurie Gibson (wordworker1@earthlink.net)

Library of Congress Cataloging-in-Publication Data has been applied for:

Stanley, Anna
 Going Up? Generation Y's Elevator to Financial Success

ISBN-10: 0-9621972-2-X paperback
ISBN-13: 978-0-9621972-2-2 paperback   2006906831

Includes index and bibliographical references.
First Edition

1. Teenagers—Finance, Personal. 2. Young Adults—Finance, Personal. 3. Finance, Personal. 4. Parenting. I. Stanley, Anna. II. Title.

Manufactured in the United States of America.
Printed on acid-free paper.

10 9 8 7 6 5 4 3 2 1

Gift Shop

The seed of this book was planted in 1997 when my then 7-year-old son wanted to purchase real estate as an investment. Two months shy of his 14th birthday, Turner achieved his goal of buying a house. *Going Up? Generation Y's Elevator to Financial Success* is a gift to Generation Y-ers, a gift that germinated from Turner's financial goal.

My editor, Joan McColly, was a huge gift to this project. I hope to wrap her up for my next one!

My proofreader, Laurie Gibson, has already gifted millions of readers with her talents having proofread *The Color Purple* and *Mrs. Dalloway*.

My cover designer, Cheryl Solheid Staples, was already a gift to me when, several years ago, she designed the covers of my books *The Crowning Touch* and *Producing Beauty Pageants*. She has also gifted readers around the world, for years, with her cover designs at Harcourt Brace Jovanovich.

My cover and interior artist, Caroline D'Arcy, has already been a gift to children around the world, as a team artist for the cartoon series, *Teenage Mutant Ninja Turtles*™.

Megan Stanley was a gift to my entire family, convincing me to be a stay-at-home mom, allowing me to help my children become successful students and entrepreneurs.

My husband, Henry, and daughter, Mia, have proven that patience is not only a virtue, but also a gift.

And, my phat cat Gracie, who walked across my keyboard numerous times as I typed this book; consider any typos a gift from Gracie.

1 st Floor

2 nd Floor

3 rd Floor

4th Floor

Start Your Own Business _____ *53*

Where Do Bright Ideas Come From? ↔ What is the Recommended Age to Start a Business? ↔ Being Taken Seriously ↔ Avoiding Scams ↔ Liking What You Do ↔ Businesses You Can Start with Little Cash

5th Floor

Create Your Niche Business _____ *109*

Advantages of Owning a Niche Business ↔ Stop Thinking You're Untalented ↔ Recognizing Your Eureka Moment ↔ Design a Dream Book ↔ How Creative Minds Found Their Niche ↔ Marketing Your Niche Business

6th Floor

Your Business Name _____ *123*

Take Time to Think of a Business Name ↔ Copyright ↔ Check Trademarks ↔ Check Domain Names ↔ Check With City Hall ↔ A Business Name Legal Nightmare ↔ A Town Name Up in Arms

7th Floor

Advertise _____ *133*

Promoting Your Business for Pennies ↔ Creating a Well-Written Press Release ↔ Television Talk Shows ↔ Cable and Network Television ↔ Television Guides ↔ Radio Talk Shows ↔ Display and Classified Advertising ↔ Internet Classifieds ↔ Yellow Pages ↔ Posters and Flyers ↔ Business Cards ↔ Grocery Store Receipts ↔ Specialty Advertising ↔ Company Newsletter ↔ Student Directories ↔ School Yearbooks ↔ High School and College Newspapers ↔ School Events Programs ↔ Testimonials ↔ Buzz Marketing ↔ Family and Friends ↔ Your Business Website

8th Floor

Set Up Shop _____ *146*

Create a Checklist ↔ Business Location ↔ Workspace ↔ Post Office Box ↔ Equipment and Supplies ↔ Return on Investment ↔ Telephone Lines ↔ VoIP ↔ Broadband Internet ↔ Caller ID ↔ Cell Phone ↔ Personal Computer ↔ Computer Printer ↔ Fax Machine ↔ Copy Machine ↔ Digital Camera ↔ Message Machine ↔ Voice Mail ↔ Answering Service ↔ Filing System ↔ Create a Logo ↔ Create a Slogan ↔ Printed Items to Get You Started ↔ Create a Website

13th Floor

Penthouse

Mezzanine

Roughly how much money flows through hands of a Generation Y-er—kids, teenagers, and young adults born after 1979? What if a Generation Y kid saves most of the money he earns, prior to his 18th birthday? How much money would he have saved? My son, Turner, a Generation Y-er born in 1990, wanted answers to these questions, so, at the age of 7, he began his financial experiment. How much money would he have at 18 if he saved and invested the majority of what he earned? Could he save enough for a down payment on a rental home by his 18th birthday? At that moment, Turner mapped out a 12-year financial plan.

The motivation to save money was in front of him nearly every day when Turner read headlines (in the *San Diego Union-Tribune*) about the hot national housing market and in magazines such as *Money* and *Kiplinger's*. He wanted to buy a rental property that would rent for more than the monthly mortgage, taxes, and insurance costs combined. Turner had the ambition and drive to see his financial experiment through. Not only did he achieve his goal, Turner also learned about various types of investing, including Roth IRAs, Certificates of Deposit, stocks, even mutual funds—all of which he included in his financial plan. Not the typical Generation Y teen, Turner began 9th grade with a net worth of *over* $50,000.

A 2005 study conducted by Alloy Media + Marketing and Harris Interactive research firms reports Generation Y spenders—nearly 70 million consumers, according to the U.S. Census Bureau—are responsible for more than $175 billion in consumer spending per year. According to a recent survey of 2,000 young people ages 12–19, performed by Teenage Research Unlimited, on average during 2005 teens spent $91 a week—including money from allowance, work, and money given to them by their parents. In a research poll conducted by MarketResearch.com, typical 8- to 14-year-olds spend—from allowances, jobs, and gifts—about $1,294 a year (approximately $25 a week). Fifteen to 18-year-olds spend nearly twice that amount. These polls show that today's Generation Y-ers are living for the moment. Saving for a house is not their goal; instant gratification is. So, exactly when did marketers begin to figure out that teens, particularly girls, were America's choicest target market? When the 1997 movie *Titanic* became the top grosser of all time, realizing that teenage girls bought all those movie tickets! As a result, retailers started pitching teens everything from eyewear to computers.

In February of 2004, at the age of 13, Turner purchased his first rental property in Flour Bluff, Texas: a three-bedroom, two-bath, two-car garage home in an excellent school district. A year later Turner became an angel investor and loaned his 12-year-old sister, Mia, $7,000 toward the down payment and closing costs on a rental property near his. I'm not telling you this to boast about my children but to coach you on how any Generation Y-er can make such an investment. Now that Turner is in the penthouse of investment knowledge, he'll be sending down your elevator to financial success so that you, too, can meet him at the top. Going up?

☼

Why is money called dough?
Because we all knead it.

1st Floor

Become Financially Successful

"To do a common thing, uncommonly well, brings success."
~Henry John Heinz

This book is not about getting rich quick. It's a vehicle to help Generation Y—kids, teens, and young adults roughly aged 12 to 28, begin and develop their own money management programs so that they can have a strong financial future. It is critical to the future wealth of Generation Y that, as soon as they are able to earn their own money, they learn to manage their money and to develop the savings habit. With cash in the bank, when an opportunity arises, they'll be ready to pounce, whether it is a winning stock in the stock market, a hot real estate property, or a new business venture. And, with time on their side, young people have a big advantage since they can begin to invest earlier.

To Become an Employee or Employer?

Deciding to run your own business, known as "making a job," or to work for someone else, known as "taking a job," is up to you. A teen who works at a pet grooming salon (employee) doesn't have to worry about all the details of running his own business. A teen who owns his own pet grooming business (employer) tends to all the details of running his business but also reaps the financial rewards. According to the Federal Reserve Survey of Consumer Finances, people who run their own business (and survive) tend to build wealth faster than employees do.[1] Most teens who use their skills to create products and services needed in their community earn at least 25% more than teens who accept typical entry-level jobs in today's marketplace. Whether teens "make a job" or "take a job," the most important things they take away from a job are references — which help them build a strong résumé (more about résumés can be found near the end of this floor).

Dreaming of Starting a Business

According to *Entrepreneur* magazine, 70% of the teenagers polled want to own a business during their lifetime.[2] That's even a higher percentage than discovered in a survey conducted by Capital One and Consumer Action, which, revealed that 40% of [adult] Americans dream of starting a business but 55% don't know where to begin.[3] Capital One and Consumer Action have partnered to develop a free guide called "Micro Business Basics: Building A Sound Financial Foundation." The free booklet summarizes all aspects of starting a small business and offers a guide to various resources available to small business owners, and can be found on http://www.consumer-action.org/english/articles/micro_business_basics_english/. This guide is worth the time to read before starting your micro business — a small company run by the owners with few or no employees.

What it Takes to Become an Entrepreneur

Do you want to work for yourself? Can you work the long hours it takes to make your business successful? Are you organized? Can you learn to be organized? Do you want to be financially independent? Do you have a great idea? Do you think you have what it takes to become an entrepreneur?

While some people have the drive to be successful entrepreneurs, others don't have the drive necessary to succeed on their own—and should focus on being successful in their careers. There's no shame is working for someone else and focusing on maximizing your income at your job. Do recognize, however, that people who have the drive, the passion, and the fortitude to succeed—no matter what—are natural entrepreneurs. These people have a strong, overwhelming desire to be successful—to create true financial freedom.

Know When You're a Natural Entrepreneur

When you watch QVC, a national TV retailer, do you look at the show and say, "My goal is to get a product into the hands of millions of people on that show!" If so, you are a natural entrepreneur—even if your product is never sold on QVC.

Jasmine Lawrence, 14, from Mount Laurel, New Jersey, could have been a model in teen magazines. Many teen girls are employees for product lines. But not Jasmine. Jasmine, a 14-year-old CEO, created an all-natural hair care product and has established distribution channels and negotiated prices with suppliers for her successful company, EDEN Body Works—before she has even attended her prom! In 2004, at the age of 12, Jasmine founded EDEN Body Works after being selected to attend a business camp sponsored by the National Foundation for Teaching Entrepreneurship. Now EDEN Body Works natural hair oil products are sold to retailers, beauty/braiding salons, and barbershops for their use and resale to their customers. In 2005 Jasmine's company had gross revenues of $15,150. Jasmine's future plans include the addition of e-commerce capabilities via www.EDENBodyWorks.net.[4]

Making a Job

If you are more than excited about starting your own business, take the steps necessary to make your business a reality. Excitement alone won't see you through a successful business if you don't have a business plan.

Don't worry if you don't have a clue what kind of business you want to operate. Make a stop on every floor of this elevator ride, and, by the time you reach the Penthouse, you may be surprised to discover a niche that could be turned into a successful money-making operation.

Advantages of working for yourself:

- You are your own boss.
- There is no upper limit to what you can earn.
- You can set your own prices and give yourself raises.
- You can make better use of your skills and knowledge.
- You have more opportunity to use your skills and talent.
- You will have more flexible work hours.
- You'll have more freedom to choose your work.
- You'll have opportunity to introduce a new product or service.
- You can generate higher income by staying active in promoting yourself and your business.
- You'll get all the benefits of your hard work.
- You can begin working at a younger age than the Federal child-labor laws allow.

Disadvantages of working for yourself:

- Nobody is taking care of you.
- You are not paid for sick or vacation days.
- You are the bill collector for both fast- and slow-paying customers.
- There may be gaps between money earned.
- You have to network and market yourself.
- You may have less interaction with people than when you're an employee at a pizza parlor.
- Your income can be uncertain.
- You might need to work longer and harder to realize a raise.
- You might have to work long hours to earn a profit.
- You need to stay active to generate income.

Taking a Job

If you feel that being an entrepreneur isn't the path for you, you can apply for a retail job in a business such as a mall shop, ice cream parlor, hardware store, grocery store, gift shop, fast food restaurant, the list goes on. Service employment that may interest you could include working as a life guard, library page, or a newspaper deliverer.

You can get employment ideas by looking in the Employment section of your daily newspaper or by visiting your local yellow pages. Google "Employment for Teens (name of your city and state)" to see any websites that list employment for teens in your area. Try visiting www.Careers4Teens.com. This website was created by Ephren Taylor, 17, when he noticed that the teen employment rate in his area was near zero. Ephren's site offers services tailored to teens. As of this writing, the Careers4Teens.com domain was for sale and may be operating under a different name by now. Teens4hire.org allows young job seekers to surf listings from more than 1,000 businesses. If you're interested in a cool job like a secret shopper, visit www.Groovejob.com, a site that uses ZIP codes to find jobs by area.

Page through the U.S. Department of Labor's *Dictionary of Occupational Titles* (www.occupationalinfo.org) to see which jobs attract you. For detailed information on teens and jobs, visit www.youth2work.gov, the U.S. Department of Labor's website for young workers. For Generation Y-ers with at least a bachelor's degree, you can find a list of positions that the Bureau of Labor Statistics put together by visiting www.salary.com, a leading provider of employee compensation data and software.

If you are undecided what your dream job is, visit www.fabjob.com, where lots of interesting jobs are posted, such as Professional Organizer, Videogame Designer, Etiquette Consultant—even how to become a Doula! If you're still not sure what you want to do, considering finding temporary work with a temp agency. It's a great way to get a feel for different types of jobs available and to see if your skills match.

If you do choose to become employed, boost your take-home pay by minimizing withholding, that is, the amount that Uncle Sam takes out of your paycheck. Most teens claim zero allowances when they fill out their W-4 form, but, as a single person with a job, you are entitled to claim one—even if a parent lists you as a dependent on their tax return. As of this writing, a teen who earns $5,150 or less is exempt from owing any income tax (exception: if he has investments or self-employment income).[5]

Advantages of working for an employer:

- You work for someone else.
- You generally have a set work schedule.
- You don't have to network and market yourself to seek work.
- You will probably work at the same location all the time, so it might be simpler for you.
- You may have more opportunity to socialize with people.
- You have a set pay for a set work period.
- You may get extra work hours if you ask for them.

Disadvantages of working for an employer:

- You work for someone else.
- There is a limit to what you can earn.
- You're limited in the hours that you work.
- Your personal potential is limited.
- You won't have the freedom to hire someone for a job when you're not available to work your shift.
- You might have difficulty asking for a raise.
- You might not get a raise if you ask.
- You have to schedule time off in advance, and you might not get the time off. (Regarding your own business, you may have the same problem in either scenario.)

Your Résumé

If you search for a job, you will need to compose a résumé. A résumé is not just a past history, it's an advertisement to sell your most important asset—you! "A résumé is a calling card," says Cassandra Jennings-Outlaw, a veteran M.B.A. recruiter who works at a telecommunications company in New Jersey. "If a résumé has an error, this indicates the applicant's lack of attention to detail." Likewise, "If the duties are not written in complete thoughts, that tells me the applicant will probably work in that manner as well," says Cassandra.[6]

Make sure that the top half of your résumé is great, because if it's not, the rest probably won't be read. Your résumé should make the person reading it *want* to interview — and hire — you. A well-composed résumé will say that this is your dream job and no one will work harder or be more dedicated than you. Don't pad your résumé with meaningless phrases such as "results-oriented." ResumeDoctor.com suggests that, instead, you give specifics. The online consultant looked at 160,000 résumés and found that more than half used vague statements, such as Communication Skills, Team Player, Organizational Skills, Interpersonal Skills, Driven, Detail-Oriented, and Highly Motivated. Visit the www.resumedoctor.com or www.rockportinstitute.com for more helpful tips on writing a successful résumé.

Send a Cover Letter with Your Résumé

Find out who is in charge of interviews and include that person's name on your cover letter. Do not be lazy and say, "Dear Hiring Manager," or worse, "Dear Sir." Know who you'll be sending your cover letter and résumé to. If you must, hire a proof-reader to ensure that your cover letter (and résumé) are error-free. Well-written cover letters and résumés float to the top of the stack.

Your Education

Understand that school will help you later in life, with or without your business or employment. People want to do business with people who, at the very least, graduated from high school. What if you do drop out of high school to run your successful business; then, later on, it goes belly-up? Now you want to work for someone else because you don't want to negotiate the day-to-day issues of operating a business. It will be difficult to find good employment without, at the very least, a high school diploma. If you keep learning, you will be better tomorrow than you are today.

Make Education Your Top Priority

Your education should be your top priority. If your grades drop, you should not be working, at least until your grades improve. Be smart and use your business to help you with your education, and vice-versa. Operating his business at an early age helped my son, Turner, create an excellent time management schedule for himself. If parents think that their children are too busy with school and other activities to operate a business, parents should just let them give it a shot. If grades don't improve or, worse, drop, running a business at this time is not for this Generation Y-er.

Leslie Shoup, 17, is the owner of Leslie's Xpresly Sportswear in Orrville, Ohio, formerly known as Xpresly Sportswear. She is also a student by day, with her sights set on majoring in banking and accounting. At night she transforms into a talented entrepreneur. Leslie's company does custom imprinting and embroidery of logos and artwork on jackets, hats, shirts, and jerseys. Leslie realizes the importance of a strong education and knows that it can benefit her future business growth.[7] The Census Bureau has estimated that college graduates earn about $1 million more over their lifetimes than individuals with only a high school diploma.[8]

If You Don't Like School

In his book *Rich Kid, Smart Kid*, author Robert T. Kiyosaki reminds us that there are seven different types of geniuses:

1. Verbal-linguistic (the genius that our educational system currently uses to measure a person's IQ)
2. Numerical (the genius that deals with data measured in numbers)
3. Spatial (the genius that many creative people — artists and designers — have)

4. Physical (the genius that many great athletes and dancers have)
5. Intrapersonal (the genius often called "emotional intelligence")
6. Interpersonal (the genius found in people who can talk easily with others)
7. Environmental (the genius that emanates from humans to the things around them)

Unfortunately, our education system only recognizes one—verbal-linguistic. If you are thinking of dropping out of school, as Mr. Kiyosaki once had, realize that "getting through" high school and/or college should be part of your lifetime learning experience—whether or not you are a verbal-linguistic genius. Then you can work on bringing out the true genius in you!

On the next floor, Operate a Business, you will learn how to create a successful business plan, where to obtain licenses and permits, where to register your business name, and how to set prices on a service- or product-based businesses, just to name a few.

2nd Floor

Operate a Business

"If you are failing to plan, you are planning to fail."
~Tariq Siddique

It is not easy to start a business. You need to find time to learn about legal issues. You need to create a business plan. You need to be able to balance your family, school, and business responsibilities while sharpening your business knowledge. How will you manage it all? In one word, organization. "You can balance it all if you are, or learn to be, organized," says Turner.

Learning Time Management

Understand that operating a business while going to school is stressful. Taking care of your education while running a business requires an act of balance. Time management is a talent at which people can become skilled if they have the desire to learn. The sooner you learn to balance work with, for example, school, family, and friends, you can realize success in all aspects of your life.

Athena Yang, 17, of Houston, Texas, and owner of Bean Pillows, Inc., finds that time management is her biggest problem. Athena finds it very hard running a business, going to school, and trying to maintain a social life all at the same time. To help herself become time-management savvy, she plans everything out on a huge desk calendar. She writes everything on it, from the orders she receives and ships out, to her clients' contact information. This is how Athena stays organized and successful.[9]

Choosing a Business

When deciding what business you wish to operate, whether it is product- or service-based, keep in mind that it doesn't need to be a unique idea. Something that you enjoy doing is really all you need. Deciding to perform a common job, like babysitting or lawn mowing, is a great start. And, if you approach these businesses differently than from your competition, your efforts could result in a lucrative money-making business for many years to come. "Don't copy your competition," says Rob Marsh, vice-president of creative services at LogoWorks.com. "When your competitors zig, you should zag."[10] "Having a business is very different from having a job," says Christian Erickson, founder of Biz4Kids.com, an Atlanta-based company that teaches kids about entrepreneurship. "Having a business is about setting goals, planning your business, and accounting for the money that comes in, the money that goes out, and the assets that you have."[11]

Market Research Questionnaire

If you're still not sure of the type of product or service that might best benefit your community, write a Market Research Questionnaire. On this questionnaire you could ask questions that could fill in a customer need, such as questions about their lawn, garage cleaning, window cleaning, pet care, or, if you are computer-savvy, computer help. If you drive, you might offer dry-cleaning drop-off or pick-up, or even an errand service. Make your questionnaire match your abilities by looking at what you are capable of doing, and then create your questions. Then go door-to-door and ask people more about their specific needs. You might find they are looking for help strictly in weeding because their lawn care provider doesn't weed. Or, someone might need a window washer. Working couples may need a grocery shopper or a tutor to help their children with reading. You can spark potential customers with your Market Research Questionnaire. Whatever your abilities are, integrate them into your questionnaire.

Mind Your Own Business

The Small Business Association (SBA) and JA Worldwide—a program that uses hands-on experiences to help young people understand the economics of life—have joined forces to launch the site www.mindyourownbiz.org, a site which supports entrepreneurship among teens. The site serves as a small-business gateway for young entrepreneurs, with resources and information essential to realizing dreams of business ownership. It offers information from deciding what business to start to handling success.

Create a Checklist

It is best to rely on a checklist, rather than your memory, while starting your business. Your checklist should include any item that pertains to getting your business started, such as creating a business name, getting it registered, obtaining licenses and permits, a list of office equipment and supplies, etc. Mark off each item as you take care of it. A checklist has proven helpful in keeping business owners organized. Then keep all of this material organized and accessible (under the bed isn't it).

Licenses, Permits, and Certifications

Next, visit your local City Hall to obtain the necessary licenses and permits needed for the type of business you want to run.

Food preparation businesses are usually required to have an inspection and permit. Retail businesses need a tax resale license. Most cities and states require a vendor's license for people selling merchandise, new or old, for example, at a flea market. Retail businesses (or any businesses) run out of the home, need a license to operate a home-based business. Christian Alf, 17, of Tempe, Arizona, started an after-school rat-proofing business, charging $30 to climb on roofs and cover openings with wire mesh. Business started to boom and Christian hired three employees. Then, an article appearing in the *Arizona Republic* about his business caught the attention of the state commission. This is when Christian became aware that state law requires those doing structural pest control on other people's property to be licensed, and he had to cease doing business.[12]

If your business requires you to knock on doors, you will need to seek permits in the area in which you wish to do business, the perfect time to find out if that neighborhood has a "No-Knock Registry" ordinance. If you plan to sell used books in your driveway every weekend, as one teenager does, be sure to check your city ordinances and make sure you are obeying any local laws. If your business is babysitting, look into CPR and First Aid certifications through the American Red Cross. A pet care provider will benefit from having Pet First Aid and pet obedience training. If you are renting an apartment and plan on running a home-based business, check on local zoning ordinances. It may be that your landlord's real estate taxes will change from residential to commercial, which are higher — or that you may be prohibited from running a business in that apartment at all. Fortunately, most local ordinance laws permit home offices, without any tax changes to the landlord.

Online or Offline?

Generation Y-ers are not afraid to take their business online. They consider being "online" an extension of their business card. Many Generation Y entrepreneurs have even designed their own websites to promote a product or service that they sell. Joshua Motta, of Olathe, Kansas, is such a success story. At the age of 16,

13

Joshua began Net-Avenue.com, an online shopping mall, followed by Merchantfront.com, which helps online merchants set up an e-commerce site. Just recently Joshua became the youngest person ever to be employed by Microsoft®.[13] Peter Grunwald, of the Internet research firm Grunwald Associates, estimates that about 2 million sites have been created by kids ages 6 to 17.[14] It is cool for young entrepreneurs to say, "Go to my website."

There are several places to learn how to build a website, including America Online's Hometown. This site is geared to 13-year-olds and up, but even younger kids are using it. Kids can also learn HTML (computer coding used to create Web pages; short for "hypertext markup language") at schools and camps, and even buy software to help them design pages. "Once your business is on the web, you are in a worldwide market," says Priscilla Y. Huff, author of *Build a Successful Small or Home-Based Enterprise*. "Be aware of language and cultural differences as you post your content and ads."[15]

A Business Plan

A business plan, a game strategy for your business, is a written document that defines where you want to go with your product or service and how you will get there. Your business plan must contain the answer to the question, "What makes you think you can do this better than present competition?"

Business Plans Help Businesses Succeed

Many new businesses fail, not because they were bad ideas, but rather because of lack of proper planning. Say you decided to provide a home carpet cleaning service. You simply say to yourself, "I'm going to price my service at so-and-so amount per job, advertise my service on flyers, post them in various neighborhoods, rent a carpet cleaner, and go for it. How difficult is this? I don't need a business plan!" Then you gain some customers, rent the carpet cleaning machine, and find that renting the machine is too costly and that you won't be able to make a profit. Had you written a business plan, you would have known this because under your "cost analysis" you would have written down the cost of renting the carpet cleaning machine and would have calculated the income and expenditures didn't match. In a Web poll conducted by *Inc.* magazine, 52% of business owners said that they had a business plan when they started their companies.[16] Is it any wonder that, according to a business failure legend, between 80% and 90% of new businesses fail within five years? Don't be one of the 48% of business owners who started their business without a business plan!

Think of a Business Plan as a Magnifying Glass

In many instances the business plan can be even more important than money needed to get the business off the ground. It might just be the magnifying glass you need to see if your product or service is needed, or if there are people—the market—willing to buy it. A business plan can reveal just how good your business idea really is, or just how weak. Without a business plan, you have no written goals to measure any failure or success. The act of writing down your plan triggers questions you often don't think about otherwise. These are typically the very questions potential investors or customers would ask regarding the strength of your business.

Write Your Business Plan

Once you decide on the type of product or service you might consider offering, write the business plan. After answering all the questions that need to be answered, you'll be able to look at it to see if you can really turn it into a business. Whether you will finance your own business or will need a loan to get started, it is important to have a business plan. Consider entering your business plan in the Junior Chamber International's Best Business Plan Competition, open to all entrepreneurs between the ages of 18 and 40. This year's winner received $5,000!

Finding Help Writing Your Business Plan

The Small Business Administration (www.sba.gov) provides a guide to writing business plans. Visit www.entreprenuer.com and click on "Business Plans" for excellent information to guide you in writing your business plan. Visit http://www.villiscareview.com/CreationsExtrodinaire.htm for a sample business plan for a teen business. While not meant to be a template for a business plan, it is an example of what a business plan looks like. This website features 17-year-old Lennie Hall's business plan for his company, Creations Extraordinaire, featuring jewelry, picture frames, and candle holders. You can browse through sixty sample business plans from Palo Alto Software (www.paloalto.com), maker of Business Plan Pro. You can also invest in business plan software at office supply stores, or try www.bplan.com.

Adjusting Your Business Plan

Expect to make adjustments to your business plan throughout the duration of your business. Continually fine-tuning a business plan shows that you are staying on top of the marketplace. When Blake Henderson of Jonesboro, Georgia, was a fifth grader, he created the Bike Handler™, a device that hooked onto the back of a bike to help adults teach children to ride. Originally Blake had spray-painted the device with paint from a hardware store. Now, at the age of 14, Blake has adjusted his business plan and started having the Bike Handlers painted at an automotive body shop. His production cost increased to $1.91 per unit, but he feels it is worth it because his customers are satisfied.[17]

Posting Your Business Plan on Websites

There are many groups that allow you to post your business plan on their websites. Doing so can provide you with opportunities, including reviewers' feedback. Posting your business plan on their websites also allows potential investors to learn about your company for investment consideration. Reputable sites like www.businesspartners.com, www.angel-investor-news.com, and www.cloudstart.com will allow you to post business plans for investor consideration.

Customer Awareness Plan

To get your business off the ground, you'll need customers. You can begin by writing a plan on how you will generate customers. Printing up business cards and brochures, which many people can do themselves, is a good start. Will you post them on neighborhood doors and at local business offices and stores? Remember to include your free promotional efforts, such as press releases sent to newspapers and magazines, advertising on free Internet classified advertisements and bulletin boards, and on your own website. Information about setting up your own business website can be found on the 4th and 8th Floors.

Product Potential Research

Jesse Walter, an 18-year-old from Covina, California, came up with a business idea to generate a line of clothing for body boarders. After creating his company name, Premiere Clothing America, Jesse spent a lot of time doing research. He ran advertisements in body-boarding magazines to see what the outcome would be. Only when the response showed interest did Jesse start making some t-shirts. And, rather than open his own store, Jesse wholesaled his new clothing line through area surf shops. During PCA's first year of business, Jesse's company made nearly $125,000. Now in his 20s, Jesse added other products to his line, including sweatshirts, jackets, bags, cargo shorts, and pants.[18]

Prototype

If you have an idea for a product, and you don't see anything like it on the market, it's time to consider hiring a designer to build a working model—a prototype—of your idea. While it's generally hard to present a prototype to a corporation unless you are already an established vendor, an invention consultant can help you reach your goal. Take It to the Market (www.takeittothemarket.com) is a seminar series that you might look into. To find a broker to help you, visit the non-profit inventor's support group, United Inventors Association (www.uiausa.com). You can find a comprehensive list of professional prototype developers at www.thomasnet.com (use the keywords that would describe your prototype).

Sometimes, one-stop shopping for your prototype isn't the best thing for a start-up company. One sourcing agent told an entrepreneur that he could have a prototype of his travel mug made in China, but that he would have to pay for a patent search of $4,700—even though the entrepreneur already did a patent search on his own! Often such one-stop shopping bundles a "package," a take-it-or-leave-it deal. Companies that do patent searches and locate prototype makers have a great incentive to find nothing in the patent search because, finding something, after all, could mean the end of the deal. It's a straight-out conflict of interest, and entrepreneurs can't win.

Plenty of companies build prototypes without the bundling package—at cheaper prices. A number of domestic shops can produce models quickly for under $1,000 using inexpensive materials. One such prototype company, Stratasys, based in Eden Prairie, Minnesota, asks clients to upload a computer-aided design drawing onto its website. A machine that acts like a 3-D printer transforms that drawing into a model using layers of molded plastic. Within a week, Stratasys delivers prototypes. While you still would have to pay a CAD engineer between $50 and $75 an hour to create the design, the total cost of about $2,000 is still less than a $4,700 quote from a sourcing agent. Another similar firm in Atlanta, Quickparts, uses similar technology and is also reasonably priced. (Search www.thomasnet.com for contact information for hundreds of design engineers and prototype makers.)

Product Licensing

You may have invented a product you're sure will sell millions. Getting your innovation on the shelves of a major retailer that prefers not to buy from one-line, underfinanced inventors, is a big challenge. When you try to get the product on the shelves of a big-name national retailer, you will most likely encounter a lot of resistance. Instead of going at it alone, your best bet is to make a connection with a company that already sells to your target customers.

Licensing your product to a company that could sell it on their shelves is the easiest way to get a product on the market. Take, for example, Todd Basche, the 50-year-old winner of Staples' 2004 Invention Quest contest. Todd created The Wordlock, a combination lock that uses letters instead of numbers. Instead of the numbers 4225, for example, the lock could spell "moon." While winning a contest sponsored by major companies such as Staples and Procter & Gamble is a great way to have your product introduced to a big market, it isn't the only way to go. It's worth noting that Staples accepts ideas from inventors as potential licensing candidates *anytime*. Visit Staples' website (www.staples.com), go to the section marked "vendors," and click on "product submissions." You can find licensing information on many company websites by following a similar format, or by e-mailing the company with product submission questions.

Patent

Before you license your product, you will need to get it patented. A patent is grant issued by the Patent and Trademark Office, giving an inventor exclusive rights to sell his/her invention for a term of 20 years from the date the patent was filed in the United States. Before you present your product idea to any company, be certain that your product is patent pending. Otherwise, no major company will even talk to you about your invention. Build the product first, get it patented, then present it for licensing potential. Entrepreneurs who come to the table with market research, sales figures, and strategic plans have a better chance of getting their product licensed. "A finished product with sales is much more valuable," says Mike Burns, CEO of Banshee Products, a Sacramento toy company that licenses products.[19] Since 1995, www.FromPatentToProfit.com has been educating inventors and small businesses on the methods of inventing and patenting. Topic information include designing, patenting, manufacturing, marketing, and licensing of a product.

If your invention has previously been disclosed, you will find it out by doing a patent search on your product. A patent search will determine if your invention has already been invented. If not, you can proceed with your patent.

Protect Your Product Idea

Before you get your product idea out to a licensor, you need to make sure that it has the "wow" factor. To find out if it does, you will need to show your idea to those with whom you network, which might include teachers, family, friends, and neighbors who already are business managers or owners. Just make sure everyone signs a confidential nondisclosure agreement that will protect your idea. For sample confidential agreements, go to the United Inventors Association website (www.uiausa.com) and click on the "Novice Inventors" box.

You can perform your own patent search. If you do find a product very close in design to your invention, it is best to obtain qualified professional legal counsel to advise you on future plans. The U.S. Patent & Trademark Office (www.uspto.gov), Japanese Patent Office (www.jpo.go.jp/) and European Patent Office (www.european-patent-office.org/) have databases for patent searching. Begin your patent search using keywords, words in the title, description of product, etc. Another useful site, www.freepatentsonline.com, allows you to print full-text of U.S. patents to aid in your patent search. Two other sources to check out are the International Licensing Industry Merchandisers' Association website (www.licensing.org), which has listings of licensing agents and a wealth of general licensing information, and *License!* magazine (www.licensemag.com), which provides a marketplace of properties available for licensing at http://tracker.licensemag.com.

If you find performing your own patent search, preparation, and filing mind-boggling, hire a professional from the start. A reputable patent attorney is someone who has expertise, experience, and advanced resources, and can provide you with quick results. Hiring a professional is generally the path most inventors choose.

Manufacturing Goods Overseas

If you are looking for a manufacturing source in Asia, start with your state's commerce department. Import and export assistance is available, and staff members can help you set up a manufacturing plan. It is recommended that you use a sourcing agent to find a foreign manufacturer if this will be your first time. The agent usually has an overseas office that can get samples and oversee production so that you will get the product you expect. You can begin your agent search by visiting these websites: Buy-Thai (www.buy-thai.com), GroupChina (www.groupchina.com), Product Sourcing International (www.product-sourcing.com), and ProSavvy (www.prosavvy.com). Another helpful direct sourcing site is BizEurope (www.bizeurope.com).

When starting your manufacturing search, look to a midsize overseas manufacturing partner with good references, since larger, more established manufacturers might be too costly at first. Whether you use a sourcing agent or go at it alone, get references and do background checks to make sure your international manufacturing partner is legitimate, and thoroughly investigate information and sources found online. You can find more information about overseas outsourcing by visiting the Global Outsourcing Institute (www.goinstitute.org), The Outsourcing Institute (www.outsourcing.com), and The Outsourcing Network (www.outsourcingnetwork.net).

Obtaining a Passport

If you're planning a trip abroad in the future, apply for a passport. You can make the process easier by looking into the guide, "Passports: Applying For Them The Easy Way," from the U.S. Department of State. You will learn how, when, and where to apply. You can obtain a copy of the guide by sending a $1 check or money order to Federal Citizen Information Center, Dept. 324M, Pueblo, CO 81009. Or call them at (888) 8-PUEBLO and charge it. To order the guide online, visit www.pueblo.gsa.gov. If you're not in a rush, many post offices can process your passport application via the mail.

Know What Your Time is Worth

Before you come up with the price package for your service or product, have an understanding of what your time is worth—or what you would like it to be worth. In an ideal world, you would work eight hours a day, five days a week, and take a month-long vacation—and still make enough money to spend and save. If this work schedule were to work out, then you would have 1,920 hours of work a year.

Whatever your yearly income goals are, divide them by 1,920, and that's what your hourly pay is. If you want to make $100,000 per year, then divide that by 1,920 to find out that you earn $52.08 per hour. If it's $400,000 that you want to earn per year, then you will have to earn $208.33 per hour.

Coming Up With Your Price Package

Properly pricing your work is one of the keys to maintaining a successful business. While every business wants to be competitive with its pricing, you don't want to underbid your work. Consider all the facts before stating your price packages.

To come up with your price packages, use the standard pricing formula: materials + labor + overhead + desired profit = estimate for customer. What will your materials cost? What are your overhead expenses (phone charges, advertising, and

22

supplies)? You may need to find out how much other professionals in your business are charging to see if you're in the same price range. Otherwise, your price might be so high that no one will buy, or so low that you can't make a profit.

Setting Prices in a Service-Based Business

Pricing a service-based business is fairly standard once you get into a routine. You have rates for a variety of service jobs that you provide, maybe even a different price for the same service during holidays. If you provide pet care, your half-hour service, which might include feeding, brushing, and walking the dog, would be priced differently than "babysitting" the dog for the entire day. If the job is extremely demanding, the job probably doesn't fit the pay — unless you already have a high fee. For example, if the pet care job also requests services above and beyond what you usually perform, for example, your client wants you to walk the dog for a half hour in addition to all the other services, the job will take you twice as long. You will need to adjust your rate to reflect compensation for the extra services. "You're not an elephant," says business writer and network marketing expert Michael K. Duffey. "Don't settle for peanuts!"

In the pet care industry, the pay you earn for selling your time, labor, and experience working with animals should be at least the going minimum wage rate for half an hour. Double the price if the time goes beyond and up to one hour. As you gain experience, you'll be able to charge more because you are an experienced professional. If you're not sure how to price your service, ask an adult to help you determine your pricing. My son, Turner, charges $12 for each 30-minute visit. (Typically adult pet care providers charge $15 to $25 per visit, more on holidays and in larger metropolitan areas.)

To be competitive, Turner provides extra services at the same price, gaining customer confidence and business. They include watering plants, bringing in mail and newspapers, adjusting draperies and lights, turning the TV on during the day — off during the night, spending extra time with the pets, picking up yard droppings, taking trash cans to curbside, even cleaning leaves out of swimming pools. He makes his clients feel they are getting their money's worth by hiring him. On the other hand, be firm with clients who want really "special" or "over and above" services for no extra charge.

Setting Prices in a Product-Based Business

Maggie and Allie Cawood-Smith, 12-year-old twins from Auburn, California, are co-founders of Beet Lips, homemade lip balm they create from plants grown in their garden. The sisters carefully consider the costs of all the ingredients that go into producing their product. Since they grow most of their herbs, the girls' main expenses come from packaging, display baskets, and advertising their product. They primarily advertise on their website, www.beetlips.ourfamily.com, which has helped them attract customers. After all this was considered, the twins added up how much it cost to make the lip balm, looked at the prices of similar products in stores, and set their prices below what others were charging. The girls now sell their lip balm to stores for $2 each, making about a $1.50 profit.[20]

When Emily Manassero of Oceanside, California, was 11, she wanted to buy a horse. To come up with the money, she started her own business, The Bread Barn. In order to set the price for each loaf of bread that she baked, Emily had to determine the cost of each loaf. She made a list of all the ingredients, then estimated the cost of each ingredient. After it was all added up, her average cost per loaf of bread was 50 cents. Next, Emily had to figure out her operating expenses. These costs include everything from electricity and office supplies to a telephone, answering machine, rent, and advertising. When these costs were added up for the month, Emily had her monthly operating expenses. Finally, Emily set her bread prices at $3.00 and $3.50 per loaf, which allowed her a net profit of 100% per loaf.[21]

Keystoning

Many business owners use a formula for setting prices that is known as "keystoning." Keystoning is the practice of doubling the cost of goods. Say you have a small, independent bookstore. You purchase books to resale at your shop. When you purchase those books from a publisher (who is the wholesaler), you are the retailer. You will typically get 50% off the cover price. This means that if a book has a cover retail price of $15, you will only have to pay $7.50 per book. In turn, you double the price that you paid, that is, sell the book for $15, which is a 100% markup. This markup generally leaves the business owner a reasonable profit to pay for his expenses and labor. Do keep in mind that if you are starting a retail business of any kind, you will need to apply for a taxpayer ID and a reseller's permit. A taxpayer ID and reseller's permit allow you buy goods at wholesale cost and not pay sales tax on the goods. Your customers will pay the sales tax when they purchase your product.

Need More Help Pricing?

Setting a price for your product is both an art and a science — and a little bit of guesswork. When you set your prices right from the start, you'll be able to afford staying in business. If you're still not sure how to price your product and need more help, access Dinkytown's free Profit Margin Calculator (www.dinkytown.net/java/ProfitMargin.html). It can help you determine the selling price for your products to achieve a desired profit margin. By entering the wholesale costs, and either the markup or gross margin percentage, the site calculates the required selling price and gross margin, computing the best price for your product or service. This helpful site also gives you definitions for wholesale cost, markup percent, selling price, gross margin dollars, and gross margin percent.

If you need to find global pricing for your U.S. price, visit www.xe.com. When you arrive at the site, place the U.S. currency amount in the left box and on the right, for example, Canada as the country you want a price conversion equivalent. Click the conversion box and you'll find your Canadian price. There is no set rule what your converted price should be. When you factor expenses such as global shipping and long-distance telephone calls, you may need to add to the converted price figure you find on the conversion site to balance costs. That's why you'll see many price versions for a $19.99 U.S. price, for example, prices ranging from $23.99 to $29.99 in Canadian dollars. There isn't a set rule.

Develop a Financial Map

A financial map is an excellent guide that will help you see, in advance, how much money you will need to operate your business, when you'll need it, how much you'll need to make to break even, and how far you need to go to get to the profit point. No matter how good your idea is, if you do not succeed in a business started with borrowed money, you'll still owe it. A financial map will help you see clearly the financial details before they happen — or don't.

Setting Up a Budget

It is important to know that things are not free. If you're in the lawn mowing business, it's OK to borrow your parent's lawn mower. When you're out of gas, you need to buy gasoline and to calculate the cost of gas refill into your budget. If you don't own a lawn mower, calculate the cost of renting one. What about advertising? Do you plan to purchase a classified ad in your town newspaper? That expense needs to be added. Write down all the supplies that you will need to operate your business, then budget for any expenses that might surface during the year. A Starting Costs Calculator can be found on www.entrepreneur.com/calculators or Palo Alto Software's site www.bplans.com/common/calculator/startingcosts.cfm. This calculator will help you calculate your start-up costs before you start your new business. It will help you evaluate how much capital you will need to start your business. You can also get more information from the Small Business Resource Center. It can provide you with a library of downloadable files, with a focus on home-based business. You'll find a couple of dozen files available on topics ranging from writing a business plan to preparing a budget. (See www.allbusiness.com.)

Marketing and Adjusting Product Line

To survive in your business, you have to continuously market and adjust your product line to keep up with customers' needs. Take for example, Erica Gluck, 7, from San Diego, California, who had the idea of selling fresh-made pasta to earn money. Erica found a farmer's market in San Diego and knew she had the perfect spot. Later she added a booth at another location in San Diego, and sales of Erica's Pasta grew. After 7 years in the business, sales began to dwindle. Erica, with the help of her father, designed brochures that educated people on the health benefits of eating pasta. Erica also added artisan breads, pesto, and flavored oils to her product offerings. Now you can find Erica's Pastas at three farmer's markets in the San Diego area. To be in the right place at the right time, in an ever-changing business market, Erica continues to look for non-traditional places to do business. Erica recently launched a website, www.Pastapress.com, to showcase her business, which now includes writing and publishing pasta cookbooks and teaching pasta cooking classes.[22]

Getting Your Product on Store Shelves

It isn't easy to get a product on the shelves of a chain store, however it can be done. When Maya Kaimal, 41, from Woodstock, NY, created her own line of Indian sauces, she knew she had a needed-by-the-market niche product. So, Maya began talking to distributors and within six months (and after modifying each recipe about 30 times before she was satisfied), her three sauces were in 50 stores. But it wasn't until her distributor began selling her products to Whole Foods Markets did her company reach national status. A year later Maya introduced her fourth flavor sauce. Soon, her sauces were sold at Williams-Sonoma. Shortly after, a Williams-Sonoma representative (who had discovered her sauces at a food show) asked Maya to create two blends exclusively for the store. How did Maya get her product on major store shelves so quickly? She found her industry's main organization, the National Association for the Specialty Food Trade, and it guided her through the ins and outs of her business.[23]

Mass Market on QVC and HSN

Did you know that QVC, which stands for quality, value, and convenience, is one of the nation's leading TV shopping retailers? QVC introduces 250 new products every week to viewers across the United States. If you want to get your product on this home shopping channel, it's not impossible to do. QVC doesn't only work with agents; it also works directly with inventors who wish to land a QVC contract on their own.

According to Abby Schaefer of QVC, "QVC does everything it can to find products, and although QVC certainly accepts products brought in by third parties, it is absolutely not necessary to hire an agent in order to have your product evaluated by QVC. If you have a great product, it will sell itself."[24]

Inventors can submit a picture or brochure of their products, along with an application, to QVC by mail or at a national QVC Product Search trade show, which takes place at various locations at least once a year. Vendors who attend the QVC Product Search events can present their products in person to a QVC buyer. Visit the QVC Product Search website at www.qvcproductsearch.com for an application and more details on becoming a QVC vendor.

Once you submit your application and photo, if QVC is interested, they'll request a sample. Once you pass QVC's rigorous quality assurance requirements, a QVC buyer will work with you to create a sales strategy for your product. A purchase order will be written, and you will ship your goods to a QVC warehouse. Then, it usually takes three months to go from purchase order to on-air appearances. If you have any questions, contact QVC's Vendor Relations department at (888) NEW-ITEM or e-mail them at Vendor_Relations@QVC.com.

HSN (Home Shopping Network), another mass marketing outlet, featured 22,000 new products in 2004. HSN sells products in a broad range of categories, some of which include jewelry, apparel, electronics, home accents/furnishings, sports/fitness equipment, and cookware/food. If you think you have a product that would appeal to the 85 million households that each of these retailers reaches, ask yourself the following questions:

1) Is it easy to demonstrate the product's features or benefits on television?
2) Is the product not available in other places?
3) Does it make a person's life easier or solve a problem?

To have your product evaluated for possible airing on HSN, fill out a vendor application and mail it in along with a catalog, brochure, picture and/or a sample. The HSN (www.hsn.com) application is available through its Frequently Asked Questions page on its website.

Getting Your Product in Catalogs

U.S. catalog sales are over $100 billion a year, so you have the opportunity to sell to a large market. You compete more easily because catalogs offer a level playing field for the smallest start-up and the biggest corporation. Unlike store distribution, you only need one product at a time. You save on packaging because, unlike point-of-purchase sales where the package helps sell the product on the store shelf, the package has no bearing on the sales of an item in a catalog. You keep your risk low because only a few catalogs now require a nominal advertising fee to sell your product (most catalogs won't charge you anything to advertise your product). Catalogs offer start-ups national exposure, offering your company instant credibility. Finally, catalogs provide an ideal opportunity to test the market to see how well your product sells.

Although you need just one product to sell, catalog houses are very selective choosing products to feature in their catalogs. To be considered for catalog inclusion, there are several hoops a product developer must jump through. The catalog company will want to test-market a product (maybe a small batch of 100) before including it in a complete run. If the test shows potential, they will purchase a large quantity (1,000 or more) for their full-scale mailings. As long as your product sells, they will continue to order large quantities to sell. In order for the catalog company to receive the largest discount on quantity purchases, they must deal as close to the original source as possible, such as the inventor, patent owner, manufacturer, or publisher—not a middleman. Finally, the product must be new and unique.

Qualifying for Mail Order Acceptance

You must look the part of an established, professionally operating business—even if you only have one product. This means you should have stationery with a company name that coincides with your product. Approach the catalog company in a professional manner by typing all correspondence.

It would be in your best interest to test-market your product yourself before offering it to a catalog house. This will allow you to see if you are, in fact, offering a "winner" or a "loser" to the company. Offering them a product that will sell shows your professionalism, and the mail order company will want to do future business with you.

Pricing Your Product for Catalogs

It is essential to properly price your product for catalog mailings. If your product is priced too high, customers won't buy; if it's priced too low you won't make a profit. Look at a variety of catalogs that you feel could be a suitable match for your product. You may find that some catalogs specialize in low-priced ($10 or less) items, while others offer products in a higher range ($50 or more).

Selling to Catalog Companies on Credit

Selling to catalog houses isn't like the conventional mail order business, where you would deal with cash. With catalog houses, transactions are conducted on credit. This means you'll need invoices to send to your customer after shipment has been made. Don't mail the invoice with the goods; typically, billing is processed at a different location from where the goods are shipped.

There are variations on credit terms. The best one will be "Payment due EOM (end of month)" or "2% discount within 10 days." It is up to you to decide if you will ship prepaid or bill your customer for the shipping charges.

Creating a Simplified Product Price Structure

Prices are usually set in quantities such as a gross (a group of 144 items; 12 dozen) or 100, 500, 1,000, 5,000, etc. While these price structures work best for wholesaling to the retailer, it is not recommended to use these price structures when trying to find a catalog to sell your product. Instead, give them your best price from the start. For example, if your product is priced 100 @ $4.25 each; 500 @ $3.75 each; 1,000 @ $3.25 each—give them your 1,000-quantity price, even if they order only 100 units for the test period. Be sure to tell the catalog company the good deal that they're getting, as the price you've given them is your lowest price for the 1,000 unit order. This shows the catalog company that you are serious about doing business with them, and that you are confident that your product will sell.

Creating a Promotional Package

Catalog company buyers are very busy, so make your presentation a quick hook to the reader. What you should include in your promotional package is a cover letter, an attractive flyer describing your product, a color photo of the product, advertising copy, and a sample of your product (only if you think it will impress the buyer). To find out if your mail order product will ever get off the ground, visit the Tilberry Direct Marketing site at www.catalogrep.com. There you will find 14 criteria to judge whether your product has potential to be a catalog winner.

Mail Order

First-time entrepreneurs find it easiest to start a mail order business from home, and grow it into a full-time venture — complete with an outside facility or office. Starting a mail order business from home is a good way to test your business, allowing you a financial safety net by saving money on rent, utilities, and much more. Lisa Hammond, from Las Vegas, Nevada, longed to run a creative business — one that sold items that were meaningful to her, such as necklaces, sculptures, art, and books. Lisa finds creations that she likes, then tracks down the artist, author, or designer, to purchase the products at wholesale prices. So, in 1996, Lisa gathered venture cash of $30,000 by tapping her credit cards and savings, then created Femail Creations. Lisa had a lot to learn about producing a mail order catalog on her own, and fortunately, photographers, printers, and other vendors graciously offered her the guidance she needed to produce her first catalog.

While sophisticated catalogers use extensive research to select prospects, Lisa's method was simple: to find customers like herself. That's when she pulled out a favorite magazine of hers, called the publisher, and asked to rent their subscribers' list. Artists and designers also helped Lisa with her mailing by providing her with the names and addresses of customers who had previously purchased their art.

Working within her means, Lisa mailed out the first Femail Creations catalog to 30,000 people — a small number in the world of mail order. Yet, determined to make up for that weakness, Lisa offered 24-hour customer service. Not having a budget for hiring a customer service representative, Lisa spent many nights sleeping on her home-office floor — surrounded by her products — prepared to answer customer questions and taking shipping information.

Lisa's company has grown to five employees, and, she now outsources orders and packing and shipping operations to experienced people, avoiding numerous headaches. Lisa's online business (www.femailcreations.com) and catalog sales have steadily increased to a $7 million mail order empire, and she is continuously on the lookout for new products to feature in her catalog and website.[25]

Best and Worst Mail Order Months

Only you can find out the best months for selling your mail order product by testing. Generally, months for mail order ranking best-to-worst (based on most types of businesses and products) are January, February, October, November, March, September, August, April, December, July, May, and June. (While several rankings slightly differed, they all stated January as being the best month and June the worst.) If you have a company that sells baked goods, your best months may be during holiday seasons, beginning with December (Christmas). It is wise to know this rule-of-thumb, because, you should run your major tests (advertisements or product testing) in the months that are less responsive than the months in which you expect good business — a way of waking up new (and old) customers in the less-responsive months.

Toll-Free Number

Toll-free phone numbers allow customers to order more easily, which will increase product sales. But will it increase your profits? Toll-free means that the caller doesn't pay for the call; you do. Some mail order businesses have found that using a toll-free number is not profitable, while others have found that it is what makes their business profitable.

Your Shipping Needs

To find the best prices for your shipping needs, compare prices of leading and regional carries, including FedEx, DHL (formerly Airborne Express), and the U.S. Postal Service, and then visit www.redroller.com. To use the site, enter the start point and final destination and soon, you'll receive a comparison chart listing the shipper, delivery time, and best price. RedRoller also allows you to print shipping labels for free.

Shipping services vary, so know your vendor—and ask questions. For example, DHL charges customers for a 5-pound package if the weight is not included on the air bill. Therefore, have preprinted air bills with a 1-pound weight on hand. (The poundage will be adjusted if the package weighs more or less.)

Drop Shipping Products

Drop shipping is an arrangement between a business and the manufacturer of a product whereby a mail-order or Internet merchant accepts orders and then pays a manufacturer to ship the products to the customer. A drop shipper is an e-tailer's solution to order fulfillment. The association allows e-tailer owners Kim and Linda O'Neill to carry "virtual inventory." Running an office supply store from a two-bedroom condo, they didn't have space to store office supplies to fulfill orders. Yet, after 10 years of business and over $2 million in annual sales, they continue to drop ship products directly from the distributors. Not having a brick and mortar store allows the O'Neills to offer products at a much lower price since their overhead is much less. "Being a virtual e-tailer, drop shipping from distributors, gives us access to dozens of warehouses with hundreds of millions of dollars of inventory without putting one cent out there before the product is purchased and paid for."[26]

Drop shipping information can be found on eBay's Solutions Directory (www.ebay.com). Click on the "Services" link on the top of any eBay page. When you arrive on the Services page, click on "eBay Solutions Directory." Scroll down and click on "Sourcing." The Sourcing page lists certified eBay Solutions providers that offer drop shipping. *The Drop Ship Source Directory* (www.mydssd.com) is a subscription service, and is updated monthly. The *Thomas Register* (www.thomasregister.com) is a free search engine for finding drop shippers. A well-respected directory of drop shippers is www.WorldWideBrands.com. For $69.95 you'll get a lifetime membership to the directory. This directory isn't just a list; these drop shippers have agreed to drop ship for small businesses.

Are You Game for Business?

The business-based board game Cashflow 101 inspired 30-year-old Ed Patisso to launch his business, Real Estate Equities, in Mineola, New York. The company, which Ed started in 2002, offers solutions for homeowners in pre-foreclosure, mortgage financing, and other real estate services. Although Ed took accounting courses in college, nothing helped him learn how to manage risk. Ed admits that before he played Cashflow 101, he didn't really understand a balance sheet or income statement. Ed, who still plays the game often with gaming and other business groups, had sales for this year of $250,000. So who created this ingenious game? Robert T. Kiyosaki, author of the book *Rich Dad, Poor Dad*!

You are now entering the 3rd Floor, Raise Start-Up Cash. If start-up money is what you're looking for, you're on the right level. You will find many ways to raise money for your business, including grants that don't need to be repaid.

3rd Floor

Raise Start-Up Cash

> *"A bank is a place that will lend you money*
> *if you can prove that you don't need it."*
> ~Bob Hope

You may find that, after adding up all of your expenses, you don't have enough savings to cover your business start-up costs. Many businesses start out the same way—needing outside funding to get the business up and running. A well-drafted business plan is your best tool to help you not only see how much money you will need to begin operating your business, but also help you raise the money that you need to start your business.

When starting up your business, it does not pay to be in a hurry to grow. Joe Shambro, 17, from Granite City, Illinois, took his time developing his business, Shambro Recording (now known as Grey Street Recording), a recording studio that commands up to $500 for a half-hour recording session.

When Joe started his company, he took what he had as a hobbyist—microphones, processing equipment, digital and analog recorders—and used them until he could afford better equipment.

As his recording business grew, Joe continued to minimize his costs by renting equipment that he needed until he made enough money to purchase more without getting a loan. Starting as a minimalist kept Joe on a successful business path without going into deep debt early in the start-up process. No longer a teen, Joe reinvests earnings into his company and has made his business even stronger.[27]

Calculating Start-Up Costs

In his business plan for Bike Handlers™, Blake Henderson estimated that his start-up costs would be $941. To break even, Blake calculated that he would need to sell 120 Bike Handlers™ at $20 each. The Ewing Marion Kauffman Foundation (www.kauffman.org), one of the country's premier resources for entrepreneurs that offers innovative programs to support new businesses at all levels — from elementary students to high-growth entrepreneurs, was so impressed with Blake's business plan that it awarded him a $1,000 college scholarship. Blake's parents were also impressed with his business plan, and loaned him $1,000 to start the business.[28]

Your Personal Savings

If you need to find funding for your business venture, begin by looking at your own savings account. Entrepreneurs should always expect to fund part or all of their new business from their own savings. You won't have to pay anyone interest on your own money, nor will you have to convince anyone of your business idea. Daniel Dawson of Center Point, Oregon, and his co-host, Jacob Ghena, both 19, used their personal savings for their new business venture, hosting a talk show. Both Daniel and Jacob saved on operating expenses by doing all the production themselves. They did, however, need about $100 for each show they hosted to cover small expenses, money which they drew from their own personal savings.[29]

Sell Something Personal

At the age of 21, Terri Bowersock, now 47, decided to start a business selling used and consigned furniture. In order to come up with the start-up money that she needed, she sold her childhood bedroom set and her mother's old living room furniture. The money was used to rent store space, buy a sign, and set up shop. Ten years later she opened her second store. Now Terri owns one of the largest chains of furniture consignment stores in the country. Terri's Consign & Design Furnishings brings in annually over $36 million in revenue with 14 stores nationwide. Terri also launched a used-furniture company online, www.eterris.com.[30]

If you have something big to sell, like a piece of furniture, used computers, and other electronics, log on to www.livedeal.com, where you can post a local classified ad for free. Contact local stores for consignment sales policies. Other places to sell personal belongings include www.amazon.com, www.ioffer.com, and www.craigslist.org. If you have books to sell, www.half.com charges no listing fee, but takes a commission from the selling price at the time of sale.

Loans from Family and Friends

Many young entrepreneurs starting their own business venture ask family and friends for loans. While it's not always a good idea to borrow from family or friends, if you do, treat the loans as you would if it were from a bank. Draw up a financial agreement stating when, and how much interest, you will be paying back on the loan. For example, if you've borrowed $100, you could promise to pay $20 a month for the next five months, with an extra $5 in the last month's payment to cover interest. For larger loans, Circle Lending can act as an intermediary between the business owner and their family or friends who have loaned them money. Get their free guide, "Financing Your Small Business: How to Borrow from People You Know" online at www.circlelending.com.

Customers as Investors

Finding a customer who believes in your business venture can be the key to getting a loan or investor. This customer will not only loan you money, he'll probably continue being a customer. If someone invests in your business, typically that means the investor gives you money now in exchange for a share of whatever money you make in the future. Kassidy Briles, 13, owner of a butterfly hatchery, had a twist in a customer relationship. Kassidy's first customer was a businesswoman who invested in her butterfly hatchery by giving her larvae, then purchasing several butterflies in cages at wholesale prices to resell in her own shop.[31] More information about Kassidy and her butterfly hatchery can be found on the 5th Floor, Create Your Niche Business.

Learning to Barter

Bartering, the trading of goods or services, has been around since before money was exchanged. Last year alone, companies exchanged $8.25 billion in goods and services, according to the International Reciprocal Trade Association.[32]

Try bartering for raw materials instead of spending money to purchase them. Bartering makes better use of your resources and lowers your cost of doing business. For example, a teen could offer to clean the local copy shop once a week in exchange for free printing services. If you need advertising from your town newspaper, offer to barter your services. Offer to deliver newspapers, wash company cars, or provide lawn care service in exchange for free display advertising. You will be providing the service as often as needed until the "cost" of the display advertisement is met. You should try to trade for something before you buy it.

Bootstrapping

Bootstrapping is a means of finding creative ways to support a start-up business until it becomes profitable. Bootstrapping may include negotiating delayed payment to suppliers and advances from potential partners and customers. When Michele Hoskins, an ex-schoolteacher and divorced mother founded Michele Foods, she didn't have funding. "If you want something badly enough," says Michele, "you can and will dream up a way to finance it." And dream she did. Michele created her own interest-free loan of bootstrapping her business by asking wholesalers for longer payment terms: 45 days rather than the standard 30. Simultaneously, she asked retailers for shorter terms, giving them a 2% discount if they paid their bill within 10 days. Michele's products now can be found in more than 10,000 food stores nationwide, including Stop & Shop, Super Wal-Mart, and Albertson's — bringing in an annual revenue of nearly $8 million. [33]

Bootstrapping can also include other creative ways to support the start-up that doesn't involve getting a loan, such as working a side job to support the business, using savings earmarked for your venture, using credit cards (wisely), even creatively bartering for goods and services that will get your business up and running. If you anticipate that your start-up business will be using a high volume of color prints, www.freeprinters.com will give you a free printer. The catch is that you would have to agree to purchase toner supplies from their company, on a regular schedule for a defined period of time, typically for two or three years. Getting a color printer for free, and then paying for the toner supplies as your business succeeds, is one way of bootstrapping your business — without borrowing money to finance your business up front.

Bootstrapping At Its Best

Fred DeLuca, then 17, was a recent high school graduate in 1965, looking for a way to pay for college when he founded a sandwich shop in Bridgeport, Connecticut. Fred didn't have any money, so a family friend loaned him $1,000. Then he borrowed his dad's car, drove around town, and found a vacant store to rent. To further bootstrap his business, Fred put ads in the newspaper saying, "Student needs refrigerator," and he would buy old refrigerators for $10 each. Ten years later, he owned 32 sandwich shops. Three decades later and 25,818 stores later, Fred's Subway chain is one of the largest privately held businesses in the world—not to mention that Fred is worth at least $1 billion.[34]

When Marc D'Amelio founded his urban streetwear label, Madsoul, in 2000, all he had was $1,000. In order to score his first sale, Marc went after the buyer of the New York Knicks, having met him from his previous job as a clothing sales rep. Before approaching the buyer, Marc asked a screen printer to create sample T-shirts for him for free. In return, Marc promised the company the contract if he closed the deal. Marc then presented the offer to the buyer representing the New York Knicks. Liking the T-shirts, the buyer ordered 3,000 to sell at Madison Square Garden—for a total of $30,000. Marc then returned to the screen printer and offered to pay $15,000 for the run—but only after the Knicks paid him. Showing proof of the New York Knicks' T-shirt order, the vendor agreed to bootstrap Marc's 3,000 T-shirts![35]

Selling your product before it is produced has always been a popular bootstrapping method. That's exactly what Bart Snow, owner of Rainbow Express moving, did when he started his business. He received payment, in advance, from his first customer. Then he had the money to begin operating his moving business. As more customers paid in advance, Bart was able to expand his business, never having had to borrow start-up money. "Since it often takes weeks or months to collect money from sales, financing a business from sales revenue is really an exercise in advance planning," says David Worrell, business writer for *Entrepreneur.com*. "The savvy entrepreneur should know not only how to pay for today's expenses, but also how to pay for the next three to six months of overhead."[36] For additional understanding of how bootstrapping works, read *Bootstrap: Lessons Learned Building a Successful Company From Scratch*, by Kenneth L. Hess. It will help guide you through an amazing way of starting your business on a shoestring—without going into debt. For more ideas visit *Inc.com* to find entrepreneurs' tips, strategies, and success stories of starting up a business on a shoestring at www.inc.com/keyword/bootstrap.

Trade Credit

Trade credit, also known as bootstrapping, is when a vendor or supplier is willing to give you credit on the merchandise they sell that you need. In the previous bootstrapping example, Michele Hoskins (of Michele Foods) needed food products from wholesalers. She was able to purchase the food products, create her baked goods, sell them, then pay off her trade credit—all without incurring interest on the money she owed. Had she thought of charging it all on her credit card, she would have incurred lots of interest had she not paid of her tab within the month. Another example: say you need shipping material that includes boxes of various sizes, bags, package filling, envelopes, and other paper or shipping products. This usually means that you have an extended period of time to pay your bill, usually 30, 60, or 90 days from the time of the invoice. Many suppliers have only the 30-day invoice period. Michele Hoskins was not afraid to ask for—and get—an additional 15 days to pay her bill.

Vendor Financing

Vendor financing is an option worth considering. When Ayana DaSilva of Montclair, New Jersey, wrote to *Black Enterprise's* James C. Johnson, she wanted to know if there was another way that she could finance a hair salon business besides business loans and grants. Vendor financing could be an option to consider. "Find a company that produces hair salon products, and make arrangements to borrow money from them," says James. "In return, you would be obligated to buy the supplier's products."[37]

Stakeholder Financing

When a customer pays you in advance for something that you are going to deliver in the future, this is known as stakeholder financing, very similar to bootstrapping. After receiving those funds, you can use it as seed capital. It's not as far-fetched as it sounds—many entrepreneurs use this method of financing. Construction workers often get paid, in part, before starting a job.

They, in turn, pay for supplies that they need to get the job done—often in advance. This kind of financing can be used across industries. An auto detailer can request payment in front, then purchase the supplies that he needs to get his business up and running.

Stakeholder financing benefited entrepreneur Kenya Lordana James, 12, of Atlanta, Georgia. When Kenya found her business niche in 2002 as founder and editor of *Blackgirl*, she wanted a magazine that focused on promoting positive messages and imagery among African American teens, while offering insightful coverage of history, culture, lifestyle, and entertainment news. Discovering that her $1,500 savings (from her previous bakery business) wouldn't be enough to publish the first issue, she included stakeholder financing into her business plan. To come up with the money that she needed to make her dream a reality, Kenya focused on pre-selling print advertising. Kenya approached businesses that she frequented and offered them a substantial discount for early ad purchases. Kenya was able to launch the first issue of *Blackgirl* with her savings and the money she made on sales of advertising, and has been in business ever since.[38]

Sell Gift Cards and Certificates

When retail gift cards became popular a few years ago, Colleen Stone, CEO at InSpa Corp., a Seattle day-spa chain, saw what prepaid gift cards could do for her business. Accounting for more than 25% of InSpa's incoming cash flow, "It's like borrowing cash from your customers," says Colleen about gift cards.[39] Since gift cards often go unredeemed for nearly a year, businesses that sell them can use that cash in the interim—like an interest-free loan from next year's customers.

Sell Stock in Your Company

Angeil Brown, 20, of Houston, Texas, along with nine of her friends, decided to start a photography business. They needed to buy supplies, such as cameras, film, and developing equipment.

Not having any luck coming up with money needed to start the business, one teacher gave them a great idea: sell stock in their company. That's when the partners sold shares of their new company to interested parents, friends, and teachers for $1 each. In return, stockholders would evenly split 10% of the photography business profits.[40]

Be careful when you issue your company stock. Craig Newmark, founder, of Craigslist, heavy-handedly issued large amounts of stock to employees, not thinking it would be worth anything. It was a big mistake because e-Bay was able to buy a 25% stake in Craigslist from a former employee.[41]

Borrowing from Banks

It has never been easier for young people to borrow money from a bank. There are several options available. Young Americans Bank (YAB) in Denver, Colorado, is the only FDIC-insured bank in America that caters solely to customers under the age of 22. YAB is one of a growing number of lenders serving youths across America. While these lenders make it easier for teens to get loans, they do often require an adult co-signer.

Call on community banks in the area where you will offer your business. Many smaller banks take pride in helping small business owners, no matter what their age.

Borrowing from Credit Unions

Another option available for teens borrowing start-up money is from a credit union. To date there are 20 youth credit unions across the country. The San Francisco Youth Credit Union Program (YCUP) was started in May of 1997 and has monies invested by over 20 young people ages 6–18, and the help of the local Community Economic Development Association and the Federal Credit Union. The YCUP has over $6,000 in assets and offers loans up to $100 to its members.

Dollars for Dreams is the youth branch of Alternatives Federal Credit Union in Ithaca, New York. It offers members (with an adult co-signer) loans up to $500 with a maximum payback term of two years at 10.5% interest.

Micro Loans

You could be eligible for a micro loan. You can jump-start your business or expand an existing company with a loan from the U.S. Small Business Administration and their Micro Program. The loans, up to $25,000, are made through selected nonprofit lending organizations. Before you can apply for the loan, other sources of financing—including personal assets—must be used first. Most of the loans made under this program are less than $10,000. For more information about micro loans for start-up business owners or other business loans, call (800) 827-5722 or visit www.sba.gov.

Person-to-Person Money Lending

Similar to micro lending institutions, Internet-based, person-to-person lending sites are an alternative to big banks. One, named Prosper, set up shop in the San Francisco Bay area last April. Zopa, a one-year-old British service with a membership base of nearly 70,000—60% lenders, will be setting up shop this summer in California. Person-to-Person lenders offer consumers better rates than they can get from traditional lenders and banks and, for investors, higher yields than those offered by the same.

When Erica Lyn Townshend's dog Buddy had a wounded paw, the vet gave him a plastic cone collar to prevent him from chewing on the wound. Not wanting her dog to wear the collar, Erica sewed an elastic strap onto a long sock, placed the strap around the dog's body, and put the sock on his leg—dubbing it the Strock. Then she set out to make Strocks in her home using a sewing machine.

Then, Erica quit her job at IBM to form her Longmont, Colorado company, Best Buddy Pet Products. Not having luck with her first two calls to two veterinary hospitals, Erica's luck changed with her third call at another veterinary hospital. Part of a 600-location chain, the head doctor at the clinic recommended the Strock to the board of directors.

Erica now needed money to mass produce, but both her local bank and the U.S. Small Business Administration turned down her loan applications due to her past credit history among other reasons. Hearing about Prosper.com, under the username All4Buddy, Erica landed a $9,500 loan from a group of 77 individual lenders.

Erica did not win her first loan request (with Prosper) of $25,000 — with an interest rate of 12.5%. On her second try, she requested $9,900 — with an 11% interest rate, but, that too, was denied. Finally, on her third request, $9,500 — with an interest rate of 13%, was accepted. [42]

To apply for a loan, borrowers sign up for a free membership in Prosper, which performs a credit check. Borrowers then post loan requests on Prosper's site, listing the loan amount (up to $25,000), the maximum interest rate they are willing to pay, the intended use of the loan, and the duration of the auction (up to seven days). Your credit score and income ratio will also be posted on your site. Borrowers then wait for lenders to offer loans at interest rates at or below the borrower's requested rate. If the loan is funded, Prosper deposits the cash in the borrower's account in less than one week. Prosper receives 1% of the loan amount up front and lenders pay an annual fee of .5 percent.

Entrepreneurial Grants

Entrepreneurial grants are monies that are given to entrepreneurs and not required to be paid back. Beware, however, of any person or organization promising to find you a small business grant for a fee. Grants can also take the form of a contest. Every year Whirlpool promotes its Whirlpool Brand Mother of Invention Grant, giving prizes of up to $20,000 to winners for innovative ideas.

The Green Bay Area Chamber of Commerce Small Business Council (SBC) and Partners in Education (PIE) provide business-oriented middle and high school students with the opportunity to put their business aspirations into practice. Students who have a

46

unique, needed-by-the-marketplace business idea, and who submit the best business plans, have the chance to win grants up to $500 each.

Another organization, Trickle Up, provides a grant of $700 in two installments ($500, then $200) through community agencies to low-income entrepreneurs. For more information about this grant, call (866) 246-9980 or visit www.trickleup.org.

Youth Entrepreneur Venture offers grants in the range of $50 to $1,000 to any student in North America, ages 8 to 18. They award grants to teens who start businesses emphasizing community service. When Jeffrey Rodriguez and John Serrano, now both 20, owners of Latin Artists in Brooklyn, New York, needed start-up capital to get their custom airbrush studio and community art center up and running, they applied for a grant from Youth Venture. Upon being awarded a $1,000 grant from Youth Venture, Jeffrey and John agreed to fulfill a community need, which they did by offering free art lessons to neighborhood kids.[43] To find out if your area provides grants to young entrepreneurs, contact your city's Chamber of Commerce. It might be able to direct you to different organizations that offer such grants.

Federal Grant Agencies

In the year 2000, Miller Harris, 37, fulfilled her dream of a career in perfumery. To obtain money to start her self-titled perfume and boutique, Miller combined her savings with a government grant to open her first shop in the Mayfair section of London. Now, Miller sells more than twenty scents, along with oils, lotions and candles. Recently a Miller Harris boutique opened inside Saks Fifth Avenue in Manhattan, which, to date, makes five shops — including two in London, one in Paris and another in Tokyo.[44]

Over 1,000 grant programs are offered by the 26 Federal grant-making agencies. These programs fall into 21 categories defined by the Catalog of Federal Assistance, and include agriculture, arts, business and commerce, community development, consumer protection, disaster prevention and relief, education, employment, food and nutrition, health, housing, law, legal services, to name a few. Visit www.grants.gov and select from their grant categories to learn more about the agencies that offer related grants.

Agricultural Grants

Joshua Onysko, now 29, is the founder of organic skin and body care company Pangea Organics in Boulder, Colorado. When Joshua started his company in 2001, he began making soaps using palm kernel oil instead of soybean oil. Palm kernel oil, a vegetable oil obtained from the fruit of the oil palm tree, is often found in soaps and other skin care products. Realizing that palm oil is one of the most destructive oils on the earth in terms of habitant annihilation, Joshua wanted to create a product that didn't depend on an ingredient that could trigger a clearing of rain forests, making way for oil palm plantations.

Joshua sought out an agricultural grant that would enable him to finance a soy-based skin and body care product for consumers while, at the same time, save threatened habitat species. With the help of an annual $100,000 grant from the Western U.S. Agricultural Trade Association (www.wusata.org), Joshua has been able to extend Pangea Organics' reach to 14 different countries. U.S. consumers can find Pangea Organics in natural food stores like Whole Foods and Wild Oats.[45]

Research-Oriented Grants

The Small Business Innovation Research (SBIR) and the Small Business Technology Transfer (STTR) are programs that give grants to research-oriented businesses. The SBIR program grants up to $100,000 to small businesses who spend six months researching the public benefits of their product. The STTR program offers the same, only they request that you spend one year on researching the merits of a new technology. Information on both programs can be found at www.sba.gov/sbir/indexsbir-sttr.html.

Rural Business Grants

States with lots of farms are making more grants available to businesses through a program funded (primarily) by the National Science Foundation called EPSCoR (Experimental Program to Stimulate Competitive Research). This program is designed to encourage scientific research in rural areas. There are 15 states, in addition, where businesses are also eligible for grants—although rules differ from state to state. South Carolina lets you do practically anything with its grants, which run between $3,000 and $20,000. Vermont, on the other hand, prefers companies that do crucial experiments or buy a piece of equipment. Charlotte Gruner of Casper, WY, founder of the software company Pronghorn Scientific, was the recipient of a $5,000 EPSCoR grant, which she used to attend a conference for grant writers. Since that initial grant Charlotte has received over $1 million in additional federal grants. Charlotte believes that had she not received EPSCoR's initial grant, she never would have received other funding.[46]

Look for Equity Investors

Equity investors become part owners in your business when they loan you money. They also share the business risks and its financial success. Who can become an equity investor? Any person who is willing to invest in you and your business when you are looking for start-up cash.

When James Carpenter, 16, began giving private lessons from his home to would-be cheerleaders preparing for tryouts, his business grew faster than he had expected. James wanted to expand, offering summer camps for cheerleading. Not only did he need to rent a studio, but also he needed to hire instructors, purchase their uniforms, and other business supplies. The start-up money he needed totaled $3,000. James' parents became equity investors when they invested in his business.[47]

Angel Investors

Angel investing has been around for many years. Angel investors are individuals, such as family or friends, and even some organizations, that provide funding to get businesses through their development phases, often for a large equity stake of 25% to 40% or more. This means that they typically will own 25% to 40% of your company. Angel investors are typically people who have money and are actively looking for true "ground floor" investment opportunities, usually a business opportunity within his or her community or a business that was recommended by another investor. Angel investors cannot be found in the Yellow Pages. If you know of a wealthy relative or a local organization that sponsors youth-related programs, present your business plan to them in a professional manner. According to the University of New Hampshire's Center for Venture Research, the pre-eminent entity conducting research on angel investors, angel investors contributed more than $22 billion to 48,000 entrepreneurial ventures in 2004.[48]

When is the best time for an entrepreneur to seek angel funding? When a business is at the go-to-market stage. By this point you will have a working prototype that you are able to show to the investor so they can see how it works. This is also a good time for angel investors to advise entrepreneurs on what not to do.

Probably the most famous angel investment was the $100,000 check that Sun Microsystems co-founder Andy Bechtolsheim made out to Google's Larry Page and Sergey Brin. Once Google's incorporation papers were completed and filed, Larry and Sergey used the check to move out of their dorm room and into the marketplace with Google. Amazon.com, the Body Shop, Kinko's, and Starbucks all got their starts with the help of angel investors.[49]

Look for Angels Close to Home

Look to friends and family to invest in your business. That's what Carolina Brauschweig did in 2004 when she created her company, CMB Sweets. But before she approached her father for a $15,000 loan, Carolina bootstrapped CMB Sweets through her own personal savings and side jobs. Only when she put all of her own personal resources into her business did she accept a $15,000 loan from her father.[50]

Abbey Fleck of White Bear Lake, Minnesota, was only 8 years old when she created the Makin Bacon® dish. One Saturday morning Abbey watched her dad cook some bacon in the microwave. Noticing the bacon grease splattering inside the microwave, Abbey thought that there must be a cleaner way to cook bacon in the microwave. By the end of that day, she had the answer. She drew up the sketch of her idea and showed it to her dad. Not long after, Abbey and her father came up with the Makin Bacon® dish.

The Flecks presented their Makin Bacon® dish to big retailers like Kmart and Wal-Mart, but were turned away at first. However, when they struck a deal with Armor Bacon, they got their wish—a national distribution agreement with Wal-Mart. But what they didn't have was the cash required to make the 100,000 dishes Wal-Mart required.

Abbey's grandfather became an angel investor. To come up with the cash, he took out a loan on his farm to give Abbey and her dad the money they needed. Abbey's company, A de F Inc., which she co-owns with her father, brings in royalties of more than $1 million every year selling Makin Bacon® dishes.[51]

Attracting Capital and Funding

There are several sites on the Internet that can help you learn more about attracting capital and funding for your start-up business, such as www.TannedFeet.com, www.StartUpBiz.com, and www.BarryMoltz.com. Angel Capital Association, a nonprofit organization, publishes a directory of investor groups by region.

Grow Your Own Money Branches

Grow your own branches if your money tree is dried-up. When Galit Strugano, then 23, and her mother watched the 1999

Academy Awards show, Galit noticed that many celebrities were wearing sparkling eye makeup. Sparkling makeup was not popular back then, so Galit figured that in order to wear such makeup, most women applied the glitter to a makeshift base of Chapstick or Vaseline on the eyelid—often with disastrous results.

Galit, at the time, was a makeup artist/food server, and her business money tree was dry. That's when her mother helped Galit create her own money branches. Galit's mother persuaded a chemist they found through the Yellow Pages to not only take a chance on the young entrepreneur, but also to waive the expensive lab fees. The chemist agreed to charge Galit only what she could afford. Their next effort, finding a packaging company, turned out fruitless. That's when Galit got creative and bought jelly bean jars from a craft store and had her mother's friend redecorate the caps. Working on her own from home, Galit was able to place her sparkle sets at several trendy stores in the Los Angeles area. Business proved successful, as each store sold out of the product, girlactik, in the first month.[52] You can find celebrities like Lindsay Lohan and Alicia Keys glowing with girlactik. Galit sells her products in boutiques, beauty stores, and on www.girlactik.com. In all, Galit was able to get her glamorous makeup line to market with start-up capital of $1,800, all financed by tip money that she had saved.

On the 4th Floor, Start Your Own Business, you will learn about many business opportunities. I have included several business ideas that will aide you in your pursuit of a perfect business to operate, no matter what age of a Generation Y-er you are.

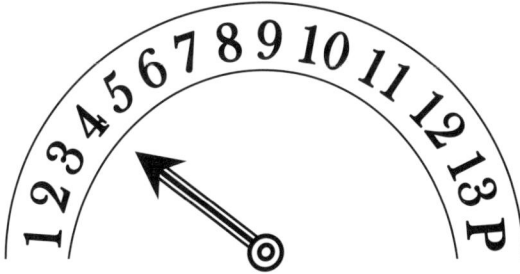

4th Floor

Start Your Own Business

"If you're going to be thinking, you may as well think big."
~Donald Trump

Generation Y-ers—the new face of entrepreneurship—are starting their own businesses earlier than any past generation. These young entrepreneurs have come a long way from running lemonade stands. Today, people as young as 13, sometimes younger, are starting and running full-fledged service and manufacturing businesses. IKEA, the worldwide retailer, was started in 1943 by a 17-year-old Swede named Ingmar Kamprad. You could be the next Ingmar!

Building your business vision slowly and staying focused on your goals should be your first concern. Your business goal should be to attract more customers than just your relatives and friends. You want to reach the public. Don't be afraid to start small, keep an eye out for new ideas, and try, try, try again.

Where Do Bright Ideas Come From?

Great business ideas come from many places. For business ideas, focus on your personal experiences, hobbies, interests, and talents. Youngsters with inventive minds should not be afraid to come up with creative, innovative ideas for a new business, the kind no one has thought of yet. At the same time, don't discount tried-and-true businesses like lawn care and babysitting. A combination of both can make an ordinary idea into extraordinary one. Know that success doesn't come from one brilliant idea, but from a bunch of small decisions. The "Teen Entrepreneur Guide to Owning a Small Business," at www.sba.gov/teens, is a Small Business Association website that answers questions like, "Where do great ideas come from?"

To really ignite your creative spark, brainstorm with friends, family members, and mentors—people who bring a varied array of talents and opinions to the table. Since young minds are often untainted by the "it can't be done" mentality, you can allow yourself to think, "What if?" You can't force creativity, but you can allow it.

Exercise your way to a more creative business mind. The beneficial effects of exercise on the ability to think creatively comes from Rhode Island College researchers, led by department chair of marketing and management David Blanchette. Published in the 2005 *Creativity Research Journal*, sixty adults (ages 18 to 27) took the Torrance Tests of Creative Thinking three times. These tests ask participants to look at abstract images and descriptions of situations and then to create alternative explanations, descriptions, and ideas. The test takers performed the same task once after being sedentary, once after 30 minutes of exercise (at a heart rate of 140 beats per minutes doing an exercise of their choice), and once more after 30 minutes of exercise followed by two hours of rest. Their findings were that exercise resulted in significantly higher Torrance scores on the total number of ideas the test takers came up with, the ideas' originality, and how well the test takers could elaborate on the ideas. Creativeness didn't stop when exercise ended—positive effects of exercise on creativity was just as high two hours after exercising![53]

What is the Recommended Age to Start a Business?

To peg an age to any of the businesses listed below is absurd because people mature at different times. Kids, teens, and young adults differ in height, strength, and even need for adult supervision where applicable. If I had told my son, Turner, that he needed to be older than 7 to begin his pet care business, he might never have started a business at all! And he certainly would not have become the owner of a rental property at 13!

Luke Lannini and Kevin Corcoran, both 14, of Tucson, Arizona, are the owners of Warp Speed Computer Repair. Although most of their customers are within biking distance, some of their customers have to bring their computers to Luke and Kevin because the boys can't drive. For now, the under-age-for-driving entrepreneurs have had to adjust their service so that their clients come to them. That will change in the future when the boys are older and have driver's licenses and cars to drive.[54]

Being Taken Seriously

Underage people tend to not be taken seriously. Sometimes adults think that teens are inexperienced and unprepared, so they don't consider a teen and his business seriously. Teens need to work extra hard to show that they are capable of the business they are running. Adnan Mohammad, 14, of Brooklyn, New York, and owner of Unlimited Web Solutions, has the answer for his biggest problem, a lack of consideration by adult clients. He suggests that teen entrepreneurs hire adults to accompany them to meetings, as well as dressing in business attire, which shows your clients you mean business.[55]

When Devin Lazerine began publishing *Rap-Up*, a hip-hop and R&B magazine, at the age of 15, he knew that his age would be an issue. Devin sent e-mails to everyone rather than use the telephone, so that people in the industry would not know how young he was. One time, however, Devin returned home from school to learn that his mother had intercepted a phone call that came to him from the marketing manager of the group Destiny's Child. His mother had made the mistake of telling her that Devin wasn't in to take her call because he was still in high school.

"The marketing manager was shocked," says Devin. "She thought I was just a teenager who wanted to meet Destiny's Child." Devin convinced the group's marketing manager that he was for real, and the fact that he had been featured on VH-1's "FanClub: Destiny's Child" program convinced the marketing manager that he was serious.[56]

Avoiding Scams

Do you ever see advertisements trying to sell you vending machines? They tell you to invest a certain amount of money and promise you that you can make more than $7,000 per month. There are vending machine companies that even promise to line up 25 locations eager to have the machines installed.

One young person in Maryland saw the candy vending machine offer as the perfect way to earn money. And before she invested in the business, she did her research. She called the Better Business Bureau to confirm that there were no complaints against the company. She even called the referrals the company provided her with, and they told her that they were making loads of money. She event went to Alabama to visit the company selling the vending machines. When everything checked out, she purchased the 25 vending machines.

Unfortunately for the young investor, this is when everything fell apart. The investor went to deliver the machines to each of the 25 locations provided by the company, and every one turned her down. The "referrals" turned out to be bogus because they were paid to lie. This scammer paid $200 to someone to pose as a satisfied customer. Another similar scammer had spent $30,000 on a voice changer and satellite phone to disguise his voice and location when he talked to unsuspecting customers.

Fraudulent business opportunities are common, with nearly a million incidents in 2004 alone.[57] Other scams to look out for, besides the proverbial "stuffing envelopes," include medical billing systems, DVD rental machines, and Internet kiosks. No company can offer guarantees, so walk away if they do. If something sounds too good to be true, it probably is. If you have suspicions about an offer or you think a story is a hoax, start your research by looking it up at www.snopes.com or www.urbanlegends.about.com.

If you are convinced that a business is "the one" to buy into, run the opportunity past your banker or a friend with business experience, as well as a lawyer, who can spot fine-print limitations and loopholes in any contract the company may ask you to sign. Also check with someone in your state attorney general's office who has experience with scams. Furthermore, never trust a business opportunity that isn't licensed by its state.

It's possible to make money with vending machines. In fact, one teen who worked at a golf course was given the blessing to install one vending machine in the clubhouse. He made a sizeable income from that venture. Several years later, one vending machine at a time, this Generation Y-er has over 70 vending machines scattered throughout his city, earning him a fortune— one vending machine at a time.

Liking What You Do

Running a business because you want to make money is an admirable ambition. But make sure you are passionate about the business you've chosen to operate. Passion is what creates breakthroughs when a business encounters obstacles. You need a combination of both ingredients to make a success of yourself and of your product or service. If you are working just to earn money, it will show in the work you do. If you don't like what you do, choose another business to operate that is in line with your interests. If you love what you do, money will follow. Harvey Mackay, a famous entrepreneur, said, "Find something you love to do, and you'll never have to work a day in your life."

Businesses You Can Start with Little Cash

Below is a list of businesses Generation Y-ers can operate, most with little (or no) cash. While many websites have included age ranges for various jobs, I try not to recommend ages for any of these businesses, as a responsible person of any age can operate the same business. Generation Y-ers can decide what businesses would be appropriate for them by weighing their likes, dislikes, talents, hobbies, dreams, and personal goals.

Acting or Modeling

If you are a ham on stage, consider becoming a professional actor or model. To see if you have what it takes to enter these finicky businesses, visit established agencies. Take acting courses. Get involved with junior theatre.

As an actor, you will need an agent. Getting an agent is probably the single most important thing a professional actor can do if he or she wants to act. An agent will represent his talent: you, the client. The agent will submit you for roles and try to get you seen by casting directors. He or she will take at least 10% of your gross pay from every job that he or she books for you. You will also need a professional portfolio, at your expense. This portfolio will include a number of recent photographs. A quality talent agency will allow you to obtain your own needed photos, or it can recommend a photographer. Do not affiliate with an agency that will only take you if you sign up with a certain school or if money is required up front.

Modeling agencies have "open calls," a time when new models can see an agent. He or she will tell you if you have potential, if they have space for your look or abilities, and if you can be marketable. Due to the number of people who visit talent agencies, representatives are blunt, so don't let one rejection send you to a 5 a.m. newspaper delivery job! If you do get asked to be a part of the agency's team, there are several things you need to know.

As a model, you will need both an agent and a portfolio, as previously mentioned. If an agency really wants you on board, and you don't have the money to pay for the portfolio, it may front the money, then take it out of your first earnings. As a model, you will go on "go-sees," that is, go and see if a particular job matches your look or talent. (Underage actors/models need a parent or guardian to accompany them on "go-sees." In the event they are hired for jobs, a parent or guardian will—at that time— sign work contracts and agree to have the actor/model at the job site on time, usually at 8:00 a.m. the next day!)

Both acting and modeling jobs are short-lived careers, so it is very important to save and invest as much money as you can while you are working. As an actor or model, jobs may cease entirely after your first assignment, continue sporadically, or be in full bloom. However your acting or modeling career ends, remember that it is only a temporary job, even if you do make it to A-list actors or supermodel status.

There is an old saying in the show business industry, "You can make a killing, but you can't make a living." Actor David Spade has some sound financial advice for anyone in the acting industry, and the same should apply to the modeling industry: "Acting is fleeting," says David. "You should save your money." Furthermore, it can only help your future if you continue your education through college while acting or modeling. Even actress and model Cindy Crawford has a college degree!

Few people can become A-list actors or supermodels, but it is possible to have a successful acting or modeling career even if you are not very tall or thin. Nowadays consumers want to see what clothes or beauty products look like on someone "just like them." As a result, there are acting and modeling opportunities for people of all heights, shapes, sizes, and looks.

Pricing Your Acting or Modeling Jobs

As a beginning actor or model, you don't have much say about what you are paid. You will most likely be paid by the full day or half-day wage, less agency commission. As you obtain more work, you will have better work to choose from, at a higher pay.

Most actors and models have expenses to cover even before they land their first acting or modeling job, so this is one type of job that may take some time before you will realize a profit—if ever. The operating costs generally include a portfolio, clothing and accessories, acting and modeling classes, hair, makeup, SAG (Screen Actor's Guild) and AFTRA (American Federation of Television and Radio Artists) union dues, and travel expenses. Once you're employed you will need to pay your agent's commission, and keep your portfolio up-to-date.

Promoting Your Acting or Modeling Career

When you begin your acting or modeling career, your agency will use some of the proof photographs from your portfolio to create your composite card. This card includes your name, stats (hair color, eye color, height, age range, etc.), various poses in a variety of outfits, as well as a full head shot. This card will be distributed by your agency to various businesses they serve. You will be required to take composite cards to your auditions and go-sees, leaving them with booking agents. If you model, you might be expected to hand out composite cards to area businesses. If the businesses want to hire you, they will contact your agent, who is listed on your composite card, to book you. As a model, you may get work on your own and be paid directly for the work. It is best, however, that you take out a commission to give to your agent. This shows your agent that you are a fair business person and that you expect them to work as hard for you as you do for them.

Looking At Your Bottom Line

Kelsey Lewis, 10, of Lancaster, California, is a child actress. Kelsey began her acting career at the age of 4, appearing in several TV commercials. At the age of 7, Kelsey had her big break, appearing in pop singer Pink's music video for a song called "Family Portrait." Last year Kelsey had her first film role, co-starring in the made-for-TV movie *Samantha: An American Girl Holiday*. In 2005 Kelsey's earnings totaled $14,000. Unfortunately her work expenses, for the same year, were $12,000.[58] Make sure you weigh your options after viewing your balance sheet. Would you be better off if you had a job that had fewer expenses, allowing you to keep more of the money you earned from your work? In Kelsey's example, it may be worth it to her to spend $12,000 while earning $14,000. Although she only saved $2,000 last year, her bigger goal is to be hired for a prime acting position that will generate a big paycheck.

Creating Your Own Acting or Modeling Agency

If an acting or modeling career doesn't pan out for you, consider creating your own acting and/or modeling agency, as Shelley Barrett did when she was 21. Shelley was not a professional model. After college she took a receptionist job at a modeling agency and soon found there was a real need for a boutique modeling agency. She set out to create one. For 10 years, Shelley has owned and operated Shelley's Management Group, comprising three modeling and acting agencies. After gaining firsthand experience working with models on their hair and makeup, in 2002, Shelley identified a niche in the market for innovative, quick-fix, multi-purpose solutions. The synergy of fashion and beauty naturally merged in Shelley's businesses. ModelCo's Lash Wand Heated Eyelash Curler was then launched. Shelley is now the creator of over 70 beauty products, with the likes of Paris Hilton, Kylie Minogue, and Elle Macpherson telling the world that they love her products. Now that has the "wow" factor![59]

Many small businesses and marketers want to get their products or services in celebrities' hands but don't know how. The *Celebrity Black Book* (www.celebrityblackbook.com), edited by Jordan McAuley, is the solution. It provides contact information for nearly 55,000 celebrities, including their representatives, companies, and addresses.[60] According to a survey found in *Entrepreneur* magazine, 72% of 'Tweens—youths between the age of 10 and 13—say seeing their favorite celebrity use a brand makes them want to use it.[61] So, if you are marketing to this group, look for celebrity endorsements, as do the Scissor Sisters Samantha, Caillianne, and Chloe Beckerman. The sisters—Sam and Cailli, 26, are twins; Chloe's 23—have created a promising fashion start-up, designing women's wear, handbags, and accessories. The sisters ship samples to celebrities like Sienna Miller and Lindsay Lohan — a practice known as "gifting" — hoping the celebrities are photographed wearing their designs.[62]

☼

Artist

If you are a painter, it is not impossible to become a famous artist and earn an impressive income, as Olivia Bennett, 16, from Southlake, Texas, has. From the moment Olivia held a paint brush, she had the flair of a talented artist. By the age of 6, Olivia was painting vivid canvases of flowers in bloom. When a neighbor saw one of her first paintings, she offered to buy it for $50. At age 11, Olivia was paid $350 for a painting that she had for sale at a local fair. Not long after, Olivia and her parents were towing her paintings in a trailer to festivals across the state.

By the age of 14, Olivia was earning thousands of dollars per show. That's when she had the idea to use part of her sales money to open her own gallery, The Olivia Bennett Art Gallery. Who are some of Olivia's customers? President Bush and Sharon Osbourne are two of many customers who own her artwork, which today fetches from $500 for a signed print, up to $75,000 for a large canvas. Now 16, Olivia spends her days studying biology, teaching an art class, running her gallery — and painting.[63]

Pricing Your Artwork

You need to keep an accurate tally of the time you spend creating your masterpieces and figure out what you would like to earn per hour. At a minimum, you should be earning minimum wage. Once you become an established artist and your work is in demand, you can set some awesome prices, as Olivia does with her work.

Promoting Your Artwork

Selling your artwork at fairs is a start. Contact the Chamber of Commerce in the city where you want to sell your art to find out when, where, and who manages the fair. As you obtain a bigger inventory of wares, consider selling your artwork on the Internet, either on your own website or at another artist's online gallery. Eventually consider opening your own gallery. Or, if you wish for a smaller space to sell your art, rent space in front of a business that will allow you to set up a kiosk to market your artwork. Offer restaurants an opportunity to place your artwork in their establishments. In exchange your contact information can be prominently placed on or near your work. (Always place contact information on the back of your artwork so that admirers can contact you for future business.)

☼

Auto Detailing Service

If you are a tidy and detail-oriented person by nature, an auto detailing service is a natural for you. Detailing cars is, nevertheless, hard work. If the work doesn't scare you, then auto detailing can be very rewarding. To begin in this business, it is recommended that you start by detailing your own family and friends' cars. As you improve at it, you can move into an auto detailing business. You will soon discover differences between amateur and professional auto detailing. You will learn what materials work best, which ones last longer, and how to select and purchase supplies for your business.

Starting an auto detailing service is not difficult, nor does it require much money. There are many websites you can visit if you Google "How to Start an Auto Detailing Business." Several sites offer helpful, free information to help you get started on your business. Auto Detailing: Secrets of the Experts (http://www.web-cars.com/index.html) is one such site.

To get additional auto detailing education, visit The Detail King at www.detailking.com. This website provides educational information that will guide you to success in the auto detailing business. You can also visit an auto products store and learn what products are available and how to use them.

Pricing Auto Detailing Services

Most auto detailers have three price packages: Just Clean, Real Clean, and Extra Clean. A quality auto detailing service, 2 Clean Auto Detailing, Inc., has a helpful website, http://2cleanauto.com/detailing.htm, that includes the various services each package offers and its prices. Keep in mind that 2 Clean Auto Detailing, Inc. is an established, professional service, so your prices shouldn't equal those of a professional at the beginning. Look at their site to learn what parts of vehicles are cleaned in the various packages offered and how the prices change from one package to the next.

Promoting an Auto Detailing Service

Start out with word of mouth to family and friends. Offer to clean their cars, at a discounted rate, to boost your experience and knowledge. Then ask these people for recommendations, or better yet, have them put in a good word for you through printed testimonials. Pass out coupons and special discount flyers (with those printed testimonials) in your neighborhood introducing your service.

When you promote your auto detailing service, state how your service will be different from other services. Nicole Baran, a 15-year-old from Wheat Ridge, Colorado, made her auto detailing service, Interior Car Detailing While You Work, well, just that. Not only would Nicole detail her customers' cars, but for extra convenience, she'd do it in their workplace parking lot. The fact that people didn't have to go out of their way to have their car cleaned solidified the demand for Nicole's business. Nicole knew that her service had to be cheaper or better than her competition. [64] Another way to stand out in the auto detailing industry is to offer additional detailing options, for example, boats, recreational vehicles, aircraft, and more.

Nicole promotes her service by hanging a sign in a window of the auto she is cleaning, advertising her business. Another way to promote an auto detailing business is to attend local business conferences, during which you can distribute your business cards. And, don't forget a job well done. Your customers will spread the word. Place flyers on grocery store and office building bulletin boards. Before leaving a flyer anywhere, check with the store or office building manager for their policies on displaying flyers, as well as with your town's ordinances. Know all local laws before starting your flyer campaign.

☼

Babysitting

If you live in a neighborhood full of young kids, you have much potential in your neighborhood for a babysitting business. Though babysitting has long been a moneymaking business for teenagers, getting work isn't easy. That's why it is recommended that sitters become certified babysitters. "It's a real trend," says Julie Hunt, creator of the instruction video "Babysitting 101: Your Complete Guide to Becoming the Best Babysitter" (www.smartkids101.com/babysitting101.html). The site www.babysittingclass.com ($17.50 per class) covers child-care safety, age-appropriate games, and techniques for babysitting kids who have special needs. It also teaches sitters how to market themselves, prepare for an interview, and determine how much to charge. For other certification options, check with the YMCA (www.ymca.net) or Red Cross (www.redcross.org), which offer babysitting classes and certification at some branches.

If you are under 18, it is recommended that your parents meet the family before you start any babysitting job. Once you are hired, you will have a huge responsibility taking care of children. You can be a well-informed babysitter by having an emergency spiral notebook containing important information and emergency numbers. There are many babysitting guides on the Internet that will give you all the information you need, from safety on the job to getting picky eaters to eat.

Pricing Babysitting Services

The going rate for babysitting ranges between $4 and $10 per hour on weekdays, slightly more on weekends. It also depends on how old you are, how much experience you have, if you are CPR and First Aid certified, how many kids you are caring for, and what area you live in. For example, teen babysitters in the Washington, D.C., area command $12 to $15 an hour. You can also use your state's minimum wage as a starting point and go up from there. If you are still uncertain what to charge, Google "What Do Babysitters Charge?" on the Internet. You'll get some ideas what people charge in different parts of the United States.

Promoting a Babysitting Service

Post business cards or flyers on bulletin boards (local churches, banks, post office, Laundromats, community centers, and grocery stores). Talk with apartment building owners and real estate offices. People just moving to the area are always in need of this type of information. Let local families know that you are available to baby sit. Your parents might let their friends know of your babysitting service. If you are 18 years or older, you can register your services, for free, on www.4sitters.com/Sitter-Sign-Up.htm. Not only can you register your business on this reputable site, but you can also look for job postings. Another site to register your services is www.sittercity.com. If your town's elementary and middle schools put on plays and musicals, contact the editor of the printed program and ask how much a display advertisement or line advertisement costs. It might be worth it to advertise in a production program since young families, many of whom have small children, attend these events.

☼

Book Publisher

Christopher Paolini was only 15 when he began writing *Eragon*, his debut fantasy novel that can be found in bookstores — and on bestsellers lists — across the country. Not only did he write this incredible fantasy, the first of his *Inheritance* trilogy, he self-published it because he wanted financial and creative control.

With help from his father, the book was formatted in Adobe PageMaker for publication. Together they determined how wide the text block would be, how much space would occupy the top and bottom pages, what the chapter titles should look like, how the cover should be designed.

In time, the book was discovered by New York publisher Alfred A. Knopf, after Christopher sold over 10,000 copies on his own through self-promotion by making more than 130 presentations at bookstores, schools, libraries, and fairs around the United States. How did Knopf discover Christopher's book? One of those 10,000 copies landed in the hands of author Carl Hiaasen, who showed it to his editor at Knopf. Soon, Christopher was offered a mid-six-figure contract for the trilogy. *Eragon* was also recently optioned for a movie.[65]

Another minor who wrote and self-published a book is Alyssa Huckleberry, a teen from San Diego, California. At the age of 17, Alyssa took matters into her own hands. Not only did Alyssa write a 268-page novel, she also paid to have it published. Now she is preparing for book signings at various Barnes & Noble bookstores. What was Alyssa's version of the Great American Novel? A mystery called *Rescuing Racei*. It is full of fantasy and wizardry. With the proceeds of summer jobs, Alyssa spent just over $600 to publish her work through iUniverse. It is an affordable form of self-publishing that allows authors to pay to print books on demand. Alyssa's first printing consisted of both paperback and hard-bound versions, selling for about $20 to $30.

Alyssa was clever at writing her book. "My brothers and sister really helped me just by listening to the story. And they were my target audience," says Alyssa, whose book is tailored to adolescents. Alyssa asked her siblings what they thought would happen next in the story line. When they told her what they thought should next occur, Alyssa wrote something completely different so the book was not predictable.[66]

Looking for a Book Publisher

If you're looking for a publisher, you'll need to find an agent. Most publishers only accept agented work, so look in the front of books you like to find out who the author's agents are. You should also check out www.writersmarket.com. Publishers get many submissions, so make yours look good. To prepare a great manuscript, read *Eats, Shoots and Leaves: The Zero Tolerance Approach to Punctuation* by Lynn Truss and *Every Page Perfect: A Full-Size Writer's Manual for Manuscript Format and Submission Protocol* by Mary Lynn. Also, contact the Writer's Guild of America (www.wgaeast.org or www.wgawest.org). More help can be found at the nonprofit organization of independent literary and dramatic agents at the Association of Authors' Representatives, Inc. (http://www.aar-online.org/mc/page.do). For further information, visit www.writerswrite.com.

There was a time when it was easy to get a book published. The market, unfortunately, has shifted. Unless you are a celebrity or have an eager audience of book buyers willing to buy your book, most publishers won't even look at your manuscript, no matter how great your idea. Because of this shift in the publishing industry, many writers are turning to self-publishing, and earning even higher profits.

Publishing Your Manuscript

If you've always dreamed of having a book published, you can do it—if you know the steps to take, according to Valeria Gray, associate senior editor of Mira Books (www.mirabooks.com). If your "thing" is mysteries, read as many as you can, and write down what was best about each one: the characters, the setting, the plot, etc. Meet other writers. If you don't personally know any, ask at your library about local writing groups or local writing classes. You'll get feedback about your work as well as learning about agents, how to self-publish, and more. If you want to become an author, read *Bird by Bird* by Anne Lamott. Christopher Paolini recommends three books for you to read: *The Writer's Handbook* (Writer, Inc.), *Story* by Robert McKee, and *Characters and Viewpoint* by Orson Scott Card. Furthermore, Paolini recommends that you write about what excites and moves you the most. Be persistent and disciplined and be humble enough to accept editorial criticism and learn all you can about your craft. If you are a 'Tween or teen Generation Y-er with an idea to write a book, you're in luck! Newbery Honor winner Gail Carson Levine, author of *Ella Enchanted*, comes to a young writer's rescue with *Writing Magic: Creating Stories That Fly*—a how-to-write guide for kids.

Pitching a Book Idea to a Major Publisher

The benefit of pitching a book idea to agents and editors is that it can teach you a lot about the publishing industry. The first question they will want to ask is, "What is your platform?" A platform, essentially, includes all the ways that you, the choice writer for this book, are capable of reaching your "pre-existing" target market of book buyers. A platform creates enhanced interest in you and what your book is about, allowing you to stand above the rest. If you think of a platform as an entire wheel, you have many spokes in the wheel that make a platform possible. Each "spoke" can represent a way in which you can reach your target, i.e., have you achieved expert status in the media that enables you to easily promote your book? The stronger the spoke, the more powerful the wheel. Other "spokes" could include receiving endorsements or testimonials from leaders in the industry, a list of subscribers from your eZine, pre-arranged book speaking engagements with schools and book stores, awards you may have received on the subject you have written about or as a writer, any work featured in magazines and newspapers, even credentials that show you are the best "expert" to write this book. A platform shows a publisher many angles—ways—that your book stands a strong chance in a crowded marketplace. Simply put, a platform is what makes the difference between getting the six-figure deal or not getting a book deal at all. Know that it takes time to build a platform, so plan ahead.

Publishers want an expert on the subject and a ready-made audience of book buyers, so, if you don't have a national presence with speaking engagements, your chances of being published with a major publisher are slim. The lesson in pitching your book to an agent or editor is that you need to have a way to market and sell your book. So, before you consider approaching a major publisher or self-publishing your book, develop a marketing plan. Determine who will buy your book, how you will reach your audience, and the ways you will market your book.

Traditional Self-Publishing

If you're interested in self-publishing because you want creative and financial control, you have two primary options: self-publishing and print-on-demand (POD). If you choose to self-publish, it will involve establishing your own publishing company, contacting a cover designer, designing the interior of the book, and purchasing an International Standard Book Number (ISBN) — a unique identifier for books intended to be used commercially. Then you can have your book printed by a book binding company — usually in large quantities such as 3,000 books, at a cost per book ranging from $1.00 to $5.00. After your book is published, you will need to get it listed with the online booksellers and with the large distributors if you want your title to have a chance of being picked up by bookstores.

Print-on-Demand

Print-on-demand (POD) companies charge a set-up fee ranging from $300 to $1,000. Most POD companies will lay out your book, assign an International Standard Book Number (ISBN), print books on an as-needed basis, and get them into the inventories of the major distributors and online booksellers. POD or traditional self-publishing can allow you to transform your manuscript into a hardcover or trade paperback book — a paperback book that is typically of better production quality, larger size, and higher price than a mass-market edition—in a matter of weeks. It can take over a year for a big-name publisher to transform a manuscript into a book, and author royalties are low. Publishing yourself gives you a better opportunity to time the market and to make a hefty profit. However you choose to self-publish, an excellent book to read is *The Complete Guide to Self Publishing*, by Tom and Marilyn Ross. The revised 4th edition can be found in bookstores, on Amazon.com, or their website www.SelfPublishing Resources.com.

Non-Traditional Publishing

People who want to go directly to market with their book (and make a lot more money) don't need a traditional publisher. If you don't want to go the traditional publishing route, the URL that will lead you to a one-stop, do-it-yourself publishing shop is www.lulu.com. With Lulu.com, you upload your book and pick a design template. Lulu.com then lets you sell your book through Amazon.com, Barnes and Noble, Borders, or Lulu.com—not having to print a single copy until an order is placed (because your book only exists digitally). This on-demand technology requires no start-up cash, just a book that has potential to sell. Talk about bootstrapping your business!

How did Lulu.com come to exist? Bob Young established the business through personal disgruntlement. In 1999 Bob wrote *Under the Radar*, a book about Red Hat (shaking up of the software establishment). The book sold 20,000 copies, but Bob was irritated by the sloppiness of its editing. In addition, the publishing company had an additional 7,500 copies they were going to destroy. The book listed for $27.50, so sales were over $500,000. What was Bob's return on a half-million dollars in sales? A meager $2,752. "Why do we need gatekeepers for content?" Bob wondered. "Why can't authors go directly to the market?"[67]

Lulu.com isn't the only direct-to-market publishing option. Xlibris (Random House, www2.xlibris.com) and iUniverse (Barnes & Noble, www.iniverse.com) have been doing something similar. Even Amazon.com has its own program, BookSurge

71

(www.booksurge.com). At Xlibris, iUniverse, and BookSurge, authors pay an up-front fee of $300 to $1,600, book prices are set by the services, and royalties range from 10% to 25%. At Lulu, no money exchanges hands until a book is purchased. The book design and layout are free, and authors set the prices for books. Excluding Lulu's charge for production, the book royalty rate is 80%. To date Lulu has approximately 40,000 titles available, doing $1 million a month in sales.

Publishing Contests

If you would rather test the publishing waters by entering your writing in a contest — preferably one that gives writers feedback, you can find many book publishing/writer's contests on the Internet. But the granddaddy of them all, The Sobol Award for Fiction (www.sobolaward.com), is designed to discover new fiction writers from the United States and its territories. This contest is available to unpublished novelists 18 and over (19 in Alabama and Nebraska, and 21 in Puerto Rico) who do not have literary representation. This unique nationwide talent screener's goal is to discover and introduce new writers to the publishing industry. The 2006 Sobol Award for Fiction contest, for example, presented $100,000 to the winner; $25,000 and $10,000 to the runners up; and $1,000 to each of the seven remaining finalists. For submission information, visit their website, or write:

Sobol Literary Enterprises, Inc.
450 Seventh Avenue, Suite 2100
New York, NY 10123

Pricing Your Published Material

Look on the Internet at various booksellers and see what prices books similar to yours, in story and size, sell for. If you are self-publishing, keep in mind that the larger your book order, the less each book costs to produce. Consider the wholesale discount (usually 50%) off your cover price, because you will be wholesaling them to booksellers. After those factors are considered, include a realistic profit for yourself, and hopefully your cover price will be the right price.

Promoting Your Published Book

Now that the writing is done and the book is published, it is time to sell the book—over and over again. "Self-publishing offers the potential for huge profits," states Marilyn Ross, author of *The Complete Guide to Self-Publishing*. "Self-publishing can be the road to independence." A book is a great example of doing the work once and getting paid for it forever. I call the royalties "interest" on my investment—the time I spent writing the book.

Promoting depends on the type of book you publish. I have self-published two books on the subject of pageantry (beauty pageants), so I promote my books in an industry magazine, *Pageantry*. I also make appearances at pageants and set up booths to sell to pageant contestants and audiences. Furthermore, my books are listed with Amazon.com. If your books are sold on Amazon.com, you have an opportunity to receive its best ranking—5 stars—on reviews if your writing is excellent. "To help reviews come in, give away complimentary books to various people," says Marilyn Ross. "In return, ask that your reviewers read your book and rank your book, which, hopefully, will be 5 stars!"[68] This promotional effort will be a great tool for selling books on Amazon.com.

Alyssa Huckleberry promoted her book, *Rescuing Racei*, at local farmer's markets, on websites for Barnes & Noble and Amazon.com, at book signings at Barnes & Noble, as well as the school assembly circuit.

Julia York was only 9 when she wrote *The Kid's Guide to New Hope*, a book that shows other kids all the cool things to do in New Hope, Pennsylvania. Julia promotes her book on local talk shows and speaks to school groups about her entrepreneurial experiences. Julia's book is also sold through gift shops and convenience stores around New Hope.[69]

Bibi Schweitzer of Larchmont, New York, was 11 when she wrote and self-published *Avoiding Homesickness: Surefire Ways to*

Beat the Sleep Away Camp Blues. Bibi has sold over 1,500 copies of her book, mostly by mail order and in downloadable form from http://www.homesickness.org. Now a college student at the University of Pennsylvania's Wharton School of Business, Bibi has revised and updated the book several times.

Children's book author Wendy Reed, of Jacksonville, Florida, wrote, illustrated and self-published the picture book, *Little Lilly's Polka Dot World* (www.littlelillypress.com). Although her book is selling well at children's boutiques and at major online bookstores, Wendy promotes her book by regularly visiting kindergarten classes. "I read the book and talk to the kids about being an author and an illustrator," explains Wendy. During her visits, she gives a book to each child—having found that giving books to the kids is the best way to market a book. Not only do the kids sleep with her book, they tell their friends about the inhabitants of an imaginary polka dot world.

Collaborating to Write a Book

If writing a book by yourself seems too daunting, collaborate with friends to complete a book project. Eleven members of the Young Entrepreneurs Society (Y.E.S.!), a for-profit organization based in Whittier, California (founded by Sharon Cook, Ph.D.), did just that. In 1999 they wrote and published *Millennium Mischief*, a story of how a misadventure in the future almost changed the Millennium Rose Parade. Once published, the book was sold at the Norton Simon Museum of Art, the Getty Museum of Art, and Vroman's bookstore in southern California.

☼

Cleaning Service

People hire maid service to have freedom, independence, and time for family and friends. Stress is the number one issue with dual-working couples, and to come home to a messy house compounds the issue. People are capable of cleaning; it's the time they usually don't have. For you it means a business opportunity.

For the thousands of maids cleaning homes, it is a multi-million-dollar industry.

Twenty years ago maid service would have been considered a luxury. Now it is a necessity, even in families with one breadwinner and a you-name-it-activities parent! With this in mind, approach neighbors to see if they could benefit from your house-cleaning services. Families usually sign up for weekly or bi-weekly service, so if you can handle only once-a-week clients, hire a team of friends to become your employees if you're hired for multiple jobs. Your client may ask that you clean their home while they are at a soccer game, or when they are home. Some families only need bathrooms cleaned. Others need laundry service: washing, drying, folding, ironing, and putting away. Yet others want everything done, which might require you to team up with a friend to complete the job. Some may want just their garage cleaned, while others want it overhauled. (If you do specialize in a garage cleaning service for homeowners in your community, by the time you get all the garages cleaned and straightened up, it will be time to start all over again.) And while on the subject of cleaning, you can also run a Parking Lot Pickup service. Simply contact local businesses and offer to clean their parking lots at night or on weekends. All you need to get started is a broom, some garbage bags, a pick-up stick, and rubber gloves.

Pricing Cleaning Services

A typical full-day maid service charges around $50 to $65 per house, per day. As a beginner, your town minimum wage could be your starting point. Or you might just set a price for whatever service you will offer. For example, you might charge $8 to clean a bathroom. Test your pricing on the first few homes. You can adjust your pricing on subsequent jobs when you learn the ropes. If you perform a Parking Lot Pickup service, you can charge for the lot or by the hour.

Promoting a Cleaning Service

Call on people you know at first. You can also post flyers and business cards at the local recreation center, grocery stores, and bank lobbies. Give out flyers at soccer and baseball games. For a nominal price, purchase an ad in the season's ending game program book. Once you develop clients, invest some of your money in a classified ad in your local newspaper and Yellow Pages. Of course, offer your cleaning service to the newspaper in exchange for advertising.

☼

Curbside Home Address Reflective Painting Service

Offer a reflective home address curbside painting service to ensure that in an emergency, police, fire, and ambulance services can find the home quickly. Vivid address numbers can also aide delivery people who may otherwise have difficulty locating faded or non-existing numbers. To get this business started, you will need cans of black and white reflective curbside spray paint, and number stencils, all of which can be purchased at a hardware store. As with any new business you start, visit your local City Hall for proper permits and licenses. Consider visiting your local fire station to get any tips and recommendations to help you get this business started.

Pricing Curbside Home Address Reflective Painting Services

Prices can range from $10 to $15 per curbside. You can charge more in larger cities. Always guarantee your work against immediate fading or rain runoff.

Promoting a Curbside Home Address Reflective Painting Service

Create a flyer or brochure informing the community of your service. Knock on doors, leaving your flyer and business cards, and advertise in local newspapers. This service will greatly help the community, so send a press release to the newspaper in the town you want to serve. Include with your press release photos of yourself next to a curbside address that you just completed, maybe a before and after shot. Make sure that you mention in your printed material that house numbers are best seen when they are clearly visible from the street. Your prospective client's mail carrier may know the address, but an ambulance driver won't. A reflective home address curbside painting service can be coupled with other services you offer. Your lawn care clients might hire you to paint their curbside address numbers.

☼

Desktop Publishing

If you enjoy writing and have an eye for graphically interesting copy, desktop publishing might be the business for you. As a desktop publisher you could type résumés (promote your credibility by becoming a certified résumé writer through The National Résumé Writers' Association at www.nrwa.com; 877-843-6792), cover letters, invitations, restaurant menus, newsletters, flyers, brochures, business cards, typeset display advertisements for small businesses, design logos, even design websites (more on website designing at the end of this floor). You can also take on tasks for other small business owners and produce their letters, mailing labels, special flyers for upcoming promotions, etc. The more computer skills you have, the more you can offer. If you don't know much about desktop publishing, a host of information can be found on the Internet by Googling "How to Learn Desktop Publishing." Make sure that whatever you publish for your clients is accurate and has correct spelling and grammar. Become familiar with Quark Xpress, Adobe Pagemaker, and Adobe Illustrator software.   Visit   www.desktoppublishing.com, www.desktoppublishers.com, and www.dtpjournal.com to see what they offer in terms of technology and style.

Pricing a Desktop Publishing Service

People getting started in this business find the most difficult aspect of starting a desktop publishing business is setting prices and estimating jobs. Before you can calculate how much to charge for specific projects, you need to know how much your time is worth. That's your hourly rate. (See "Know What Your Time is Worth," on the 2nd Floor, Operate a Business.) One basic formula is Salary + Overhead + Profit/Billable Hours = Hourly Rate. This rate may need to be adjusted based on market conditions, but to arrive at a starting point, you need to figure out how much money you want or need to make, what your expenses are, how much profit you'd like to make, and how many billable hours you can put in to complete the task.

Promoting a Desktop Publishing Service

You can begin promoting your service by printing a batch of your own business cards and flyers informing people about your services. To build a client base, place ads in local newspapers or in association bulletins, such as clubs, churches, community organizations, law firms, etc. Include an advertisement for your services in high school and college newspapers as well as your local newspaper. Many desktop publishing services get lots of work from college students who don't want to type their own papers.

When Ayanna Howard from Brooklyn, New York, was 11, she began her desktop publishing business by typing a 40-page paper for a college student who didn't have a computer. Ayanna has since expanded her desktop publishing services to include designing flyers, party invitations, and greeting cards. To let people know about her services, she relies on word-of-mouth advertising. She also puts her own logo and the signature phrase

"Designed and Published by Ayanna's Creations" on the back of her work.[70] Remember to include any contact information on the back of your work so that old and new clients can reach you.

☼

eBay Store

If you want to own a store but don't want a typical store, selling on eBay could be an excellent option. An eBay store is a place on eBay where you can display all your products in one customizable place, encourage multiple orders from buyers, and maintain a larger permanent inventory than you sell through auctions. The eBay store's directory is designed to promote all stores, and you'll also have your own web address, a Universal Resource Locator (URL), that you can use as you wish. The store's e-mail marketing tool lets you send e-mails to your customers, allowing you to announce new items or specials, or to deliver other information that could entice old and new buyers into your store to shop. *The Complete Idiot's Guide to Starting an eBay Business*, by Barbara Weltman, can help establish your online business and teach you how to sell effectively using your very own eBay store.

The Process of Opening an eBay Store

The process of opening an eBay store is as simple as setting up your initial User ID. The only requirements are that you are a registered eBay seller and have a feedback of 20 or higher, or be ID verified, or have a PayPal account in good standing. The cost of an eBay store ranges from nominal to substantial, depending on the level of business you want to operate. The three levels are:

1. **Basic**. This level is ideal for sellers who are just starting out and want an affordable, easy-to-use platform for selling. A basic store is automatically listed in the eBay stores directory and appears in every category where you have items listed.
2. **Featured**. This level is designed for small-to-medium-sized sellers who want to grow their online business. A feature store rotates through a special featured section on the eBay store's home page. It receives

priority placement in "related stores" on search and listing pages. Finally, it is featured within the category directory pages where you have items listed.

3. **Anchor.** This level is the advanced solution for high-volume sellers who want maximum eBay exposure. Anchor stores offer the same benefits as featured stores, plus your store can be showcased with your logo within the eBay stores directory pages and will receive premium placement in "related stores" on search and listings pages.

Setting Up Your eBay Store

From the eBay home page, click on eBay Stores, then on "Open a Store," and follow the steps. It is best to have your store's name chosen before you begin this process.

Your eBay store name, which will also be its URL, can be a maximum of 35 characters. It is wise to choose a straightforward name that tells buyers what you sell.

Your store name must start and end with a letter or number. It cannot start with four or more consecutive letter "A's." It cannot start with an "E" followed by a number. Finally, it cannot infringe on any other company's trademark. Your store name can be the same as your User ID, as long as it meets the store name requirements. eBay's Help Center offers advice when choosing your store name. To learn more about eBay stores, visit http://stores.ebay.com.

Staffing an eBay Store

Your eBay store will be open for business 24/7/365, whether you are asleep or awake. While it doesn't need to be physically staffed around the clock, you need to pay attention to it every day. Monitor your store closely, answer questions from shoppers promptly, ship merchandise on schedule, and deal with any other customer service issues as soon as possible. Arrange for someone else to monitor the site and take care of your business when you're on vacation. If that's not possible, you can take advantage of eBay's vacation hold service.

☼

Envelope Stuffing Service

Along with a shredding service, offer an envelope stuffing service. Many small businesses have mail promotions that keep them in contact with their customers. Often the mailing is small, so businesses usually ask an employee to perform this task. If the business owner knows of your service, he might hire you. Envelope stuffing (and shredding services) can be performed at the business or outsourced to your place of business. Do not write to envelope-stuffing businesses advertised in some magazines and newspapers. These companies generally request an upfront fee, and usually that's the end of that business road. The FBI calls them scams, so stay away from them. Small, locally-owned businesses are your potential customers.

Pricing an Envelope Stuffing Service

The rate is typically the same as that of a document shredder, around $10 to $15 an hour. If you're a fast worker, charge by the job. To stuff 1000 envelopes, seal, address (with company-provided pre-addressed labels) and bundle, you might set a fee of 15 cents per envelope, which would total $150. You'll make the same amount in less time. If you're new, or slow, charge by the hour until you build speed.

Promoting an Envelope Stuffing Service

Leave your business card with business managers or owners in their establishments. Other small businesses operate from their homes, so, in order to reach these business owners, place a classified advertisement in your town newspaper. Place flyers in neighborhoods you feel have many home-based businesses.

☼

Entertainment Business

Do you have a talent with which you can entertain groups of people? Do you play a musical instrument, act in mime, sing, or perform magic? There is a demand for such entertainment, and magician Andrew Schneider, 14, of Tomball, Texas, knows it. As the owner of Mystifying Magic, Andrew markets his magic shows to adults with children. Performing a half dozen times a week, mostly at birthday parties and corporate events that include family, Andrew makes over $30,000 a year.[71] Jeremy Scott, 17, from Racine, Wisconsin, is a talented saxophonist. A saxophonist since 1990, Jeremy averages around 150 performances a year at weddings, jazz festivals, and even on TV and radio.[72] David and Paul DiMuzio, 15 and 13, from Charlotte, North Carolina, are known as The Dazzling DiMuzio Brothers. They perform together as jugglers and on unicycles.[73] Spencer Horsman, 12, is a ventriloquist from Baltimore, Maryland. A ventriloquist since 1994, Spencer not only performs before large groups, but also he recently began giving motivational speeches. He has his sights on performing on television.[74]

Pricing Entertainment

Sara Klinger, 18, of San Francisco, California, is a performing magician. Sara charges $100 for a 30-minute show. In 1999, Sara performed over 250 shows.[75] Consider charging more if there are going to be a lot of children at an event. Also, you might charge more to attend events in local bookstores or malls as opposed to the backyard birthday party.

Pianists, singers, or saxophonists can command the same as a performing magician, more if they are well-seasoned. If you have CDs of your music, or perhaps a DVD or VHS tape of magic tricks and instructions, ask to sell them at the function you are performing at. Maximize your time and profits. Get all agreements in writing.

Promoting Your Entertainment Business

If you perform at birthday parties, ask that your magnetic business cards or company logo pencils be included in the birthday goodie bags. Post flyers on local community bulletin boards and keep a stash of business cards ready to give to people you meet.

Remember to include bartering in your advertising plan. If you are performing at an event that publishes a printed program, ask to have your advertisement included in their program free of charge. If you are required to pay for the advertising, ask for a discount. Contact the publisher of your local advertisement flyer and town newspaper to find out if that person would be interested in trading services. Offer to entertain at the newspaper's company picnic or Christmas party in exchange for advertising. Furthermore, if you are performing as a musician at a company event, ask that part of your performance agreement include an advertisement in the company's newsletter or on its website. If you donate your talents to local schools, ask that your advertisement be included in their printed materials (such as programs, school newspapers, and campus newsletters). Consider purchasing an advertisement in the school's yearbook. If there is a marquee, ask that your name be posted on this medium. This will aid you in creating business awareness. People not attending your event who happen to drive by can see your name on the marquee.

Become creative in advertising your entertainment business. If you have a separate business telephone line, advertise your business on your recorded message. If you are using your home telephone line for business, include information about your service at the end of a family voice-mail message. A singer can sing jingles about his service wherever he goes. Wear your company logo and telephone number on a T-shirt to promote your business. Magician Andrew Schneider promotes his service on trading cards, brochures, and a website. Other ideas about advertising can be found on the 7th Floor, Advertise.

☼

Flyer Delivery Service

A flyer delivery service can work two ways. One approach is to sell advertisements, publish your own flyer, and distribute it yourself. Another is to distribute a company's own flyer.

Christopher Short, 17, of Cape Creek, Arizona, self-publishes two community classified advertisement flyers through his company, C.S. International, Inc. The idea to publish two community advertisement flyers came to him when his younger sister wanted to advertise their Red Cross-certified skills. When Christopher saw a local flyer, he saw the potential in having other people pay him to advertise. Christopher and his sister sold 11 advertisements at $9 each, so their first issue was launched. On skates, Chris delivered the flyers to over 1,000 homes in their community. Advertising doubled for the second issue, and it only got better from there. After four years working in this field, Christopher is personally worth nearly a quarter of a million dollars! What is Christopher's next plan? To purchase his own printing press.[76]

Create a team of delivery people and one supervisor to distribute flyers. Professional companies that provide this service will have a team of six to eight workers, plus a supervisor to oversee the job. They also have cars and planned maps of the areas in which they will distribute. As a young entrepreneur, it's best to tackle smaller areas, with a smaller distribution—at least until you're familiar with routes and pacing.

Pricing Flyer Delivery Services

One company charges $550 for 5000 flyers, placing one flyer on every household door in neighborhoods of the client's choice. For the same number of flyers distributed, piggy back, the cost is $350. ("Piggy back" means another business—or more—will have their flyer delivered at the same address and time.)

If you want to own a community flyer and sell advertisements like Christopher Short, research similar flyers to come up with your own competitive prices and marketing strategy.

Promoting a Flyer Delivery Service

Visit local businesses and ask if they would like to hire you to post their own flyers in targeted neighborhoods. You can present (on paper) a cost comparison that shows them how valuable a flyer delivery service can be. For example, by using the post office, the business pays the cost of a stamp per flyer distributed. With your delivery service, they might only pay 8 cents per flyer distributed.

If you own a community flyer, you will have to educate area businesses about your flyer and sell advertisements, at least in the beginning. If all goes well, businesses that want to advertise in your community flyer will be calling you!

☼

Holiday Helper Service

Want to be a Santa's elf and provide people with a stress-free Christmas? Start a holiday business and tackle holiday chores. Christmas holiday helpers can perform a number of jobs, including wrapping gifts, handwriting Christmas cards, shopping for gifts, decorating Christmas trees, and hanging outdoor lights. People who can't stand the thought of straightening out knotted strings of lights and decorating a Christmas tree just might call for your services. Providing a professional holiday helping service will fill the need of many busy families. For many people, personal, hands-on Christmases are a thing of the past. They want Christmas to be fun and happy, not a chore.

If you wish to hang Christmas lights on homes, I recommend that you are at least 18 years old, or get permission from your parents. When Jamie A. Limer was a freshman in college, he hung Christmas lights on homes, earning $25,000 a year. Then he started noticing a need for products that didn't exist yet, that would aid him and others during the Christmas holidays. Now 37, Jamie founded Christmas Light Co., and created many of those products. Several of his inventions have been sold on QVC, as well as at Home Depot, Target, and Wal-Mart.[77] Expect to be hired to take down and put away lights and decorations you have put up, and incorporate that into your price.

Pricing Holiday Helper Services

Holiday helpers can earn a profitable seasonal income during the Christmas holidays if they know how to price properly. In San Diego, for example, you can earn $1 to $2 per wrapped gift; $3 for handwritten Christmas cards; $20 an hour for a personal shopper; and over $300 to hang outdoor lights. If you are to take the lights down, you'll need to double your price, or at least set it so that the put up and take down prices are included. Not sure what the going rate is in your area? Log on to Craigslist to find a host of entrepreneurs offering Christmas help and various rates.

Promoting a Holiday Helper Service

Send out press releases to your local newspaper announcing your service. If an editor has informed you that your story will run, purchase a classified and/or display advertisement in the same newspaper to run at the same time. If, for example, your press release is printed on the first week of December, continue your classified and/or display advertisement until Christmas eve (that is, if you want to work up to that time). If your holiday helper service is one of many services you offer, let your current business customers know about it. They just might give your telephone a jingle.

☼

Lawn Care Service

Lawn care services seem to be more valuable now than ever before with busy families. Can you offer more than lawn mowing, like edging, raking, weeding, and sweeping? If you're not sure how to provide good lawn care, ask your parents or another relative to show you some basics.

Dain McKeon, 13, of Colorado Springs, Colorado, wants to become a pediatrician one day. With that in mind, he realized that the best way to pay for the schooling necessary to reach his career goal was to start his own business. That's when Teenage Yard Workers was born. Dain used the income gained from his first few jobs to upgrade his equipment. With nearly 20 regular customers and a dozen calls a week, Dain's landscaping business keeps him busy year-round. If Dain has too much work, he hires help on a job-by-job basis.[78]

If you do hire other teens to work for you, keep in mind that some teens are often flakey. If one fails to do the job, you, the employer, are totally responsible. Your reputation hangs on the behavior of your employees. Choose wisely who will work for you. Information about fair hiring practices can be found on the 9th Floor, Open for Business.

Pricing Lawn Care Services

Depending on the size of the yard, you could charge between $20 and $25 per yard, less if you're younger than 12. You might charge $10 for every half hour if you include other yard services, like weeding, raking, sweeping, and watering plants. Call lawn care professionals in your area to find out what they charge for similar services. Then price yours competitively.

Promoting a Lawn Care Service

Knocking on doors works great. You can also call on people you already know and tell them about your service. Post flyers in neighborhoods where you would like to work. Keep business cards available so that you can give them to people you meet on your way home from school, in the grocery store, and throughout your day. If your lawn care service offers extras, such as weeding, be sure to include this in your promotions—at an added charge. Many lawn services don't offer weeding, so clients are left to weed on their own. Many homeowners would appreciate the extra options.

☼

Magazine Publisher

Publish your own magazine. A teen might find her own town lacking teen-related information, thus creating an opportunity to begin the town's teen-beat magazine. This magazine could direct teenagers to hip things to do in their hometown, where the popular restaurants are, teen events happening around town, which businesses give student discounts, and feature reviews of current movies. You'll be amazed how much information is available for you to print, for free, if you dig.

In the beginning you could enlist teen friends to write articles for the magazine. In time, if you profit, offer to pay for the articles. The book *How to Start a Magazine* by James Kobak, provides information about how anyone can get started as a magazine publisher.

Jasmine Jordan, at the age of 12, launched the magazine *Tools For Living*, with $300 in seed money loaned to her by her brother after he and her mother urged her to compile her poems and stories. Now, at the age of 19, *Tools For Living* has a circulation of 25,000 and annual revenues of $25,000. *Tools For Living* features such articles as "Be Your Own Bo$$!" and "Great Teen Business Ideas!"[79]

Brothers Devin and Cameron Lazerine, then 16 and 15, founded *Rap Up.com*, a hip-hop and R&B website magazine. Wanting to transition into a full-color, glossy publication, Devin pitched his idea to a few publishers. To his amazement and delight, a publisher interested in doing a magazine based on Devin's website called him. They were interested in the concept of publishing a hip-hop magazine targeting a 12- to 18-year-old suburban demographic, an idea that Devin had already been thinking of doing.

Five years later and two publisher changes, *Rap-Up* is a full-color, glossy publication, with a national circulation of 200,000,

88

distributed by Time-Warner. Furthermore, each month 80,000 copies are sold at Wal-Mart, Barnes & Noble, Borders, Safeway, and other retailers. [80] More information about the Lazerine brothers and how *Rap-Up* came to be the successful magazine that it is can be found on the Internet (www.rap-up.com).

Pricing Magazine Advertisements

To begin setting prices for your advertisements, you will need to consider many things. Will you be doing your own typesetting? How much will it cost to print your magazine? What will be your magazine's circulation? Will you charge a subscription fee or will your magazines be distributed for free to homes and businesses? To have an idea of what other similar magazines' advertising rates are, request their rate cards. The more you can do for your magazine, like typesetting and layout, the more costs you can absorb. This allows you the option to offer competitively priced advertisements. However, until the magazine is successful, you may have trouble getting paying advertisers.

Promoting Your Magazine

Your magazine will promote itself if it is distributed for free to the public. You should be making your money through advertisements. With permission from managers or owners, you can place your magazines in several area businesses, including grocery stores, book stores, clothing stores, barber and beauty shops, dry cleaners, just to name a few. You could also place them in high schools, colleges, and public libraries. A team of deliverers can distribute them to homes and businesses if local ordinances allow this.

Creating an eZine Online Magazine

When we think of magazines, we usually think of glossy color pages. But a magazine need not be tangible. An eZine is a magazine available online and can be published for free. Yahoo (http://groups.yahoo.com) will host your eZine for free. Furthermore, Yahoo takes care of all your subscription requests. To build your directory, use one of the list servers found on the Groups listing. Yahoo will provide you with subscribe and unsubscribe e-mail addresses at no cost. The only drawback is that each posting will contain an ad for the service.

Don't let the fear of writing intimidate you from creating an eZine. If your eZine's focus is on an area of your expertise, you can write about what you know. To freshen up on your writing and grammar skills, log onto these sites for guidance: 11 Rules of Writing: http://www.junketstudies.com/rulesofw/; Exploring English: http://www.shared-visions.com/explore/ english/; Simpler Words and Phrases: http://www.smart biz.com/sbs/arts/tpl5.htm.

When creating a title for your eZine, consider that many eZine listing sites present their eZines in alphabetical order. The closer your eZine title is to the beginning of the alphabet, the further up the list your eZine will appear. Your title should tell the reader exactly what your eZine is about, so adding AAA to the front of your business name won't do it.

When you first launch your eZine, you may want to publish just once a month. When your subscription rate increases, consider producing a bi-weekly or weekly eZine. This would be the ideal time to begin selling advertising space, say, once you have 1,000 subscribers. You might sell ad space for $30 for every 1,000 subscribers; $50 for every 2,000 subscribers, and so on. Since competition is fierce for ad sales, you may begin offering ad space that allows the buyer to purchase two weeks of advertising for $60, and get the third week for free. For further information on publishing your own eZine, read *eZines: A Complete Guide to Publishing for Profit*, by Tom and Marilyn Ross. Or visit www.ezine-tips.com and click on "eZine-Tips Experts" for free, professional advice about eZines. There are several eZine websites that can help you with your eZine: www.e-zinequeen.com (tell-all instructions); www.constantcontact.com (an eZine distribution service); and www.1shoppingcart.com (an eZine distribution and shopping cart service).

Bridging an Online Magazine to a Tangible Magazine

When you bridge an online magazine, that is, go from an online magazine to a tangible one, you are in an advantageous position, unlike a beginning tangible magazine publisher who doesn't already have online presence. Your online magazine can serve as the beginnings of a prototype—a mock-up of how the actual magazine will look—to show to potential advertisers and investors. It is essential to have a printed prototype of your magazine when approaching potential advertisers and investors. Not only will it aid you in obtaining their support, it can help you secure a national distributor. Cynthia Good, 46, and Genevieve Bos, 41, are the co-founders of *Pink*, a magazine for professional women that was launched in June 2005. Although *Pink* didn't start out as an eZine, they credit their prototype for helping secure their national distribution contract with Kable News Co. "We showed them a prototype, gave them our résumés, and talked to them about our vision," says Genevieve.[81]

Online magazine publishers and editors benefit from bridging their online magazine to a tangible one because they have an already-established customer base. If it's a strong one, you have excellent ammunition—your platform—to present to advertisers, investors, and distributors, along with your prototype. Florentina Abramov, a 16-year-old who attends Physical City High School in Flushing, New York, is the owner of *Graffiti* magazine, a two-year-old magazine that began as an online eZine. Now in print, *Graffiti* comes out four times a year and is operated by a staff of volunteers ages 13 to 22. *Graffiti* addresses cultural, social, and political issues, giving young writers the chance to express their ideas and political opinions.[82]

How much work you will need to do on your online magazine in order to prepare it to become a paper-based publication depends on your magazine goal. Check these resources for help with launching a tangible magazine:

Advertising Age (www.adage.com)
Folio: Magazine (www.foliomag.com)

The Editor in Chief: A Management Guide for Magazine Editors,
    by Benton Rain Patterson and Coleman E.P. Patterson
Starting and Running a Successful Newsletter or Magazine, by
    Cheryl Woodward
*Launch Your Own Magazine: A Guide for Succeeding in Today's
    Marketplace* and *Samir Husni's Guide to New Magazines,
    Vol. 21,* by Samir Husni (www.mrmagazine.com)
How to Start a Magazine and Publish it Profitably, by James
    Kobak

Associations :
Western Publications Association (www.wpa-online.org)
American Business Media (www.americanbusinessmedia.com)
Magazine Publishers of America (www.magazine.org)
*Audit Bureau of Circulations (*www.accessabc.com*)*

☼

Metal Polishing Service

Many families don't bother using their brass pots and pans and silverware because they are simply too busy to keep up their care. A metal polishing service can be a profitable business, because busy people don't have time for such details. If you offer a metal polishing service, your clients should provide all the necessary tools, including cleaning gloves. (They should also assume responsibility for the polish used.) For brass cleaning tips, visit http://doityourself.com/clean/brass.htm. Here you'll learn such tips as rubbing olive oil on brass after polishing it to make the it look brighter. Visit http://interiordec.about.com/od/silver polish/ for silver polishing tips.

Pricing Metal Polishing Services

Ten to fifteen dollars per hour is a reasonable price to request, with a minimum of one hour service. That means if you have a polishing job, and it takes you only 35 minutes to complete, you will get paid for the full hour. Or price each job by the piece.

Promoting a Metal Polishing Service

Start by informing family and friends of your service. Knock on doors in your area and let neighbors know about your service by leaving your business card and a flyer. Your flyer could feature a photo of you polishing a brass pot and could also include silver and brass polishing tips. People who know about your service might dig up pieces that need polishing, especially prior to holidays. You'll be the shining star!

☼

Music CD

Are you a talented musician? Do you have music in you to share with the rest of the world? Consider recording your own CD. Katie Glassman, the 1998 National Junior Fiddle Champion, wanted the world to hear her music. During her senior year of high school, Katie wanted to record a CD of the Texas-style fiddle music that won her the NJFC award.

To come up with the money needed to pay for recording costs, Katie put on two concerts and earned $4,000, but still fell short of her goal. In search of more money, she went to Young Americans Bank in Denver, Colorado. Thanks to a $2,000 loan from YAB, Katie recorded her first CD, *Who Walks In*.[83]

Pricing Your Music CD

Visit any music store and look at the music in your genre to see what the price range is. Next, see how much it costs to record and produce each CD. Other expenses need to be factored in, for example, the design jacket printing, and the photography for jacket cover. If you can't afford a professional to design and print your CD jacket cover, you can design and print your own with Easy CD Cover Creator (www.softpedia.com/get/Authoring-tools/cover-editors/Easy-CD-Cover-Creator.shtml). After all your costs are figured out in your business plan, add a reasonable profit to the total to see if it comes out to the cost of a similar CD. If it doesn't, go back to the drawing board and see where you can adjust expenses to balance the costs.

A family member might be capable of taking a quality jacket photo. But what about typesetting and printing for your jacket cover? If you cannot do the typesetting for your jacket cover, ask your local printer if he is willing to barter with you for this service. For example, offer to detail his car in exchange for your CD cover-printing services. Or work in his shop until you are "paid up." Look at all your expenses and see if they can, in fact, be bartered. When goods or services are traded, it is best to have all agreements in writing, even if the amounts are under $100.

Promoting Your Music CD

Katie Glassman promotes her CD, *Who Walks In*, on Ludiker Music, http://www.ludikermusic.com/fiddlecd.html and on her own website, http://www.katieglassman.com/products.htm. CDs can be sold in local book and music shops, as well as gift shops. If you have a CD that has a Christian theme, contact Christian music and book stores to carry your CD. Set up booths at fairs, art shows, and other special events. If you entertain at an event that presents a program book, ask to have an advertisement promoting your CD included in it. You should also arrange to set up a booth after (or during) the show to sell your music. Many people would be delighted to purchase an autographed CD!

☼

Pet Care Service

If you love animals, why not start a business devoted to these wonderful creatures? A pet care business could be a dream-come-true job for anyone who loves pets. Pets are a big business, and animal lovers spend billions of dollars each year catering to their birds, cats, dogs, fish, etc. According to the American Pet Product

Manufacturers Association's 2005 National Pet Owner's Survey, in 2004, pet owners spent $34.4 billion on their pets, up from $17 billion in 1994.[84] People want excellent care for their pets, and they are willing to pay for it.

A pet care business can be a lucrative business. "It is also a huge responsibility," says Turner. "If you have a pet, then you know pets are a big responsibility. When people go out of town, they usually need a dependable person to take care of their pets." Be sure to know your abilities. Walking a poodle sounds simple enough, but what about a Great Dane?

How will you operate your business? Will your parents and siblings be available to help you when you need it? It is helpful if your family is supportive of your business and able to cover for you in the event you get sick in the middle of your job. Will your parents or guardians help you to manage your bookings? When the telephone rings during a school day, and I'm home, I am able to take client calls and book jobs for Turner and Mia. When I am not home, clients leave messages on our family recorder. Customer calls are returned by Turner and Mia when they get home from school. You will need to check out local zoning laws through the county clerk's office in case you are planning on hosting pets in your home.

Pricing Pet Care Services

Dog walkers earn on average $15 for half an hour of service, per client. (This price is based on one or two dogs from the same client; three or more pets, add $10 or $15 to the cost.) Turner started his business charging $5 for half an hour visit. Now, his fee is $12 per visit, still competitively priced. For daily dog sitting (8- to 12-hour periods), he is paid between $75 and $100 per day, extra on holidays. This fee includes constant supervision and play with a pet, the same care that a babysitter provides for a child. Turner also handles multiple pet jobs when necessary, or hires helpers to work for him.

Promoting a Pet Care Service

Place flyers in selected neighborhoods introducing your pet care service. Send a press release to your local newspaper. Include a picture of yourself next to a pet you are currently caring for. If you don't have a client's pet to pose with, have a picture taken with your own pet. Or, offer to care for a friend's pet in exchange for posing for a snapshot with their family pet. You can obtain free advertising on the Internet promoting your pet care service on the website www.4sitters.com. Another website to promote your pet care business is www.petsit.com.

Post your flyer or business cards at pet businesses, including boarding kennels, veterinary offices, pet supply stores, and dog training centers. Attach rows of your telephone number so that potential clients can tear one off while leaving your main flyer on the board. Or, include a small envelope attached to the bulletin board with loose business cards inside. Get permission from management before placing your material on their board. If businesses are reluctant to help you, offer a finder's fee for every client obtained through their location.

Promote your pet care business on custom keychains. Often clients will hand over a single key to their home. Rather than risk losing it, immediately hook it onto a key chain, preferably one that features your pet care business logo and telephone number. Return the key on the keychain to your client. Now your client cannot "forget" your telephone number.

Do you have experience cleaning aquariums? Maintaining aquariums will make you stand out from all the other basic pet care providers. If you do maintain aquariums, include this information in your promotional material. Let doctors' office staff know of your services. You will have steady customers because there are very few doctors, nurses, or staff personnel who want to take on the additional responsibilities of managing the fish tank!

☼

Pooper Scooper Service

Dealing with pet waste is one of those topics that every pet owner must face. This may not sound like a cool, glamorous business, but this service is in great demand. Many working professionals just do not have the time to pay attention to small details like picking up after their dogs. Managing dog waste can be a profitable business for any person. Believe it or not, if you look on the Internet, you will find that quite a few pooper scooper services exist. According to Sterling Quick, president of the Association of Professional Animal Waste Specialists, about 300 pet waste removal companies exist in the United States and Canada.[85]

A pooper scooper is a cashless start-up business that can immediately realize a profit. You can learn more about the pooper scooper business by reading *The Professional Pooper Scooper: How to Start Your Own Low-Cost, High-Profit Dog Waste Removal Service*, by Matthew Osborn. Visit his site at www.pooper-scooper.com.

As for what you will need to begin your service, absolutely nothing. Your client can provide you with plastic trash bags and a trash can to dispose of the waste. If you would, however, prefer to own a device that helps with your service, the Scoop & Sack It, also known as the SASI Scoop, is a pooper scooper invented by a 10-year-old boy living in Broomfield, Colorado. Never pleased with his job of cleaning up after the family's dogs, he complained about the length of time it took, the mess, and the pain in his back from bending over to get the job done. For a 5th grade social studies class project, he was required to invent something new or improve an existing idea. That was the motivation Aaron needed to finish his scoop. The device uses standard grocery store bags, and even allows wheelchair bound, elderly customers the ability to pick up after their pets.[86]

Pricing Pooper Scooper Services

It may not sound cool, but the money you can make providing a pooper scooper service can be very lucrative. Services start around $12 to $15 a week (one visit), depending on the number of dogs and the number of times the yard needs scooping. Cleaning up after a dog that weighs over 65 pounds should start at $15 per visit. A typical yard costs $15 per week. If you perform services on six yards in one neighborhood in one hour, at $15 per yard, you'll gross $90 for one hour of work that week. Multiply your clients and you, too, could be purchasing a home like one of Yucko's Pooper Scooper worker's did. Within one year of working for Yucko's, she was able to buy a house of her own.[87] Imagine what investments you could make if you owned the company! You could charge $15 for the first visit during a week, followed by a sliding scale. A second visit would be an additional $13; a third, $11; and a fourth, $9. Or you can keep it simple and charge the same rate for each service you perform.

Promoting a Pooper Scooper Service

It takes time to create awareness, so beginnings can be modest. Then, again, if you're in a neighborhood with busy, dual-working parents with kids and dogs, you could be making a small fortune right from the start.

Begin promoting your service by letting dog owners you know about your service. You can also post business cards and flyers in grocery stores, vet clinics, and any other place that offers a bulletin board. You can advertise in the Yellow Pages under Pet Services and Dog categories. You might ask your Yellow Pages publisher if they would create a Pooper Scooper Service category if there isn't one. It's always best when you're on the leading edge of any business product or service.

Contact condominium complexes and apartment building managers to inform them of your service. Keeping the city parks clean is a big concern of your city parks manager, so make him aware of your service. If you also provide cat litter box service, posting flyers and business cards on bulletin boards in apartment and condominium complexes can be a boon for both you and cat owners. Apartment and condominium associations publish monthly newsletters. Ask the manager of the complex to include your service in their newsletter. Many managers would be happy to keep not only the exterior smelling good, but the interior as well.

☼

Snow Shoveling Service

Snow-shoveling jobs are available in many parts of the United States during snow season. If you live in Saint Paul, Minnesota, count on loads of snow-shoveling business, as it is illegal to leave a sidewalk unshoveled after any accumulation of snow. You can count on continuous business during the winter months because shoveling is never over until the spring comes. To stop heavy snow from clinging to your shovel, coat it with a spray shortening, like Pam, and you'll tire less quickly. For your safety be sure to stretch before and after jobs, and take breaks every fifteen minutes.

How many customers you get depends on how ambitious you are and how much time you have to shovel snow. Enlist a couple of friends and work the neighborhood! Many people own their own shovels, so, in the beginning, you probably won't even need to purchase a shovel, particularly if you're only hired to shovel the front walkway and back porch. If you are requested to do more, say the driveway and the 6 feet of snow drifts that accumulated against a back door and garage *overnight*, you might look into the benefits and risks of owning a snowblower.

Pricing Snow Shoveling Services

For a typical small job, teenagers charge, on average, $20 per house. More experienced snow-shoveling operators who have a vehicle and a high-powered snow thrower charge $30 for smaller, lighter jobs; $40 and up for larger, heavier jobs. Since a snow-blower provides quicker service, you would be able to provide quicker snow-shoveling service and accommodate more customers throughout the day.

Promoting a Snow Shoveling Service

Let your neighbors, family, and friends know about your service. Post flyers on neighborhood doors. Take out a classified advertisement in your local newspaper. As with any press release, a well-written one sent to your community newspaper prior to the snow season prepares clients for when they need your service. After shoveling one driveway, visit nearby homes to let them know you just shoveled their neighbor's driveway and ask if they would also like theirs shoveled on the spot. If no one is home, don't leave your promotional material on the ground because the snow will ruin it. Instead, leave your business cards and brochures in plastic door hangers. Door-hangers-direct.com [(800) 226-7879] sells plastic door hanger bags, a unique and high-profile way to deliver your message to your market.

☼

Trash to Curbside Service

Every week Micah Jones, 13, of Valencia, California, carries a neighbor's trash to the curbside.[88] This includes hauling lawn trimmings, trash, and recycling. Trash pickup days vary in neighborhoods. This allows you to spread out jobs and add additional clients.

Pricing Trash to Curbside Services

A weekly trash-to-curbside job can command $6 to $10, maybe more, depending on the amount of trash to be hauled. If you need to return the empty trash cans the following day, add at least 50% of the take-out cost to the tab. For example, if you charge $8 for trash take-out, add an extra $4 to the tab to retrieve the cans. Most people prefer help taking out full trash cans, while they can return the empty ones themselves.

Promoting Trash to Curbside Services

Visit neighbors in areas where you want to work to let them know about your service. Lining up several customers on the same street makes profitable sense. For every job you perform, ask customers to give out brochures, flyers, or business cards to their neighbors, letting them know of the service you just performed. You might be fortunate to line up half the street for this service that very evening.

☼

Tutoring/Teaching Service

There is a strong demand for tutoring as a result of significant changes in education during the past decade. Because of increased testing, larger class sizes, and an emphasis on college preparation, tutors are needed. Popular subjects for tutoring include math, history, and reading. Tutoring academic subjects isn't all that can be taught. If you play the piano well, tutor younger students to reinforce what their piano teacher has already taught them. If you have a talent like knitting, needlework, yoga, swimming, or computers, you might offer instructions in these areas. Nicole Knothe, during her high school years in Eden Prairie, Minnesota, ran a swim instruction program, which helped kids from kindergarten to high school with all aspects of their swimming skills.[89] If singing is your talent, giving singing lessons could be your niche. A bookworm might offer to teach young children how to read, or simply be hired to provide an hour of nightly reading to or with a child. An expert at chess might teach people how to play the game.

To become a tutor, you must have plenty of patience and good communication skills. Students who need tutoring usually lack confidence, so having patience—not to mention an outgoing personality—can help you to build confidence in your students. Also, a bachelor's degree—although not required—will add credibility to marketing your tutoring services.

Your students are beginners, so give them the respect that any professional would. Find out special things about your students and write them down in your notebook. If they are having a birthday, bring them a treat to make them feel special. If they excel in something not related to what you're tutoring, remind them of the things they are good at when they are having a rough day. Have a sense of humor around kids younger than you are. It will help to relax them, making you both feel more confident. The National Tutoring Association (www.ntatutor.org; (863) 529-5206) is a good destination for learning how to start your own tutoring service. Tutor.com is an online service that uses the Internet to connect people for one-to-one instruction. Using the Internet as part of your tutoring business, whether you plan to offer services online or develop a website to promote your tutoring, should be included in your business plan.

Pricing Tutoring/Teaching Services

The range of fees could be anywhere from $10 to $15 per hour, depending on your age and level of expertise—more if you live in a large metropolitan area. (Adult expert tutors can command between $25 and $45 per hour. A teenage tutor should not charge as much.) If you have extensive expertise in an area, you could charge more.

Promoting Tutoring/Teaching Services

Send press releases to middle or high school newspapers in the towns you want to serve. You can also benefit from placing a classified ad promoting your tutorial services in your town's newspaper. Knock on neighborhood doors and leave your business cards or flyers promoting your service. Distribute your flyer at after-school community centers and anywhere mothers congregate, for example, at a "mother & child" gym class.

☼

Virtual Store

Launching an online storefront can be a fast path to financial success. Begin by searching for a good idea. While there's always a market for professional and technical services, products generally sell better on the Internet. It is easier to sell online customers items they can see and then use. Geneva Johnson, 15, president of the Hamilton Art Gallery, Bronx, New York, sells ceramics that celebrate African American culture.[90] Geneva runs her gallery out of her home, via the Internet on her website http://hamiltonartgallery.com.

Setting Up a Virtual Store

To set up your online store, there are several websites you can visit for guidance. Google "Setting Up a Virtual Store" or "Setting Up an Online Store," and you'll find sites such as www.inc.com (Build Your Virtual Store) and www.abiogenesis.com (The Online Store: Setting Up Shop on the Web). These sites, and many others, will give you information on how to set up your online business, such as explaining the anatomy of a website, setting up a site, how much it will cost, content development, site maintenance, how to make your site appealing, incorporating a transaction mechanism (the process of collecting money online), and how to promote your website. You'll also get advice on what products can be sold profitably on the web, since not all products can. You'll learn how to register a domain name (Register.com, NetworkSolutions.com, and GoDaddy.com), set up an e-mail account that allows you to receive customer feedback, and how to affiliate yourself with another site.

Yahoo Small Business offers hosting packages. You can use their free site builder tools to design some basic web pages. You can also take a class and learn how to design websites using FrontPage. Also check out www.businessmag.com for hosting solutions.

PayPal

If you are setting up a website to sell a product, PayPal allows you to set up a free shopping cart and merchant account to accept credit cards. PayPal charges a small transaction fee but collects money from buyers for you via credit cards. It's a great way for you to accept MasterCard, Visa, and American Express without having a merchant account. For more information, visit www.PayPal.com.

PayPal recently announced that merchants who accept PayPal can now offer online gift certificates to their customers. PayPal enables online businesses of all sizes to set up customized gift certificates, offering their customers more choices when shopping for family and friends. To set up a gift certificate program, businesses need only add a "Buy a Gift Certificate" button to their websites. For detailed information about PayPal's gift certificate program, visit http://www.paypal.com/sellgc.

Obtaining a Resale Number

Before setting up shop, you will need to get a "resale number" in order to purchase goods wholesale. Your local county clerk's office can help you establish that. In return you will have to collect and pay state sales tax.

Registering Your Online Store

It can take days to register your online store, but doing so does ensure that your company is placed in the most appropriate category in each database. Some sites let you include longer descriptions of your company. Begin with WebStep Top 100 Free Listings (www.mmgco.com/top100.html).

If time is limited, you can pay a small fee for companies like WebPromote (www.webpromote.com), The Central Registry (www.centralregistry.com), Link Exchange's Submit It! (www.linkexchange.com), or PowerSolution's Site Promoter (www.sitepromoter.com) to submit your company's information to a long list of sites.

Promoting Your Virtual Store

A virtual store is marketed the same way as a brick and mortar store. You want to attract visitors so they'll place orders. You will need to get your site on as many search engines as possible. It is the starting place for Internet shoppers looking for a product or service. A search engine is a huge cyberspace Yellow Pages, and it covers the entire world. Some major search engines available— Google, Yahoo, Infoseek, Excite, and Alta Vista—are your best bet for a broad-based approach. Surfers use a search engine to find your site by entering key words. In addition to multiple search engine listings, it is recommended that you list with at least 100 directory listings. To find out more about search engines, their costs, etc., Google "Search Engines" on the Internet.

Use every possible marketing tool to promote your online store. Create cross-links with sites like yours. By doing so you'll place a link to another business' site on your home page as they place a link to your page. Link Exchange (www.link exchange.com) will help you do this. You may also consider joining affiliate programs, where your web store is linked with a larger website that contains similar products or services. You can also find out which websites are linking to your competitors but not to you. Link Tree (www.linktree.info) is a free link analyzer that helps increase your website's link popularity. Begin by entering up to seven competitor URLs and submit your URL as a comparison site, and Link Tree works with that. Once the sites are identified, it's up to you to decide where you want to be linked.

Search Engine Optimization

Some website designers perform a procedure called a "search engine optimization," in which your site is peppered with key words that would make your site clearly visible to the web's major search engines. As online shopping grows, search engine rankings can make a difference in the success of your Internet business, as 62% of U.S. search engine users look no further than the first page of results before clicking a link.[91] Ryan Pieter, 21, of Durham, North Carolina, the CEO of Broadwick Corp., a web marketing consulting firm that assists start-ups and established Fortune 1000® organizations launch brands and build sales on the web, authored *Obtaining a #1 Ranking in the Search Engines.*[92]

☼

Website Developer

Teenagers are tech-savvy. They have time to explore their computer gear, do not fear it, and want to be challenged. They seem to learn the inner workings of the computer without reading manuals. Thousands of teens are becoming website developers. Brad Ogden, 17, of Detroit, Michigan, is the owner of Virtual Webpages. Brad operates a web design company that has an annual income of *over half a million dollars*! While he enjoys an occasional Friday night football game with friends, Brad spends most of his time in his home office or with one of his clients.[93] You can see some of Brad's work on his website, www.virtualwebpages.com.

Learning How to Build Websites

"Building sites has grown organically, but not until recently did we promote and market it," says Jamie Riehle, Director of Product Management for Lycos, Inc., one of the Internet companies promoting website-building.[94] People start with its free service. Later, they can upgrade, for a fee.

Lycos, Inc., offers three sites: Angelfire.com, Tripod.com, and Planet.Lycos.com. If you want to build a website, this is the place you can go to for free. The only "cost" is that there are many advertisers who place their ads here. If it's an ad-free zone you are looking for, you'll have to pay for space. Angelfire is geared to teens and young adults. Tripod is designed for college-age and older subscribers. PlanetLycos is geared toward both demographics; however, it is more targeted to the 18–32 demographic.

Six years ago, at the age of 11, Lissa Daniels of Celebration, Florida, built her own website (www.lissaexplains.com) to explain HTML to other kids. (HTML is the computer coding used to create web pages.) Today, her site gets over 28 million page views and over 5 million visitors each month. At the age of 17, not only was Lissa able to buy a herself a car, she will be able to pay for her college education.[95]

Editing Your Website

Edit.com is an online service that offers do-it-yourself website editing, allowing businesses to easily update sites. For advanced changes, expert developers are available. Edit.com works with any existing website and lets you change text, links, images, and PayPal buttons as well as add new pages. Visit their website for pricing information.

Pricing Web Development Services

Contact older, established website developers to find out what they offer at what price. Compare several businesses with each other, then compare what you can offer. If you will provide web development services to small businesses, you should compare the same.

Michael Simmons and his friend, Cal Newport, founded Princeton Web Solutions several years ago as teenagers. Their Internet service and Intranet Solutions provide services for medium and large businesses. To keep expenses low, their company employs help to create a total package. They hire a development team from Kerala, India, that provides experienced graphic designers, HTML coders, Flash experts, and e-commerce specialists. As a result, Michael and Cal offer professional web development services competitively. As of this writing they charge $75 per hour, which is about half the rate of most of their competitors. Their discounted service still provides Michael and Cal with an average *monthly* income of $40,000.[96]

Promoting a Website Development Business

Promote your website design business to all business owners you know or meet. If a professional lawn care company is taking care of your family's lawn, tell a representative about your service. They might want to hire you to create a website for their lawn care business. Walk into businesses and leave your business card with the manager. It just might get to the owner, who probably has already been thinking about creating a website, but doesn't know where to start. Offer your services to other teens, for a fee, who simply want a personal website. I believe the teen market, alone, could be a lucrative business arena for any website designer. Michael Frederickson, 14, of Pembroke, Massachusetts, who designs websites for businesses, recruits "salesfriends" to pitch his services to local businesses, and gives them a 10% cut from any clients they send his way.[97]

You know you want to start a business, but you're still not sure which business is right for you. Not just any business will do. You realize that if you don't feel passionate about your business, it will never succeed. You're looking for the ideal business that fits your personality, but you don't know what it will be — yet. To help you dig deeper into your personality, visit the next floor, Create Your Niche Business. You might discover your perfect business niche.

5th Floor

Create Your Niche Business

"Do what you love to do, and find a way to get paid for it!"
~Oprah Winfrey

Find a niche within yourself and turn it into a business. What is a niche? A niche is a focused area of business that can be targeted with a focused plan. A business that focuses on a niche market is addressing a need for a product or service that isn't currently being addressed. Your goal is to fill that need. Creating a niche business allows you to be unique and not compete with other similar businesses. This offers you the opportunity to be visible in a sea of related products or services.

Can't find a niche within yourself? Then look to the business headlines—even one that seems unrelated to what you want to do—and try to figure out if you have an angle. Chances are good that you can figure what people are going to need and what you can offer. If the two match up, you have a niche idea to further investigate. It just might make you a successful niche entrepreneur!

Advantages of Owning a Niche Business

Being alone in the market can be your best advantage. Other small businesses may not be aware of your particular niche market, and large businesses probably won't bother copying you. You will become a specialist in your field. "The best thing about owning a niche business is that you don't have to be a global company to attain market leadership," says Turner. "Being the big fish in the small pond is much better than wading in a big pond where you can be eaten by the big fish!"

Stop Thinking You're Untalented

Everyone has a creative streak, and often it's just a matter of finding the right outlet. Look at all the ways that you express your inner self—that's what creativity is really all about. Consider taking an art class or music lessons to begin your search. Do you like to sew, paint, cook, write, decorate? These are all ways to help your inner self shine. Need to dig a bit deeper to find out what your creative streak is? Listen to music or take a walk in nature, writing down anything that strikes your fancy. File your notes away, then, when you're feeling creative, pull them out to inspire your imagination. It's amazing how many people create something from an idea that they had conceived years earlier. Last but not least, according to a recent Harvard study, the more joy and love you feel, the more creative you will be![98]

Recognizing Your Eureka Moment

You can discover your eureka moment—a sudden burst of inspiration—through your passions, because that's where your unique talents lie. Record your hobbies and interests on the left side of a T-chart. Then, derive a business idea from each, writing it down on the right side of the T-chart. If you're not sure what your passions are at the moment, maybe you left them in your childhood or on the table on the way to work years ago, start keeping a journal. Write down past and present desires, which can help you articulate your vision. Or, simply be in tune with

110

everyday life, as was Walt Disney. He was at a local carnival with his grandkids when he was inspired to create Disneyland. Bill Bowerman created the Nike Waffle running shoe after a breakfast of waffles. (Wherever your passions might lead you, www.tradepub.com is the place to go for free, industry-specific trade publication subscriptions that best match your skills and interests. This website offers hundreds of trade magazines organized in 32 key industries.)

Design a "Dream" Book

Document your creative streaks by using a notebook, describing each goal and placing a matching picture beside each one. Every so often, look through the book, visualizing your dream. You'll be amazed at how this can motivate you to make your dreams come true. If your documented dreams include writing a book, inventing a product, and creating a service business, why not make your favorite three happen? The simple act of writing down your dreams is the beginning of it coming to life. Every company in the world, no matter how big, started at one time as an idea which, over time, evolved into a business. Studies show that our brains are most creative when we're relaxed — sometimes asleep — which is why many of our best ideas come to us when we're asleep (or about to go to sleep). When researchers asked business people where they got their most creative business ideas, 81% named places outside of their workplace. The top three idea zones included the car, in bed, and while socializing.[99] Therefore, have a notepad and pen in your car, near your bed, and with you while socializing — ready to take note!

How Creative Minds Found Their Niche

Creative minds are never "off." They work on ideas 24/7/365 — whether they are asleep or awake! The niche stories you are about to read will show you that business ideas can come to people while they sleep, out of frustration, out of boredom, out of hobbies, out of unmet needs — even by accident.

Dream Your Niche

When 6-year-old Miranda Evarts of Milford, New Jersey, couldn't sleep at night, she thought up a game—and now it's a best seller! Miranda always loved fairy tales, and even dreamed up her own characters—mystical queens with names like the Starfish Queen, the Ladybug Queen, and the Rose Queen.

One night, when Miranda couldn't sleep, she made up a game about them—that they were sleeping, and needed to be awakened. Tremendously excited, Miranda ran into her parents' room and blurted: "I made up a game!"

Her parents listened, smiled, and felt that Miranda was on to something. Over the next few months they helped Miranda work out the rules for the game and create the artwork, which included 12 sleeping queens, and 12 kings that could awaken the queens; cards that could send the queens back to sleep; and others that allow players to steal the queens. The player who first collects five awakened queens wins the game.

To test her product, Miranda let her friends play the game. They liked it so much that they begged for copies. So Miranda's parents e-mailed Gamewright, a Massachusetts game manufacturer, and "Sleeping Queens" became the company's first-ever kid-invented game! Over 10,000 copies sold in the first three months, making it Gamewright's best-selling new game.

What's Miranda's secret to getting her game "Sleeping Queens" created by Gamewright, a company that receives hundreds of suggestions for games each year? Jason Schneider, who selects new games for the company, noted that the game had "novel quirks that keep it from being boring." Jason Schneider was amazed that someone as young as Miranda had thought up the idea for the game.[100] "Sleeping Queens" can be found in retail stores like Barnes & Noble and on www.areyougame.com. Whether you are creating a toy or game, read *The Toy and Game Inventor's Handbook*, by Richard C. Levy and Ronald O. Weingartner. It will provide you with helpful, industry-specific information.

If Your Niche is a Self-Created Product

If you end up selling a non-food product that you created and need to mass produce, you'll need to have a prototype made (more information about prototype can be found on the 2nd Floor, Operate a Business.) If you have a great product idea, a product that an already-established company is looking to market, you can search for that company through NineSigma (www.ninesigma.com). Since inception, NineSigma has provided services, information, and software to help support clients in the development, establishment, and execution of their innovation strategies. Inventors can register for a bi-weekly *Innovation Newsletter* that lists some of the products, solutions, and technologies that big companies are looking for. Furthermore, if you have a truly great product idea, this site can connect you with someone to help you co-develop your product.

Frustration Can Lead You to Your Niche

Jacob Dunnack developed the JD Batball, at the age of 6, out of frustration. When Jacob went to visit his grandmother, he remembered to bring his bat, but forgot his baseball. Frustrated, he decided to do something about it so that it wouldn't happen again. That's when Jacob created a plastic baseball bat with a removable cap for storing baseballs. Jacob, with support from his parents, submitted the idea to Toys "R" Us. Liking the idea, Toys "R" Us started carrying the JD Batball.

So how did Jacob's idea go from concept to design? Jacob's parents presented the idea of JD's Batball to Pete Wood, a Principal Designer with South Carolina-based Zzorco Consulting. Jacob's parents brought the crude design model, complete with foam and duct tape, to Pete Wood. Since the prototype would not stay together in the field, using SolidWorks software (www.SolidWorks.com), Pete converted Jacob's idea into something that could be manufactured. Pete was able to refine the model with a detailed snap-lock design and the grip for the bat in a matter of hours.

To move from the product design phase into production, Pete saved the designs of the cores and cavity details in a standard graphical file format and sent them via the Internet to Santin Engineering in Peabody, Massachusetts. They built a one-third-scale model that the Dunnacks presented to buyers at Toys "R" Us. The national toy store chain placed an order for 12,000 units as a test run. The Dunnacks and Pete Wood have since tweaked the design based on Toys "R" Us' specifications and sent it to Custom Technical Molding, a Massachusetts company that manufacturers the product.[101]

Richie Stachowski, from Orinda, California, at the age of 11, also developed a product out of frustration. Richie and his father were snorkeling during a Hawaiian vacation. Frustrated that he couldn't talk to his dad underwater about their undersea discoveries, Richie came home and designed an underwater megaphone. Using the Internet for research, his home pool as a test lab, and $267 of his savings for start-up capital, Richie designed Water Talkies™. First, Richie mounted a standard snorkel mouthpiece onto the tip of a plastic soccer-field conical boundary marker. Then, in a series of tests, Richie found that he could keep water from flooding the device by including a blow valve in the cone and a plastic membrane in the mouthpiece. A month later, Richie's invention was a complete success, allowing people to talk to each other underwater up to 15 feet away.

Under the guidance of his mother, Richie flew to Paramus, New Jersey, to pitch his new "Water Talkies" to Toys "R" Us. Richie concluded his presentation by using a fish tank to ask, underwater, for a purchase order. Toys "R" Us placed an initial order of 50,000 units, and, in the summer of 1997, Water Talkies™ were a big hit and have been ever since, reaping over half a million dollars annually.[102]

Hobby Niche

Imagine being paid for a hobby that you love to do. According to *The New York Times*, iPod lovers are turning their talent into an entrepreneurial business and are making a small fortune—some as much as $600 a day—programming iPods for busy people who don't have the time to program theirs.[103] To learn how to transfer music on both Mac and Windows platforms, *The Pocket Idiot's*

Guide to the iPod, by Damon Brown, is the book to read. This guide will show you how to put thousands of songs onto an iPod; the pros and cons of each iPod "flavor"—original, mini, shuffle, photo, and nano; how to download music legally from Internet music stores; and tips on how to create playlists.

Vintage Clothing Niche

Evan Kiley, 18, and Renold Aparicio, 19, of Corona, California, couldn't find the type of clothing that appealed to them. They were tired of seeing the skate fashion and instead wanted to see more vintage style clothing. Since the only good place to find vintage clothing was in Los Angeles, the pair decided to open Impact Clothing, their own vintage clothing store.

Before opening their store, Evan and Renold laid out the groundwork. They visited the library every day for two weeks to get information on how to start a business. They also polled kids at their school to find out what type of vintage clothing they would buy. Next, they spent two months writing up their business plan, which not only helped them see where they were heading but also helped them get a grant for starting their business. Their preparation and business plan were vital to starting their own vintage clothing store.[104]

History Niche

In 2004, when Michael Stanat was 15, he began researching his book on China's teens and how their worldview could affect American business. Nearly two years later, *China's Generation Y: Understanding the Future Leaders of the World's Next Superpower* is available at www.Amazon.com, at www.publiclibraries.com, and can be found on the Homa & Kekey Books website, featured as the "first English book to look into all aspects of China's young generation."

What motivated this senior at the United Nations International School to write *China's Generation Y*? This book was an outgrowth of a life spent visiting 27 countries with his marketing professional mother, his interest in things Chinese, and a fondness for history. His next project is a similar book on India's Generation Y. [105]

Medieval Niche

When Rick Jensen, 17, from Chippewa Falls, Wisconsin, was a high school freshman, he was tired of the grungy, "just-rolled-out-of-bed" look of the '90s. That's when he attempted to resurrect a popular fashion from the 13th century: chain maille.

Chain maille is a mesh-like material consisting of small metal rings linked together and was used during the Middle Ages to create flexible armor. During Rick's freshman year of high school, he learned to weave chain maille. One day, a female classmate asked Rick if he could make her a pair of pants out of maille, and offered him $100 for the pants.

In June of 2005, Rick won the National Federation of Independent Business (NFIB)/Visa USA "Youth Entrepreneur of the Year" award for his entrepreneurial achievements. He was awarded a $10,000 educational scholarship to apply to his college tuition. For now, Rick relies primarily on word-of-mouth advertising to promote his business, Maille Time (www.MailleTime.com). He plans to sell his maille apparel and accessories at craft fairs, Renaissance festivals, and over the Internet.[106]

Inventor Niche

On a cold and snowy day, Kathryn Gregory, at the age of 10, was out building a snow fort when her wrists started to hurt because they were cold. She fixed the problem by inventing Wristies®— fingerless gloves, wrist warmers, and glove liners all in one, keeping hands warm and fingers free—and wore them under her coat and mittens. To see if her invention would be a success, she tested them on a scout troop. Proving a hit, Kathryn applied for a patent. Starting a business at such a young age, Kathryn experienced many challenges, the most difficult one being taken seriously. Kathryn would have her mother accompany her to meetings, but the downside to that was that most people thought

116

Wristies® was her mother's idea. Not so. Kathryn and her product, Wristies®, are so popular that they have been featured in several books, including *I Want to Be A Fashion Designer, How to Be a Teenage Millionaire,* and *Girls and Young Women Entrepreneurs.* Kathryn was an inspiration on Oprah's show![107] In 1997, Kathryn became the youngest person to sell a product on QVC. To learn more about Wristies®, log on to http://wristies.com/about.asp.

Woodworking Niche

At the age of 13, Kenny Kirkpatrick loved woodworking. When an ad in a woodworking catalog for kits to make pens caught Kenny's eye, he immediately thought making and selling fine writing pens would be the perfect way to make money. Ken's Pens was born, and five years later, Kenny continues to sell his handcrafted works of art in stores across Nebraska, realizing an average profit of $700 per month.[108]

Cart Niche

Kim Simpson was only 26 when her corporate recruiter job began to sour. "I was making around $40,000 a year, and the mortgage was no problem," said Kim of the home that she and her husband purchased a few years back. "I didn't want to wear a suit anymore." After looking at her finances, Kim decided to quit her job and start her own business, running a hot dog cart. "Nobody was doing a Chicago-style dog," said Kim, "so that's where I started." Kim searched the Internet and found a cart for $5,000. Then came her permits—at a cost of $273 a year (to guarantee her corner), $95 for a license to sell food, and a $75 vending fee. In her first year of business, Kim grossed over $18,000—almost double her start-up costs.[109]

Insect Niche

Kassidy Briles, a 13-year-old from Des Moines, Iowa, likes to study insects. She created Dream Wings, a butterfly hatchery, and sells butterflies in decorative cages. To get Dream Wings started, Kassidy used the Kauffman guidelines (www.kauffman.org) to create an 18-page business plan, invested $50 of her own money, and registered her business name. Kassidy sells butterflies to many people who love the creatures and especially encourages them as gifts to hospital shut-ins.

Boredom Can Lead to Your Niche

Juliette Brindak, now 17, from Old Greenwich, Connecticut, doodles when she's bored. When she was 10, during a family vacation, she sketched five characters she calls Cool Girls. The Cool Girls have since evolved into MissOandFriends.com, a website for 'Tweens that has received more than half a billion hits. The site is aimed at girls ages eight to 12, and includes games, diaries, horoscopes, contests, and an advice column. "It's a safe place for girls to go and just be girls," says Juliette. "Miss O provides a place where girls can build self-esteem and grow." In 2005 Juliette launched a product line, inspired by the Miss O & Friends gang. A book of short stories, written by visitors to the site, was recently published.[110]

Finding a Niche by Accident

Many young entrepreneurs found their niches by accident. Take for example Chris Hass of Murrieta, California, who was 9 when he discovered his niche. He was playing basketball with some friends and noticed his teammates were missing easy shots because they didn't know how to hold the ball. To solve the problem, Chris dipped his hands in poster paint and placed them exactly in the proper positions for holding a basketball when shooting. Baskets were made and so was a new product, the Hands-On Basketball. Today, stores and catalogs across the country carry his Hands-On Basketball. Chris didn't stop there. He also created the Hands-On Football, Baseball, and other assorted balls and swimming aids.[111] Chris Hass wasn't the first youngster to find a niche by accident. In 1905, 11-year-old Frank

118

Epperson left a stick in a cup of soda outside on a freezing night, accidentally inventing the popsicle.

Fill-a-Need Niche

Don't you hate it when you try to find something in the store, or even online, and can't find what you're looking for? Does that product even exist? Would your life truly be better if you had this product to use? Can it help others? You just might be onto something. Greg and Doug Myers, two college brothers who wanted to do better on tests, developed a program that raises math scores on the SAT by an average of 90 points. The program, compatible with Texas Instruments calculators, is a legal way for test-takers to solve math problems in less time. Score Raising Programs, established in 1998, was founded because the Myers brothers realized that SAT review classes were having students memorize many formulas that could be made into calculator programs, instead of memorizing them. SRP began as a five-program set, and today it contains 22 individual files. Verbal virtual flashcards were recently added to their line to assist students in the one part of the test where memorization is necessary.[112] Visit SRP's website at www.highersat.com.

Fill-a-Void Niche

Teen entrepreneur Kayla Branscum, 16, of Batesville, Arizona, filled a void in her community. She looked around her town and thought, "What's a college town without a coffeehouse?" Thanks to Kayla, the people of Batesville now have a home away from home when they stop in her coffeehouse, Kayla's Java Café.

Although her business actually started as an entrepreneur class research project, Kayla saw the potential in operating a coffeehouse. After calculating the start-up costs for everything from paper cups and coffee, to equipment, furniture, rent, and salaries, Kayla realized that she could make a profit with her idea. After writing up a business plan, she went to the bank and applied for a loan.

119

Kayla continues to watch for new ways to respond to customer needs, such as adding pastries and deli sandwiches to her menu, thus creating more sales opportunities. Adding cold items to her menu, such as cold drinks and a coffee-flavored concoction that she created, the Dreamsicle, helps bring in even more customers to her café in search of new, tasty treats.[113]

Connect-the-Dots Niche

Scott Rock, 17, of Chapman, Kansas, is the owner The Scan Man, a connect-the-dots niche. Scott's customers send him photos they would like to scan to use on their websites or online auctions. After scanning the photos, Scott hosts the files on his site, sends them back through e-mail, or copies them onto a disk for the customer.[114] Scott saw a need, created a niche business, and is a now successful entrepreneur.

Pet Niche

Connor Casey, 12, of Tulsa, Oklahoma, is the owner of Casey's Kanine Treats. Connor's all-natural treats are a hit with all of his customers. Connor doesn't just make dog cookies, he also prints labels on his computer, and packages the goods himself.[115] You would never guess that a 12-year-old runs the business when you purchase Casey's Kanine Treats from a pet supply store!

Overlooked Niche

Has competition overlooked some niche? At the age of 12, Charles Schwab, now CEO of the investment powerhouse Charles Schwab and Co., started a chicken operation in his backyard. He felt that the neighborhood did not have access to fresh eggs, only store-bought eggs, which were old by the time they got to the grocers' refrigerators. Charles sold fresh eggs door-to-door. But he didn't stop there. He took his business one step further and sold chicken droppings as fertilizer, then killed and marketed the chickens himself.[116] Charles never convinced himself that he could do only one thing. Every business opportunity has potential angles that can serve customer needs, and Charles wasn't inhibited about extending those branches. Additionally, he was always on the lookout, and prepared, to surf the next business wave—all before his 13th birthday!

Create a Niche

Christine Keck, now 14, from Brookville, Indiana, needed to raise money to buy a horse. Two years ago, at the age of 12, out of the blue, Christine decided to sell fleece hats to people whom she approached. Christine designed fun, silly, bright-colored, Happy Hats in 14 different styles and designs. It took her less than a year to get the horse after opening her Happy Hats business. Christine enjoys her business so much that she expanded her business by selling her hats in several different locations, including craft stores, ski shops, and convenience stores, as well as at craft shows.[117]

Unmet Niche

Christopher Gilliam, 41, has a talent for looking in a place and spotting an unmet need. Christopher discovered his niche when he saw prime advertising space on the empty backs of parking garage and valet tickets. At the time, Christopher worked at an advertising company, so he pitched the concept to his company for them to offer in their line of products. When the agency didn't want to take a chance on his idea, Christopher decided to develop the business himself. He went to local garages to gauge their reaction to his concept, found a building in which to lease an office for his new business, and attended the National Parking Association's Parking, Transportation and Services Convention & Exposition trade show to meet people and show them his product. Today, AdverTickets has clients like Delta Air Lines, DreamWorks, and Sony and can be found in parking garages all over North America and in Mexico and Puerto Rico. Although AdverTickets began in 1998 with a budget of $5,000, sales are over $10 million per year.[118]

Realizing that elevator riders are a captive—and usually bored—audience, Mike DeFranza's advertising brainstorm is ending one of the last ad-free zones in America: elevators. Mike launched Captivate Network, based in Westford, Massachusetts, which shows ads on flat-screen TVs in elevators. In six daily trips of one minute each, a rider can view up to 24 hours of elevator ads annually. Captivate Network charges companies such as General Motors, McDonald's, and Sprint up to $300,000 *monthly* for repeating 10-second spots on nearly 5,600 screens. Talk about going up an elevator to financial success!

Marketing Your Niche Business

Marketing your niche business is a key business strategy for young entrepreneurs. Instead of spreading your advertising dollars thin by mass marketing a niche business, smart young entrepreneurs find specific, identifiable groups of people who are interested in their products or services. Then they hone in on that area and sell, sell, sell!

By now you probably have a business idea in mind. The next floor, Creating and Registering Your Business Name, will help you decide what to name your business, and how to check for trademarks, domain names, and other tips to ensure that the business name you choose is not being used—and is right for your business.

6th Floor

Creating and Registering Your Business Name

"The simple joy of taking an idea into one's own hands and giving it proper form, that's exciting."
~George Nelson

Up until now, you have gathered an extensive amount of information about business and are ready to make yours happen. The vital stage of your business has now been reached, and you are ready to give it a name. If you have a business name already chosen, put it aside for now. Take the time to visit this floor and, afterward, you'll be better prepared to set your business name in concrete—or create a new one.

A great name is the beginning of a great brand of business: Yours! Creating a business name can be one of the most rewarding tasks in the initial phase of your business. It should be short, memorable, easy to spell, easy to pronounce, culturally sensitive, descriptive, and easy to associate with your business.

Take Time to Think of a Business Name

Thinking up an effective business name is going to take lots of time and some hard work. Do not create a business name based on your favorite vacation spot or family pet. Obscure names won't create awareness of your business over time, won't give your business considerable value, and won't reflect the nature of your business as well as a carefully chosen name would. Do you think that department stores would have sold as many Ralph Lauren polo shirts had Ralph kept his original name, Ralph Lifshitz?

Company Name Contest

When searching for the perfect title for my book, *The Crowning Touch: Preparing for Beauty Pageant Competition,* I wanted a unique title to add to my already-chosen subtitle. As a pageant director, I held a book title contest in one of my pageants. The pageant contestant who came up with a winning book title received $100 in tickets for her guests to attend the pageant. One of my contestants came up with *The Crowning Touch,* and it proved to be a winner.

If you want to broaden your horizons, offer a "Test Your Wits with My Company Name Contest!" to family and friends. If you are trying to come up with a business name for a virtual store that sells baked goods, offer a set amount of goods to the winner. If you provide a car-washing service, offer a free car wash to the winner.

Memorable, Nonsensical Names Work

When competition is fierce in your business, a unique name can brand you. Silly company names like Google, Yahoo!, and Amazon.com work because they stand out. Good business names are easily memorable and easily typed, so this generally means they are short.

Avoid Words with Variable Spellings

Try to avoid words that have more than one meaning and words that sound the same but are spelled differently. For example, knight.com might be mistaken for night.com when spoken. Tough-to-spell words should also be avoided, such as "compliment," which could also be spelled "complement." Deliberate misspellings can work against you. Count on losing business to "The Candy Store" if your business name is "The Kandy Store." Count on getting tired of spelling it out to potential customers. It was a smart move when Bill Hargis, then CEO of the Switch Beverage Co. and creator of the carbonated juice drink, The Switch, changed the drink's name from the original name Knew Jewce. (The Switch is a skateboarding term for making moves more complicated by doing them backwards, or "switching" them.) Bill Hargis was successful in getting many soda and juice drinkers to switch to The Switch.[119]

Brainstorming for a Business Name

To get started, brainstorm. Think about all the possible names you could name your business and write them down. Look at the thesaurus and find all the synonyms for your words. Start playing with a combination of your various words. Don't worry about how things sound right now—just make a list. Then review your list and give some thought to each name. Weed out the ones you don't like and prioritize the ones you do.

Be Broad with Your Business Name

Be broad with your chosen name. When Turner named his pet care business Turner Cares…, his company name remained open for many services other than pet care, including lawn care, child care, metal polishing, tutoring, etc., all listed in bullets under the main name. "Being broad allows you not to restrict your product or service lines," says Turner.

Ian Abston, an Elkhart Lake High School student from Wisconsin, and his partner, started their business "2 Buff Guys," a company specializing in lawn care and other handyman-type jobs. During their first summer of business, "2 Buff Guys" netted nearly $10,000![120] Their broad business name told customers, "We are strong. We can do labor-intensive work!" When Eric Lupton, 17, of Boynton, Florida, named his company Cyber Surgeons, you know that his company provides an "MD for your PC," one who probably can fix any type of computer and problem it has. Cyber Surgeons grossed over $13,000 in its first year of business.[121]

Avoid Names that Literally Describe the Product or Service

When thinking up a name for a new business or product, consider the four types used: *descriptive*, which says just what the business is (The Beaded Jewelry Co.); *suggestive*, which points out a quality or attribute of your product (The Moroccan Jewelry Co.); *arbitrary*, which has no connection to what you are selling, for example, Amazon.com; and *fanciful*, a made-up word like Xerox.

Avoid names that literally describe the product or service, like Computer Consulting Company or The Pizza Parlor. Such business names limit—in consumers' minds—what you sell. If your computer consulting company or pizza parlor offers more than the names imply, people may not realize it.

Avoid Geographical Names

When coming up with a business name, avoid geographical names. Besides being easy to forget, and difficult to protect under trademark law, a geographical name may no longer fit if you move or expand your business.

Copyright

Copyright is the legal form of protection provided by the laws of the United States (Title 17, U.S. Code) to an author, composer, playwright, publisher, or distributor to exclusive publication, production, sale, or distribution of a literary, musical, dramatic, artistic, and other intellectual works, both published and non-published. The symbols that are used in copyright protection include © or (c).

According to Larry Maxham, Esq., founder of The Maxham Firm (www.maxhamfirm.com), a San Diego patent and trademark law firm that provides legal services in the field of intellectual property, "A copyright gives the owner the exclusive right to reproduce, distribute copies, perform or display the work publicly and enables the owner to prevent people from copying or commercially exploiting the work without the owner's permission. It protects the form of expression rather than the subject matter of the writing."[122]

For general information about copyright, contact the Copyright Public Information Office at (202) 707-3000 between 8:30 a.m. until 5:00 p.m., Eastern time, Monday through Friday, except federal holidays. Recorded information is available 24 hours a day. Or, if you know which application forms you want, request them from the Forms and Publications Hotline at (202) 707-9100 24 hours a day. Leave a message. You can access the Copyright Office homepage at www.copyright.gov, or write:

Library of Congress
Copyright Office
Publications Section, LM-455
101 Independence Avenue, S.E.
Washington, DC 20559-6000

Check Trademarks

After you've narrowed your names down to two or three choices, check trademarks. Make sure no one is using your chosen business name. A basic federal trademark search can be conducted online at the United States Patent and Trademark Office's (USPTO) website at www.uspto.gov. To get to the trademark section of the website, click on "TRADEMARKS" on the left of the homepage screen. Once in the Trademark section, visit the top left section called "SERVICES." In that section you will find "SEARCH trademarks." Click on that and follow the instructions to do a very basic trademark search. If your chosen name comes up instantly, try searching the name with variations to see if something else is available.

If your business is anything but a small, local service or retail business, such as a lawn care or an art supply store, you'll probably want to take advantage of trademark protection. Distinctive business names such as Xerox and Amazon.com are clever and memorable, and they usually receive protection under federal and state trademark law. Common or ordinary names, such as Henry's Hardware or Pets.com, usually don't. Therefore, it's not necessary to have a trademark or service mark for a local business. To protect your brand, a U.S. Trademark (TM) or service mark (SM) costs $325. This is inexpensive compared to trying to defend it later. Contact the Commissioner for Trademarks, 2900 Crystal Drive, Arlington, VA 22202-3513, for more information.

If you haven't reached a satisfactory conclusion about whether your chosen name is available, the next step is to use a commercial service that exists for this purpose. This service will search a number of trade name (the official name of a business, the one it uses on its letterhead and bank account when not dealing with consumers), trademark (a word, symbol, or device used in trade with goods to indicate their source and distinguish them from the goods of others), and service mark (same as a trademark with the exception that it identifies and distinguishes the source of a service rather than a product), registries and compile a detailed list of similar names and/or marks. Probably the best-known trademark search company is Thomson & Thomson, 600 Victory Road, North Quincy, MA, 02171, (800) 692-8833, www.thomson-thomson.com.

Check Domain Names

If your business will have a website, you must decide what your domain name will be. Make sure that an appropriate domain name is available and can be registered. You want YourCompanyName.com, of course, not to be already in use. Customers have come to expect a website address that is close to or a derivative of your business name. You can search for available domain names by visiting a domain name registrar such as register.com. For help with selecting and registering a domain name, click on "Choosing and Registering a Domain Name."

If your domain name is petwears.com, for example, you might want to buy petwares.com. Each domain name costs $35 per year, but you'll probably earn more than $35 a year off of each name registered. Just be careful that you do not buy a domain that could be an infringement of someone else's trademark. That could lead to the loss of your domain name, not to mention legal costs. One lady wanted to register "The Martha Steward of the Dog World" as her own name, but wisely, she didn't.

Once you purchase your domain name, don't let it accidentally expire. If you do, someone might swoop in and buy your name—then resell it or use it for a website loaded with advertisements. "I wish we would have paid for ChuckleBait.com on an automatic renewing payment," says children's book author John Scieszka of his online promotions site. "We lost the name when it expired and some business thing took it over."[123]

To ensure that you don't become a victim, keep your contact information up-to-date. This allows your registry to let you know, via e-mail, that your domain is going to expire. Don't use a free e-mail account because if you happen to not access it in 30 days, it goes away. Take advantage of automatic renewal of your domain name. Most registries offer this service, which allows registrants who buy a domain name for a year to automatically renew it, so make sure that your payment information (your credit card) is current; If your credit card will expire soon, know that automatic renewal of your credit card won't connect to your automated domain registration. Many people have lost their domains because their credit card expiration dates were extended, which caused the automated registration renewal charge to not go through for the registrar, who then tried to contact the domain owner, but couldn't because they'd changed e-mail addresses. Finally, register your domain name for more than one year, say, in three-year increments. In most cases, doing so will decrease your registration costs.

Domain Name Search Programs

Domain name search programs can help you choose variations on a business name. "Mozzle Std 2.30" is a program that can help you do so. It is downloadable for free from: http://www.simtel.net/pub/pd/54228.html. This program is very helpful when you're trying to think of a new domain name. (Mozzle's "Advanced Search" feature is very useful.)

How to Register a Domain Name

There are many services that will register your domain name, including your Internet service provider or the people who will house your website. The best way to do this is to go to Net Solutions, the oldest, biggest, and most reputable registrar (http://netsol.com). Click on "Learning Center." Then click on "Getting Started." Under "Learning Center Topics," click on "Domain Names." Here you can learn about domain names, the benefits of a domain name, the differences of domain name registrars, and for how long you should register a domain name.

Search the Internet

Search the Internet to see if anyone else is using your chosen name. Just because it's not someone else's domain doesn't mean it isn't being used on the Internet in some other form. If you do find it being used in some form, this doesn't mean you weren't allowed to use the name. It's important that you know everything about the business name you are considering before you use it.

Check With City Hall

To obtain a license, contact the City Hall within the city where your business will be conducted. For sole proprietors—a business owned and operated by one individual, check for local assumed names (also known as DBA, which stands for Doing Business As). You will also be required to publish your business name in the local legal notices of your town newspaper unless you actually conduct business under your own name rather than the fictitious name.

A Business Name Legal Nightmare

According to "Be Smart...Be Legal," an article written by Amy Rauch Nelson for *Y&E – The Magazine for Teen Entrepreneurs*, a nightmare happened to Desi Metcalf and her sister, Sharlene, who started, at the age of 16 and 17, respectively, their own private label of surf wear and accessories, based in Whittier, California. After coming up with the idea to carry their own surf wear line, GidgetGear (in honor of Desi's nickname, Gidget), business started to take off. This is when Sharlene and Desi received a letter from an attorney notifying them that GidgetGear was violating another company's trademark on the name Gidget.

The sisters had known from the start that the name Gidget had already been registered. They thought that GidgetGear, however, was different enough to stand on its own. In the end the Metcalf sisters didn't want to challenge the name in court and donated the remaining $15,000 worth of merchandise to charity.[124] Had they challenged the name in court, I believe they would have won. The name GidgetGear, a single entity without a space between the words Gidget and Gear, was four letters longer than the word Gidget! This experience has only made these two ladies more careful when selecting their business name, so look forward to their next successful business venture. These young ladies have what it takes!

A Town Name Up In Arms

When 'Tween shop owner Margarita Olivares, of Corpus Christi, Texas, created her store, she called it "Splendora—It's a Girl Thing." She thought it was a cute, whimsical, and completely original name. Later, she learned there was a city in Texas called Splendora, with the word Splendora in many of the local businesses' names. Margarita felt that the state of Texas was big enough to hold plenty of Splendora stores.

But Texas had other plans for Margarita. An online retail search engine company with Splendora in its name soon issued a letter to Margarita, suggesting she change the name of her business or face them in court. Both Margarita and the online company had pending trademarks on their names, but Margarita eventually gave up fighting for the name due to legal costs.

Margarita left this experience on a positive note. Now called The Startup, Margarita recently opened a second store in San Antonio, Texas. She was grateful that this experience happened to her early, when she only had one store to deal with. Having to change a store's name when she had become more established or had 10 stores would have been much harder.[125]

Now that you've named your business, it's time to learn about the power of advertising. On the next floor, Advertise, you will see that having visibility in various media, at the same time, will benefit your business. As a new business with a small advertising budget, you will learn how to barter with advertising media, obtaining much business visibility for the least amount of money.

7th *Floor*

Advertise

"If you think advertising doesn't work, consider the millions
of Americans that now think yogurt tastes good."
~Joe L. Whitley

One of the toughest challenges for any new business is getting its name out in the public. This battle, also known as marketing, is one you'll wage throughout the life of your business. Business mogul Ted Turner once said, "Early to bed and early to rise, work like hell and advertise." To survive in the business world, one has to both work hard and advertise.

If you learn to become creative in your promotional efforts, you can grab your audience's attention without spending much money. Alicia Dacoba, 9, from Paw Paw, Michigan, couldn't afford to advertise her ventriloquist business. So she took her $13 puppet and alerted the local newspaper every time she performed for charities, in order to gain free publicity when she could. Alicia is now in her twenties, and her business, "Alicia and Her Live Talkin' Critters," is a full-time venture. She has been featured on

The Tonight Show with Jay Leno and even on the BBC while traveling the United States with her portable zoo.[126]

Promoting Your Business for Pennies

Before you pay for advertising, think of what you can offer to a magazine, newspaper, radio or television station in exchange for advertising. When Marc D'Amelio founded Madsoul in 2000, an urban streetwear label, with a mere $1,000, his advertising budget was non-existent. To gain advertising in a small hip-hop magazine, Marc traded some clothes from his Madsoul stock line in exchange for advertising. With other magazines, he pushed to get the line coverage in the editorial pages first, then, with incoming sales from the editorial feature, was able to purchase advertising.[127]

Creating a Well-Written Press Release

A press release is a brief text announcement of an event, development, or other newsworthy story. A press release should be short and to the point and should include the 5 Ws: Who, What, Where, When, and Why. The material should contain your business name, address, and phone number, plus the name of a contact person. If you have a website address, be sure to include it in your text. According to a recent survey, 61% of consumers discover/find new website addresses in magazine articles; 94% of businesses discover/find new websites in magazine articles.[128] Always make sure that your press release has excellent spelling and mechanics. Type and double space all press releases. This is one rule that should never be broken. The press release should not be longer than one page and should be limited to a single event. Write the press release as if it were going to be published word for word in the newspaper. Give your press release a short but interesting headline. Indicate where the press release ends, otherwise a busy editor might wonder whether there was a second page to the release. That is why reporters and writers always indicate the end of a piece with "###" or "END."

Check to see that your press release is free from typos and grammatical errors. With one typographical error, Liz Miller made a hugely embarrassing mistake in the public relations world. As communications manager for Jan Marini Skin Research, a skin care company based in San Jose, California, Liz mailed out a press release without verifying the telephone number on the press release. Liz, as it turned out, typed a single incorrect digit that connected readers to a sex phone line.[129] Poorly crafted press releases will do a new business more harm than good. Proofread very carefully.

Once you've written your press release, you need to get it to the right department. If you're not sending it to an individual editor or reporter, send it to the appropriate department, such as city news, entertainment, business, sports, etc. Send press releases at least two weeks in advance. For more information on writing press releases, visit Dr. Randall Hansen's website, http://www.stetson.edu/~rhansen/prguide.html.

Include a Photo with Your Press Release

When you submit a press release, it is important that you include a clear photo of yourself and the product or service that you are offering. Make sure that your photo is of good quality, in sharp focus, with people's faces no smaller than a thumb print. Identify each person in a caption attached to the back of the photo and always include a contact telephone number. Make sure you spell everyone's name correctly.

If you have a product to promote, submit a photo of you holding your product. If you mow lawns, a picture of you pushing the lawn mower says 1,000 words! If you design hand-crafted jewelry, include some local, well-known teens to model your jewelry in the photo. If you can't afford to pay them, consider gifting them the jewelry for their time. This gives you an opportunity to have these "models" serve as walking advertisements for your product.

Magazine Press Releases

A magazine is another medium to include in your business promotional efforts. Is your business new to the area? Do you feel your product or service can help people? Contact the editor of your town or city magazine to let them know about your business in case they would like to do a feature story about it. Or, submit a standard press release. Make sure your contact name and number are clearly visible so that you can be reached for further information. For some publications and magazines, the deadline is two months prior to publication.

Become an Excellent Writer

If you are not a good writer, become one. "There are so many kids that come out of high school and college who are used to e-mail, instant messages, and thinking and writing in fragments that they can hardly speak in full sentences," says Tim Hodgman, senior agent/team leader for the Holt Dimondale insurance agency in Holt, Michigan. "So how can we expect them to write full sentences?" The ability to deliver top-notch sales writing stems from a commitment to reading. If you read good writing, you'll develop confidence to write well. "It's like playing an instrument," continues Tim. "The more you practice, the better you'll be." [130] If business owners can't structure a letter or e-mail, how are they going to run a company successfully? The English Language Institute Hotline is an excellent place to find grammar tips. Visit their free website and browse the subject areas at http://www.udel.edu/eli/questions/g-contents.html. If you have a grammar question, send yours in. A reply will be posted.

Television Talk Shows

Talk shows are the ultimate tutorial of today's "video-oriented, high-tech world." Each year, nearly two thousand guests are scheduled to appear on programs broadcast throughout the United States and Canada. Since appearing on talk shows doesn't cost guests anything, it is probably one of the best promotional vehicles for your business. Nine-year-old Julia York promoted her book, *The Kid's Guide to New Hope*, on local talk shows.[131] Appearing on a TV talk show can provide a wealth of opportunities for promoting products and services to a wide audience, without the exorbitant expenses of paid advertising. And, when the show airs in re-runs, it's like a free commercial for your business. If there is a particular show you would like to be on, visit the show's website and click on the "Be a Guest" link. Here is where you'll find dozens of show subjects the producers are currently pursuing. Or pitch your show idea to the producers.

To give you a better understanding of appearing on talk shows, read *Get on TV: The Insider's Guide to Pitching the Producers and Promoting Yourself*, by Jacquie Jordan. If it's Oprah's show you're striving for, read *The Ultimate Guide to Getting Booked on Oprah*, by Susan Harrow. To find out about national TV talk shows, including contact information, visit http://dir.yahoo.com/Entertainment/Television_Shows/Talk_Sh ows/ on the Internet.

Cable and Network Television

If you want to reach a wide audience, contact your local cable or network television stations for their advertising rate sheet. You might be surprised how relatively inexpensive their advertising is at different times of the day.

Bartering for Cable Advertising

I was able to barter for local cable programming advertisements for my pageant on the local cable's MTV station. In exchange, the cable TV company received advertising on a music radio station, which was simultaneously set up by both cable and radio managers and myself with the idea that I would obtain both media as co-sponsors. When both teams agreed to sponsorship, I then secured a glossy city magazine and the town newspaper to round out sponsorship. In all, I was able to secure four major media, for free, to promote my pageant event. The different media enjoyed being promoted on the other sites. Often these media will work a promotional trade when space is available. It won't hurt to ask, especially if you are in the entertainment industry and need to reach a large audience. Not only did I receive promotion prior to the event to create public awareness, but also the pageant was aired in its entirety on the local cable television station.

Television Guides

Advertise your business in the local network television guide. A TV guide lasts for a week, so, if you're looking for a longer stay, stick with a monthly magazine or the yearly Yellow Pages. If you want to advertise in the cable television guide, contact your local cable provider. It might be worth your investment to purchase advertising in both network or cable television guides if you can secure advertisement next to a favorite programming evening, or even a crossword puzzle.

Small town network and cable companies might be more willing to barter advertisements in their cable television guide. Speak to management to find out what you might offer in exchange for an advertisement in their cable television guide. For example, if you are a performer, offer to perform at the cable company's picnic in exchange for advertising. A baker might bake cakes for a station party or event. Figure out what your costs will be before you offer to barter to make sure it will be worth your effort to get the "free" advertising.

Radio Talk Shows

Radio talk shows offer another avenue for promoting your business. If accepted, you can appear at the station or call in your information. If you call in your interview, the host will generally ask you to call in five minutes before air time and put you on hold until his show begins.

Radio and television station directories can provide you with the names and addresses of thousands of media leads. Though somewhat expensive, these directories can be helpful. They are also available in the reference sections of most well-stocked libraries.

Display and Classified Advertising

Newspapers and magazines sell display and classified advertising. Both can be effective media for advertising a product- or service-based business. In some areas newspaper classifieds are now free. Contact the advertising department to request a rate card. A rate card provides advertisers with advertising rates, mechanical and copy requirements, advertising deadlines, and other information that the advertiser needs to know before placing an order.

Test Your Ad Copy

Can't decide whether to use "soon to be released" or "in limited supply" in your ad copy? If you are struggling to decide which ad copy works best, check out the free website www.adcomparator.com to simultaneously test up to 15 varying aspects of any ad, website, or e-mail campaign. It will show you which combination of elements is likely to have the highest success rate.

Track Your Ads

Say you are running several ads in different publications, then, all of a sudden you receive a load of orders. How will you know which ad(s) generated those orders? You can track your orders by keying them. On each ad, next to your company name, add a letter or number code that will indicate to you where the order came from. For example, if you are advertising in the February issue of *Good Housekeeping* magazine and your business name is Creative Toys, put your name in the ad as Creative Toys-GH2. GH stands for the magazine name, and the 2 stands for February.

Internet Classifieds

There are many free online classified sites in which you can place your classified ads to sell your product or service. Craigslist has a growing presence in most major cities, and you can list ads for free. Visit www.Craigslist.org. For a huge list of other online classified sites, Google in key words "Internet Classified Advertising."

Yellow Pages

The Yellow Pages have proven to be a great advertising vehicle for Turner's pet care business. He runs a line advertisement in the business section under "Pet Sitters." In the past he has purchased a display ad in the same Yellow Pages, but felt that the line ad pulled in the same number of customers as a display advertisement did. So, Turner dropped the display and continued the line advertisement.

If you would like your listing to be near the top, create a business name that starts with the letter A. Mia is able to see her business, Affordable Pet Care, listed first in the Yellow Pages.

Posters and Flyers

There is usually no cost for displaying posters and flyers on community bulletin boards. However, request approval before posting any item on a board. Include a posting deadline date on the right corner of your poster or flyers for proper maintenance. Don't forget to take down old flyers and replace them with clean, current ones.

Business Cards

Treat your business cards as part of your advertising campaign. Always keep some with you for when you meet new people. Most businesses print their business information on the front of their business card. But did you know you can *also* print information on the back? If you provide a lawn care service, advertise your name, logo, slogan, and contact information on the front. On the back you can list the types of lawn services that you provide. Or, use the back to list your service or product prices. What you promote on the back is only limited to your creativity. Furthermore, you could have a folding business card. Lift the flap and you have even more space to get your message out.

Grocery Store Receipts

Grocery stores often print advertisements on the back of their receipts. Contact the store manager for advertising information. Grocery store receipts might be an ideal place to advertise a babysitting service, garage cleaning, lawn care, or pet care business.

Specialty Advertising

A specialty advertising company can print your business name and telephone number on several items, including pens, hats, Frisbees, t-shirts, key chains, and magnetic business cards. Imagine your business information prominently displayed on the refrigerators of an entire town! To find a company that can place your company name on products such as key chains, pens, and Frisbees, Google "Specialty Advertising" on the Internet.

Company Newsletter

You can keep old clients and new clients involved in your business via a newsletter. A company newsletter can acknowledge your business and what you can do for your clients. Your newsletter can feature the latest industry news, tips, and any other helpful information related to your business. Your newsletter could include photos of you and your product(s) or service, photos with customers, customer testimonials, and contact information. Your newsletter serves as a reminder of your business to your clients and as a vehicle to encourage new clients to give you a try. Your goal with the newsletter is to keep connected with your current clients and reach new ones.

Student Directories

Turner advertised his pet care business in a number of elementary, middle, and high school student directories. These directories have long staying power, even beyond the intended year, so his ad works for him all year round and beyond. Classmates remember where they saw Turner's pet care ad and consult the directory before they go on vacation. No matter which directory classmates look at, chances are good they'll find Turner's advertisement, because it was included in student directories several years in a row.

School Yearbooks

Contact the school yearbook staff if you want to buy an ad in their yearbook. They can give you advertising rates, copy, and deadline information. It wasn't long ago that only high schools printed yearbooks. Now, middle schools are printing them as well, some just as elaborate. Plan ahead and call in September or October to be included in the end-of-the-year yearbook. Yearbooks need plenty of lead time.

High School and College Newspapers

High school and college newspaper departments would love to sell you advertisement in their newspapers. If you do purchase advertising, remember to also send the editorial department a press release about your business. Many will give free press alongside a paid advertisement to "tell more of the story."

School Events Programs

Middle and high schools frequently stage productions that include a printed program. These programs often include ads purchased by individuals and businesses. The ads are usually not very expensive. Contact the production manager to find out how you can purchase advertising in this medium.

Testimonials

One of the easiest ways a new business can establish credibility is to get letters of reference from satisfied customers. Like an article in the newspaper, testimonials can also be reproduced and used as independent proof that yours is the sort of company with which people like to do business. Word-of-mouth advertising—testimonials—is the best type of advertising.

Buzz Marketing

How do you get people talking about your business? You advertise. You can also generate press releases and ask clients to talk you up. Using the power of word-of-mouth is what buzz marketing is all about. Getting people to talk about your business in their general daily conversation is buzz marketing at it's best. While many people aren't swayed with advertisements, they do tend to listen to what a friend recommends. "The notion of word of mouth is that people have conversations every day with each other, and certain people, between 20 and 25 percent, relate in some way or another information about brands," says Ed Keller, CEO of Roper ASW and co-author of *The Influentials: One American in Ten Tells The Other Nine How to Vote, Where to Eat, and What to Buy.* "Word of mouth marketing is the desire on the part of marketers to increase the chances that their brand or message will become part of those conversations."[132]

Tina Wells was still in high school writing reviews of fashion and beauty products when she became CEO of Buzz Marketing Group, an "organically-designed" online company that helped other companies create buzz. Tina is currently studying marketing management at the University of Pennsylvania's Wharton School of Business, applying this successful "out-of-the-box" method of advertising to those included in her textbooks.

If you want a strong buzz campaign, you must comp, that is, give freely, to generate buzz. Your chances of gaining great expose improve by giving away products or services. To get your name out in the public, you must comp a lot of products or services. This will help you to successfully generate buzz and boost demand for your product. One dentist placed a set of free veneers—over $20,000 worth of market-value dental work per set of teeth—on three of her popular, "blabbermouth" customers. Photos of these "satisfied patients" were then placed in local and regional advertisements—without compensation to the patients. When friends saw their new smiles, buzz generated—and so did sales for the dentist. Years (and an occasional original ad-run) later, still more sales are generated. If you want to start getting the word out about your product or service, comp it to get people to engage in conversation about it.

Buzz marketing can occur in many forms. If you write books, give free copies to friends to review your book, asking them to rank you on Amazon.com's website. If you communicate in an online chat room, start spreading the word there. You may want to say to someone, "Have you heard/read/seen...?" You don't even have to tell them that the product is your brainchild!

If your company puts its best foot forward, then it's time for you to begin your buzzing campaign. "Buzz should be the byproduct of any well-conceived, well-executed marketing program," says Drew Neisser, president and CEO of Renegade Marketing Group. "At the core of buzz is a product or service that delivers on its promises. Although you can generate buzz about a bad product, it will only serve to hasten that particular brand's demise. If you have a product problem, fix it first."[133]

Family and Friends

Remember to include family and friends in your promotional efforts. William Shakespeare said it best: "We are advertised by our loving friends." Give them a dozen business cards to hand out. Write their names on the back of each card so that you can track where the referrals came from. This allows you to reward those who help you secure new jobs by, for example, washing their car for free when they line up two or three new customers for your car-washing service.

Your Business Website

A business website is a smart place to advertise your business. Your own personal website gives you the perfect opportunity to display your product or service. Take advantage of the web's free pages for business advertising that are part of the benefits of a business ownership. If you want to assess your products' sales potential on the web, test your product at online auction sites. If your preliminary sales are good, then consider purchasing a domain name/URL and build a basic site. Above all, keep your website simple and easy to navigate. Information on creating a website can be found on the 4th and 8th Floors.

Mark Twain said, "Many a small thing has been made large by the right kind of advertising." Hopefully you have absorbed from this discussion some insightful information on the different types of media and benefits on advertising your business wisely. On the next floor, Set Up Shop, you'll learn about business tools and supplies that will benefit your business. You will also get tips on creating a business logo, slogan, and printed material to get your business started. You'll even find more information on getting your business website up and running.

8th Floor

Set Up Shop

"To open a shop is easy, to keep it open is an art."
~Chinese Proverb

When beginning a business, it is helpful to follow a checklist that will guide you through all aspects of preparing to operate it, from finding a location to house your company all the way to constructing a website. The "all the way" part can bog anyone down, especially when left solely to memory.

Create a Checklist

Instead of relying on memory, create a business checklist to help guide you on the path of every important detail prior to opening the doors of your business. You'll be confident when you display an "Open for Business" sign on ribbon-cutting day and are truly prepared to serve your customers' needs. The information on this floor is simply a guide. You can add or delete items on your business checklist to fit your company goals.

Business Location

While every business owner dreams of a business office in an office building suite, this is also the most expensive way to go. Instead, make an office out of a spare bedroom or corner of a room in your home. If you truly need to rent a location to house your business, call a real estate company's leasing department to help you find the right office or store location at the right rental price.

Sublease Office or Retail Space

You might check into already-established businesses to see if they have an office or corner space that can be subleased to you. The downside to subleasing space from an already-existing business is that you pay rent to the business owner, not the landlord. If the business owner that you sublease from doesn't pay her rent, she could go out of business and you could lose your entire investment — overnight.

If you really want to sublease a space, do extensive research. At the very least visit with the landlord before agreeing to a deal with the tenant. Furthermore, visit the store several times, at different times of the day, to get a feel for business activity — or lack of it. You might find that the shop isn't always open when it is supposed to be, and that the shop appears to be running low on inventory — all classic signs of a failing business. It may be that the clothing boutique you want to sublease space from doesn't have much traffic and welcomes your rental income — not to mention your business traffic — to boost their business.

Trade or Rent Office Space

Sometimes you can trade or rent office space from other business owners by the day or even by the hour if you need to meet with an important client. You might be able to provide services for free to a company in exchange for use of office space as needed. The Office Business Center Association International (www.execsuites.org) and the Regus Group

147

(www.regusgroup.com), for example, offer many business services and offices for rent on an as-needed basis. Check with local clubs and organizations. Many often have free meeting spaces available for members, maybe even members' entrepreneurial children. You can even rent a room at your local public library, as technology consultant Peter Bryant does when he initially meets his clients.[134]

Creative Business Locations

Many teen business owners find that coming up with a business location is a real problem. For instance, they have little start-up cash, so there's no way they can afford the high monthly rent of a prime location. And even if they did have the money, they're too young to sign the contracts required to rent a storefront or office. For Daniel White, 20, of Houston, Texas, owner of DEWIE Chairs for Children, finding target customers was a no-brainer. At first Daniel had a lemonade stand at the soccer field, to which he brought the chairs he had for sale, setting them out by his stand. While that worked well for a while, he realized that he needed to reach more kids (and their parents). That's when he struck a deal with a local day-care center. Daniel was able to display pictures of his chairs, constructed out of PVC pipe and canvas, as well as an order form on the front desk. He picked up the order forms once a week and delivered the chairs to the day-care center.[135]

Rent Retail Shelf Space

You might be surprised to learn that many small retailers would gladly rent you shelf space in their stores. Talk to the manager or owner and present your product in a professional manner. Since this may be a first for the store owner, ask him or her to make you an offer to have your product in the store, or make a fair offer yourself. You can even suggest a 90-day trial to see how your product sells.

Consign Products to Retailers

You can also consign your product to retailers. Retail store owners often work with limited budgets and may be reluctant to carry a new product. Consignment, however, provides an attractive alternative to the business owner. It is best to present your product in a self-contained display. One hand cream company offers its products in a stand-alone display. The hand cream representative visits the store twice a month to check inventory and restock the display. Then the representative gives the store owner an invoice at the end of the month.

Sell Products at Trade Shows

If you have the ability to deliver your product in large quantities, consider selling at trade shows. Attendees of trade shows visit them to make buying decisions, and many businesses have been launched on the path to superstardom from the halls of convention centers. To locate upcoming events, visit the Trade Show Network at www.tsnn.com.

Amazon.com

Amazon.com offers several ways you can sell your product(s) in an easy-to-navigate environment. To learn about the different ways you can sell new, used, refurbished, and collectible items, visit www.Amazon.com. Go to the far upper-right corner and click on "help." Scroll down to "Making Money With Amazon.com." Click on "Selling at Amazon.com." When you arrive at the page, read "Selling at Amazon.com is Easy." Here you will find information on the different places that you can sell your products, including Marketplace, Auctions, and zShops. If you have your own book, music, video, or DVD title to sell, visit the "Advantage Program." To find out how you can begin selling in minutes, click on the "Quick Start Guide."

Workspace

If your work is home-based, a work space dedicated entirely to your business is essential. A desk is ideal, but a table from which you can conduct business over the phone will do just fine. Avoid using the kitchen or dining room table or any other space that needs to be cleared when business ends for the day. Experiment with layouts using Ikea's (www.ikea.com) online space planner.

If your business is away from your home, for example, a window washer, while you don't actually work at home, you do run the business from home (sending out flyers, making calls to place ads, calling customers to get work, customer billing, etc.). A space dedicated to your business helps to make your business successful. But before you set up your work space, check local zoning laws, which sometimes limit the scope of home businesses.

Post Office Box

See your postmaster about renting a post office box if you don't want to use your personal or business address for your business. Prices of the boxes vary according to the size you rent. Plan in advance because many post offices have a waiting list for reserving a post office box. An alternative to a post office box is to rent a specialized mail box that allows you to use the street address of that company as your business address and the box number as your suite number. Companies such as the UPS Store will rent you such a box.

Equipment and Supplies

Buy only the office equipment and office supplies that you absolutely need when starting your business. You can always add equipment and supplies as you generate more business. Keep your receipts so that you can deduct your business purchases on your tax forms, or return items you do not use. Find the right suppliers for your business by searching suppliers by industry, product type, or location at *Entrepreneur's* Supplier Search from ThomasNet.com (www.aolsmallbusiness.com/startup).

150

If you can borrow office equipment, do so. If you must purchase office furniture, buy used, either at garage sales, from thrift stores, from the classified advertisement listings, or from the used section of an office supply store. Do not spend lavishly for your office, excessive travel, and "perks." There really is no room for excess spending in any young business. If you will initially produce the same business working from your basement as you would renting a swanky office space, work from your basement. Scrutinize every expense.

Several pieces of equipment are important for running a successful business. Suggested general equipment and supplies can be found on this floor. Not included are specific equipment and supplies that you will need for particular businesses, such as a lawn mower and weed whacker for a lawn care service or cameras and film for a photography business. It will be up to you to decide what equipment you'll need for your particular product or service business and if you can rent or buy it. But before you decide to buy or lease office equipment, or, for that matter, sign up to become a member of an association such as the Chamber of Commerce, consider the Return on Investment (for these and any other business expenses).

Return on Investment

Many big companies go to great lengths to evaluate the Return on Investment (ROI) of large expenditures, such as purchasing a computer system or a building to house their business. They calculate that buying the building verses leasing will save them money in the long run; leasing a high-volume printer verses buying one, on the other hand, would be in the best interest of their business.

Yet, smaller or newly established businesses don't always begin evaluating the ROI from their business purchases. It makes sense for smaller and/or new companies worried about cash flow to look at the ROI on every purchase—not just on technology equipment or real estate. For example, say you spent $200 on a classified ad in your local newspaper that reaches your target customer base. Your average customer spends $40, so you need only five people to respond to the ad to make it worth the investment. From the five people who responded, two become repeat customers several times over. The ROI from the $200 classified ad was worth the investment. So, rather than spending thousands of dollars on an ad that will only generate a few hundred dollars in sales, focus your efforts and spend what you know you can earn back.

Likewise, if you want to join an association like the Chamber of Commerce, but find the membership fee of, say, $250, too high, look further into this business investment by calculating the ROI if you were to become a member. For example, consider the benefits that come with membership, such as discounts of 20% on office supplies. If you spend $1,000 a year on office supplies, you could save $200 on supplies alone. Or, if you purchase informational products such as a magazine subscription or a book and learn one strategy that benefits your business — possibly translating to thousands of dollars in the future — the ROI from these publications is more than worth the cost.

Telephone Lines

A telephone is one of the biggest necessities for any business. It can save you money, time, and energy if used wisely. If you are just starting your business, you most likely will use your residential line. Once you are on the road to success, you can add a second line to be used only for your business. If you are under eighteen, your parent or guardian must be present to approve the installation of the phone line. There is a charge for the installation of additional phone lines.

When you get a business line, get a number that is easy to remember. Customers like easy-to-remember, easy-to-dial numbers. Your phone company will assist you in selecting such a number. Choose numbers that end in hundred or thousand figures, such as 000-5500, or 000-5000. Repeated or consecutive numbers work well, such as 000-1111 or 000-1234. Or choose relevant words as part of your business phone number. For example, Canadian pet care provider York Professional Pet

Sitting's telephone number is (905) 806-PETS. When you request a number, either for a personal or business line, you are requesting a personalized number. In most areas you will pay a one-time fee for the personalized number in addition to a monthly charge for the telephone service. The charges are relatively inexpensive and well worth the added cost.

If you purchase a second or business line, the entire expense of operating the phone for business purposes is tax deductible. If you do not have a separate line for business use only, you can deduct the portion you use for business from your personal line. For example, if you use your home phone line for half business and half personal use, you can deduct 50% of the phone service and 100% of any long distance calls related to business. Because these calculations can get complicated, a second line will help keep your tax records simpler. Remember that your family's use of the phone is included in the non-business usage.

VoIP

Voice Over Internet Protocol (VoIP), also referred to as Internet phone or Broadband phone service, is a way of making phone calls over a Broadband Internet connection instead the more traditional telephone networks. VoIP targets people who already have Broadband Internet. Unlimited local and long distance calling can be yours for as little as $240 per year, representing a yearly savings of over $500. Use the free search engine www.WhichVoIP.com to find a VoIP product plan that best meets your needs. WhichVoIP.com recently launched its new search program, enabling visitors to find VoIP service providers that have free calls to their country of interest (from a database of over 50 countries).

VoIP Costs

VoIP companies charge between $20 and $45 per month for unlimited local and long-distance calls in the United States. The price includes features such as call waiting, caller ID, call blocking, voice mail, and three-way calling. In addition there are many bonus features that VoIP provides. They include voice-mail messages going to an e-mail address; calls can be set to bounce from one telephone to another until they are picked up; you can manage your service online, so you can add a second phone line instantly or see all calls made; you can take the phone number—and your phone line—anywhere you go (VoIP numbers can move from state to state, as do cell phones); you can pick a New York number even if you live in Florida; you can even group call, that is, one number can call several phones—even if the phones are in different offices; and, when you travel, a phone adapter and a phone can be plugged into the hotel's Internet service to keep receiving calls from your home/business line. Furthermore, you can add a second phone number for about $5 per month. It can even be a different area code (still rings to your home/business), so, if you live in California, but do lots of business in New York, New Yorkers won't be calling "long distance," nor will you be paying for long distance calls. A weakness to VoIP services is that they don't automatically come with 911 emergency call capability, so you must register for it when you register for your VoIP service.

How to Use VoIP

VoIP can be used by almost anyone with a personal computer (PC) and access to a Broadband connection. While you don't have to have Broadband to set up VoIP, without Broadband, you'll have a slow connection that hurts the quality of the phone call, creating unbearable static or cutting off the conversation. VoIP service can be catagorized into three areas: PC to PC calls, landline to PC calls, and PC to landline calls.

VoIP users have many options for obtaining phone service connection. To use VoIP, you first need to get a VoIP phone, or download one of the many free "virtual phones," which can be installed on your PC or laptop. A good, free virtual phone application is x-lite (www.xten.com). If you prefer instead to use a standard phone, you can also purchase a small conversion box—which allows you to plug your standard phone into your

154

Broadband socket. Another option is using the Intel Universal Phone Device Interface—a new software framework and development kit that enables plug-and-play components for web-based phone calls (www.intel.com/go/software). Or, your VoIP provider will provide you with an Analog Telephone Adaptor (often called a "gizmo"), which allows you to make phone calls using a regular telephone.

Broadband Internet

Broadband is the term used to describe high-speed Internet service. Broadband Internet access is a requirement to setting up VoIP, due to the bandwidth needed to make a phone call over the Internet. If you want to set up VoIP, you need a Broadband Internet service. Why? Having Broadband Internet access allows for speed of up to 30 times faster than dial-up and has the added benefit of being "always on," so Internet access is available as soon as you start your computer.

Caller ID

Caller ID is an electronic, telephone-related device that allows people to identify most callers before answering the telephone. When a telephone rings, an electronic display registers the caller's name and telephone number. A telephone can also feature its own caller ID on the handset. Whether you have a separate electronic device that serves as your caller ID or a built-in feature in your telephone, caller ID allows numbers to be saved in a database. This means that if potential customers call and hang up, you have the information to call them back, even if they did not leave a message.

Cell Phone

If you don't want to use a landline for your business phone, look into purchasing a cell phone. A cell phone can serve as a message machine, so you won't need to buy a separate message recorder. Cell phones also have a built-in caller ID, so you won't need to purchase a separate device. A cell phone can take the place of a landline, message machine, and caller ID. Make sure you choose a company that has excellent service in your area.

Keep your cell phone nearby and charged at all times. If possible, keep a spare battery on hand. You will appear professional and capable of any job you're hired to perform if your cell phone is always operating at peak performance. Check for messages frequently and return calls as soon as possible. However, when meeting a client in person, don't have your cell phone (or pager) on.

Choosing a Wireless Company

You need to know what to look for in a wireless company. Obtain "Going Wireless: A Consumer Guide to Choosing Cellular Service" from Sprint and the National Consumers League. The guide will show you how to select the right service and calling plans, understand your contract, and how to avoid fraud. For your free copy, call (888) 8-PUEBLO or (888) 878-3256 and ask for item 589M. Or visit www.pueblo.gsa.gov to read or print out this information.

There are nearly 180 million cell phones in the United States and only five major carriers—which means competition for your business is fierce. Know that these companies will do anything for your business. If you already have a wireless contract and want to switch plans mid-contract, it can't hurt to ask your new carrier to pick up the cancellation fee. Shop for a plan that suits your needs and pocketbook. Log on to www.letstalk.com to compare different plans and to find great deals on cell phones. Log on to www.saveonphone.com, which has a calculator that helps you figure out the best long-distance carrier for your needs.

If you're on a budget and don't want to pay full price—$100 or more—for a new cell phone, buy one used at www.eBay.com or www.cellphoneshop.net. Most sellers list phones by provider, so you can be sure to get one that works with your chosen provider, but you'll still have to take it to your provider to activate it.

Furthermore, bundle your phone fees. Many companies will give you a lower rate if you combine land, cell phone, and Internet fees under their service.

Personal Computer

A computer is an awesome business tool. Smart entrepreneurs use e-mail as a way to connect with their clients. Though not absolutely necessary in the beginning stage of your business, computers allow businesses to be organized and efficient and can greatly streamline the work that you do. Business transactions, from daily notes to letters, can be stored and updated in computers. Business records can be updated frequently. When tax season rolls around, you can have a legible report ready for your accountant in moments. Remember to back up your computer data. More than 50% of small to mid-sized companies do not have formal procedures in place for backing up data hosted on laptops, leaving them vulnerable to data loss.[136]

Computer Printer

Computer printers come in a variety of styles and with a host of features. Visit your local computer center to obtain information about the printer that will best suit your needs.

Fax Machine

A fax (short for facsimile or telefacsimile) machine is essentially an image scanner, computer printer, and modem, combined into a highly specialized package. The scanner converts the contents of a document into a digital image, the modem sends the image data over a telephone line, and the printer at the other end makes a duplicate of the original document.

A very high-quality fax machine with some additional electronics can connect to a computer and can be used to scan documents into a computer, to print documents from the computer, and to make photocopies. If you have such a fax machine, you won't need a desktop copier.

Copy Machine

A desktop copier is convenient and well worth the investment. With this handy equipment there is no more waiting until the next day to send clients information. You can make copies in your home in the late afternoon and send them that same evening!

Digital Camera

It might serve your business well to invest in a digital camera. You can take pictures of your products or services and download them on to your computer for quick photo printing when you need photos. Digital cameras range in price, so visit several camera shops to compare quality and price. Check *Consumer Reports* for recommendations. Your local library should have the annual buying guide.

Message Machine

If you don't have a stay-at-home parent or other family member who can help you with bookings or other client needs, a message (answering) machine can take incoming messages. Don't assume that other family members want to be tied down to your business. Investing in a message machine can save you time and money. Having a message machine pick up incoming calls allows you to return calls at your convenience. It also helps your business by not letting you miss important calls from prospective clients, at least those who leave a message.

Voice Mail

Voice mail is a computer-based message system that goes beyond the functions of the usual telephone answering machine. In addition to taking messages from callers when you can't answer the telephone, you can send, forward, and reply to messages; send messages to a distribution list; turn your telephone number into a bulletin board or information center; give special access privileges to a secretary or a guest user such as a family member; and store messages in an archive. For information on subscribing to voice mail, call the Telephone Client Support Representatives at (617) 253-3670.

Answering Service

It may be smart to have an answering service take your incoming calls when you are out of the office for an extended period. People are more likely to leave a name and number with a real person than with a machine. However, answering services are expensive. Shop around for best prices and features before you decide.

Filing System

Sloppy record keeping results in lost time and money. Create a simple filing system and stick to it. You will find that, once your filing system is set up, filing all business literature is easy. Many office supply stores carry second-hand file cabinets at reasonable prices.

☼

Before we look at the printed items you'll need, you will need to think about the image you want to create for your business. Logos and advertising slogans need to be thought out carefully before you go to press.

Create a Logo

Does a business need a logo, one of those little symbols that you see on almost every product or service available? It's certainly worth considering, advises Jeff Kearl of LogoWorks.com. Visual cues make an impression, and people remember them.

The Importance of a Professional Logo

Your logo is usually the first impression a client has of you and your business, so it is essential to make an outstanding first impression. A professionally designed logo helps customers understand what you do. It also helps potential customers remember your product or service by identifying and remembering it through a visual image. An eye-catching logo that appears on stationery, flyers, advertisements, and a website helps to identify you, your business, and gives customers a first impression of a professional operator.

Spell Out "Work for Hire"

A "Work Made for Hire," sometimes abbreviated to "Work for Hire," is a concept of intellectual property protection in Section 101 of the 1976 Copyright Act. When a person signs a "Work for Hire" agreement, that person creates a copyrightable work but does not own it. The copyright law treats the person who hired the creator to make the work as the copyright owner.

When M.B.A. owner Bill Hargis created the carobonated juice beverage The Switch, he developed packaging with a retro look. Then he hired a design firm to create the design. A year later, the design firm claimed ownership of not only the packaging design, but the name — and sued The Switch. What Bill didn't realize was that it is standard practice for designers to own what they create and license it to their clients, that is, unless the work is performed under a "Work Made for Hire"contract between the parties. While Bill didn't have a "Work Made for Hire" contract signed, he had something else that proved he owned the design and name: Because his company was new and not-yet profitable, Bill had paid the design firm in part with shares, and the shareholder agreement the designers had signed said that all work done by shareholders was owned by Bill's company. Nearly a year later and $150,000 in legal bills, The Switch won.[137]

It is standard practice for designers to own what they create and license it to their clients, unless the contract between the parties specifically says it's a "Work for Hire" arrangement. When you seek professional help with any designs for your company, including your logo, make sure that you state, in print, that it will be "Work for Hire." Otherwise, the design firm can claim ownership of the design on any work they've done for you and sue you for a share of the business. To obtain a "Work for Hire" Agreement, visit www.creativebusiness.com. Click on "Free Forms," then scroll down to the end of the page and click on the "Work for Hire" Agreement. Permission is granted for single copy reproduction of the agreement. If you do contract "Work for Hire," do not authorize to proceed on any projects until you have a signed copy of the "Work for Hire" agreement.

Designing Your Logo

If you offer pet care service, your logo could be a drawing of a dog, cat, mouse, and turtle combined, or just a feature of one. If you offer babysitting services, a teddy bear held by a young child might be your logo. If you want a professional to help you create your logo, a desktop publisher could help you with your needs. Look in your Yellow Pages under desktop publishing. Or Google "logos" on the Internet for a host of companies that design logos. If your local high school has a graphic arts program, that could be a source for logo design. Also check with local colleges and universities for the same. You can instantly create a logo online, choosing from more than 20,000 exclusive symbols and dozens of fonts to create your logo using the easy point-and-click process by visiting www.entrepreneur.com/services/logoyes.

Create a Slogan

An advertising slogan can support your business name in announcing your distinctive brand identity. Slogans can be one word, such as IBM's "Think," or Apple's "Imagine." Or, a slogan can be a complete sentence. When Turner wanted to differentiate himself from other pet care providers, he created the slogan, "No job is too small or too tall." He created public awareness that he could handle any size pet, even a Great Dane. The slogan also suggested that, no matter how unique the pet care situation, he was the person for the job. If you need ideas on slogans, visit The Big List at www.wordtab.com. If you're looking for a real authority to help you develop a great slogan, visit www.adslogans.com. They are experts at identifying the pros and cons of slogan making.

How Do Slogans Help a Business?

Slogans help businesses develop a distinctive reputation; they even help to bring in customers. Pioneering book discounter Crown Books' slogan of nearly 20 years ago read, "If you paid full price, you didn't buy it at Crown Books." It was powerful enough to stand all by itself and induce customers to shop at that store.

Where to Use Slogans

Slogans can be used in a number of places where you advertise your business. Slogans belong on business cards, answering machine messages, business stationery, direct mail marketing pieces, address labels, company websites, business brochures, magazine or newspaper display advertisements, and Yellow Pages advertising. You can probably think of other places to include your slogan. Get creative!

☼

Selecting a printing company to produce your business materials requires some thought and research. Printing companies range from the less expensive quick printers to the more expensive elaborate ones. Some printers print only quick items, such as business cards, stationery, and brochures. Others print an array of items including calendars, books, and four-color items. If you are computer savvy and have the equipment necessary, you can print your own material.

Printed Items to Get You Started

At some point, arrange a list of items you will need printed. Though you won't need some of them until later, some will be necessary sooner. Most office supply stores sell pre-printed letterhead, business cards, and brochures that you can purchase relatively inexpensively until you know exactly what you want printed on your sales material. Even some dollar stores sell stationery and supplies that can be customized with basic word processing software. Here are some items you might need to get your business started.

Stationery and Business Cards

Initial stationery purchases might include business cards, letterhead stationery, and envelopes. Remember to include on your stationery your company name, business logo, business address, e-mail address, website address, pager, and telephone number(s). Stationery can be purchased at a reasonable price, so don't hesitate to give them to anyone who is interested in your business. Or you can make them yourself. It is smart to take advantage of one of the least-expensive forms of advertising.

If you want engraved business cards and stationery, reconsider. Thermography, a finishing technique applied after printing that raises the ink and gives the effect of engraved printing, will give you a similar effect at half the price. You will need to ask the printer to "heat set" the thermography; otherwise it will melt when it goes through a laser printer. If you're trying to cut costs, consider flat printing—the least expensive option.

What to Include on Your Business Cards

On your business card include your logo and slogan, and all the ways your customers can reach you, including your landline telephone number, cell number, post office box address, business address (if not your home), fax number, pager, e-mail address, and website address. Showing that you are reachable presents a professional side that counteracts youth. You can also advertise your product or service on the front or back of the business card.

Free Business Cards

VistaPrint, a printing company, will give first-time customers 250 business cards for free. All you need to do is pay for shipping and handling. VistaPrint makes this free trial offer available to the public because it is confident that you will find the cards an appropriate representation for your business. Visit www.vistaprint.com to place your order.

Magnetic Business Cards

Advertising a service business on magnetic business cards is smart. Any person with a refrigerator could be a potential customer. Because magnets can be used to post other reminders, your business card will be in view of potential customers for a long time.

Custom design your own full-color magnetic business cards for promotional use. A babysitter can feature her services on teddy bear-shaped magnetic business cards; a pet care provider can feature his services on dog-shaped magnetic cards. Companies that allow you to choose from hundreds of designs in stock (or you can use your own artwork) include www.magnets.com, www.professionalprint.com, and www.berda.com/magnets.shtml.

164

Invoice

An invoice is a bill or list of charges issued by a person or organization that has provided products and/or services to a customer. This formal request for payment itemizes the list of goods or services provided to a buyer, stating quantities, prices, shipping charges, and taxes (where applicable). An invoice details the amount due and other terms in regard to a product sale or service performed.

Create Your Own Invoice

You can create your own invoices with a personal computer, even without invoice software. Or you can have invoices created from your local print shop. If you do draft your own invoices from scratch, try to escape the stale corporate output of QuickBooks® by adjusting colors and fonts to reflect your personal brand. At the very least, place your logo on the invoice.

Invoice Software

You can produce invoices by using invoice software. Most small companies use accounting software to create their invoices. To locate a variety of invoice software, Google "Invoice Software" and carefully do your research.

Personalized Receipts

When your business is running profitably, you can have some personalized business receipts made instead of using generic ones. Personalized receipts show the professional side of your business, giving you that extra advantage. In the beginning, generic receipts work fine when needed. Include the same information about your company that you would on your business cards.

Brochures

A well-designed brochure educates your potential clients about your product or service and has an eye-catching layout. Brochures must be visually appealing and should tell your story. A brochure should include basic information about your business. Your business logo should be included on the cover for company recognition. The cover can also feature an eye-catching picture of the product or service. To learn about the five essentials for an effective brochure, visit http://advertising.about.com/od/brochures/a/brochureplan.htm.

Flyers

Inexpensive to produce, a flyer is generally an 8-1/2" by 11" sheet of paper with printing on one or both sides. Adding a few testimonials on your flyer can be very effective. If you don't have space on the front of your flyer for your testimonials, use the back. You can also list your qualifications, making sure to set yourself apart from other similar companies. If you want your flyer to get people's attention, use bright, cheerful colors, instead of white, to bring out the message you are trying to convey. Again, check with your town's ordinances to be sure you know and understand all the local laws before starting your flyer campaign.

☼

Even if you're not selling online, you need to have a presence on the Internet. The first question customers ask business owners is, "Do you have a website?" This gives them the opportunity to look up your business at their convenience, view the products or services you have to offer, read any testimonials that you may have posted, and become convinced about your abilities to deliver. In turn, they will be confident in doing business with you.

Create a Website

If you run a small business today, a website is a good idea. It gives your business instant legitimacy, advertises your service or product, and shares testimonials. It's a tool that speaks to your potential clients on your behalf, so it is essentially a company representative.

Constructing an excellent website takes some thought and work. But the old adage, "work smarter, not harder," reminds us why it's worth the effort. An awesome website takes most of the work out of marketing, which allows you to focus your energy on your business. David Brown, president and CEO of Website Pros (www.websitepros.com), stresses the importance of a properly designed website. Such a website would reflect the key brand of a business, while also fitting the current state-of-the-art look and feel for websites.

ISP Site Builder Software

Before you initiate this process, you need to find your Internet service provider (ISP), a company that provides individuals and other companies access to the Internet and related services such as website building and virtual hosting. Among the largest national and regional ISPs are AT&T WorldNet, IBM Global Network, MCI, Netcom, UUNet, and PSINet. ISPs also include regional providers such as New England's NEARNet and the San Francisco Bay area BARNet. They also include thousands of local providers. In addition, Internet users can also get access through online service providers (OSP) as America Online and Compuserve. An ISP is also referred to as an IAP (Internet Access Provider).

An ISP site builder software program is usually bundled in a package with your ISP membership. Although the cheapest route, many people are not impressed with this option and feel you get what you paid for. An ISP site builder software program often makes everything very "one size fits all." It is good, however, if you are on a very limited budget.

Website Developers

Many novices can benefit from a website developer, especially for the initial design. Do realize, however, that there are just as many terrible website developers as there are good ones.

Prices vary widely according to both your needs and the quality of the service. To find a good developer, visit the page of a local business that you like and check the bottom for the developer's name and link. Research a developer by looking at the current and former client list on their site. If you like the work, chances are the staff is good at what they do.

Build Your Website Yourself

If you're willing to take some time to learn new software, are decent at layout and design, and don't mind the work, you can design and build your own website. It's not nearly as hard as it sounds. For professional results, there are three excellent software programs: *Microsoft FrontPage*, *Macromedia Dreamweaver*, and *Adobe GoLive*. *FrontPage* ($120, www.microsoft.com) is the most widely used — it's fairly inexpensive, straightforward, and comes with a reasonable amount of art to get you started. *Dreamweaver* ($399, www.macromedia.com) and *GoLive* ($399, www.adobe.com) are of professional grade, very expansive, and flexible. This means that the software program is more expensive and is harder to learn; however, just remember that your website is an investment in your business.

Helpful Website Construction Websites

Like many people starting out, you probably are not sure where to begin in setting up a website. There is a do-it-yourself website, www.register.com, which will guide you through the entire process. For as little as $4.95 per month you can build a website yourself and publish it on the Internet. Then use the register.com tools to see reports that outline your site's traffic. Your site can be up and running in 20 minutes using their step-by-step process. If you'd prefer to work one-on-one with professional website designers, click on "Professional Website Design" for further information. If you want a full-fledged website store, www.webdesignplaza-site-builder.com is the site to visit. Google "How to Start My Own Website" to view many sites about website building.

Now that your shop is set up, you are ready to flip that "Open for Business" sign. The next floor, Open for Business, will guide you to your ultimate goal—selling your product or service to your customers—over and over again. American statistician and educator W. Edwards Deming (1900–1993) said, "Profits in business come from repeat customers, customers that boast about your project or service and that bring friends with them." Let's make it happen!

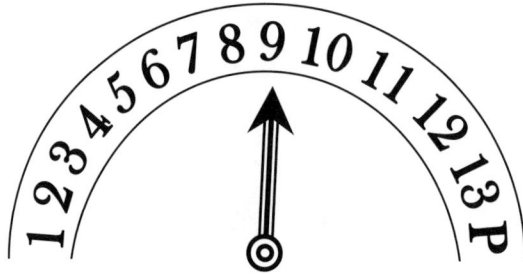

9th Floor

Open for Business

"A man without a smiling face must not open a shop."
~Chinese Proverb

To have the best possible chance of success, your business needs clear leadership, and this must come from the chief executive: you. Only if you, the chief executive, are fully committed to your business plan will it have any chance of success. You must communicate enthusiasm and commitment through your leadership to everyone involved in your business.

Becoming an Entrepreneur

You have chosen to become an entrepreneur and be your own boss. You have the drive to control your financial future and become self-employed. Whether you will operate your own unique business or work as a member of a team, you are ready for your business venture. You should not be concerned about other competitors in your chosen business. You have chosen to compete with yourself, and you believe that success or failure lies within your personal control or influence. You are officially open for business.

Rejection-Proof Yourself

You'll be better able to focus on your job of selling when you no longer fear rejection. As you mature you will discover more opportunities for working on your technique or pitch, and you'll have more confidence in your abilities as a salesperson and in yourself.

Visualize a Positive Outcome

When Turner prepared for his black belt in Tae-Kwon-Do, he knew he had to break a board. But just knowing that he had to break one wasn't enough. If you want to break a board, you don't concentrate on the surface of the board, but rather, you think all the way through to the other side. Thinking all the way through to the other side *before* you tackle a project allows you to visualize a positive outcome in advance.

Bartering for Advertising

When starting a business, you might not have an advertising budget. Instead of worrying about a non-existent advertising budget, visualize the end result of successfully obtaining advertising through bartering. Write down all the things you are capable of doing in exchange for advertising. You probably have many services you can offer a local magazine, newspaper, or printing company. I've mentioned that you could offer to clean a print shop in exchange for printing services, which might include business cards and flyers to get your business started. You can barter many services, even products, in exchange for advertising. A creator of gift baskets could offer, dollar for dollar, her product in trade for advertisements in the town or city magazine. If you produce a community flyer, exchange advertisements with other print media. This would benefit both media because dead space will be put to effective use. Bartering for advertising is a smart way to get advertising without paying for it. Revisit the 3rd Floor, Raise Start-Up Cash, for more information on bartering.

Getting Free Publicity

Send a press release to your local newspaper, town magazine, even your local radio station. Remember to send press releases to high school and college newspaper editors. Many radio stations run public service announcements (PSAs) when time and space are available. Think of a creative angle and contact your local television and cable stations for submission guidelines. Soft news—news that does not deal with formal or serious topics and events—is always a bright spot for these stations, especially when the focus is on the community's youth. If you accompany your press release with a photo of you and your product or service, you will increase the chances of having your release published. Add a title to your release to relate to current news, and you are more likely to attract media interviews. You can't effectively spread good news about your business without a stellar PR program. You can obtain free information on writing press releases, speaking to the press, and getting free publicity and other publicity tips from www.prsecrets.com, www.publicityhound.com, and www.yudkin.com/pubfaq.htm.

Give Out Business Cards and Flyers

Business cards are easily tucked away in a potential client's wallet for the occasion your product or service is needed. Because it takes up minimal space, a business card has staying power when tacked to a bulletin board. And for those "models" to whom you gifted your jewelry creations, ask that they give your business cards to people who admire your jewelry.

If you are offering a service business, distribute your flyer in neighborhoods that you would like to service. Ask permission to post your flyer or business cards on community bulletin boards.

When distributing your business flyer in the neighborhood, a reminder that placing them in door hanger bags keeps them fresh for when your potential clients view them. Otherwise, a lawn sprinkler might soak your printed material, a dog might chew it, or it may get blown away.

Meeting Your Clients

If you are operating, for example, a pet care service, you'll want to meet your clients where your services are to be provided. If you are to care for pets at their home, meet there. If a dog will be boarded at the kennel, and you are expected to walk him during his stay, meet at the kennel to go over details. If you provide another service, such as tutoring, suggest meeting at the library. If you are a sports coach, meet your client at the park or field where you will be coaching. When meeting clients, be clean, well-groomed, and neat in appearance. Don't wear a baseball cap, frontward or backward, even if you are a sports coach—unless it has your logo on it.

Confirming with Clients

If you have set up a meeting with your client, confirm the appointment the day before you are to meet. If you've already scheduled a job, confirm the service the day before your service begins. Clients who are busy packing for a trip don't need to worry about whether or not the person they hired to care for their pet will show up for the job. Your call will put them at ease, and you'll appear professional. Always confirm with your clients, even if the job is routine. You can be reminded of your job with the client by looking at your written contract, which outlines the agreement, the fee, and the agreed terms of payment prior to calling. You can leave your confirmation on the client's message machine if that person is not available to speak to you.

173

Billing Your Clients

Be prompt with billing. Billing is a tedious part of any job, but Turner has found that if he prepares an invoice before the job, billing is much easier. Create an invoice on your computer, purchase generic ones at an office supply store, or have them custom-made. Total the bill, but do not present the invoice until after the job. This allows you to make adjustments in your billing if additional service is required.

Sometimes clients want to pay in advance, in which case, you're prepared to present your bill for their accounting. Other clients choose to pay after the job is completed. Yet again some like to pay half up front and the balance after the job is completed. Customers pay in different ways. Just remember, cash beats a check, and a certified check beats a personal check. *Anything* beats a verbal IOU!

Timing Your Invoice

There is a certain strategy in timing of an invoice delivery to a client. For down payments, the first invoice should be in the client's hands immediately after the product or service has been requested. For delivering the final invoice, it should be sent within 48 hours, while your fantastic work is still fresh in your customer's mind. Never send an invoice prematurely, because no one wants to pay for unfinished work.

Instead of attaching invoices to the actual deliverables, send them separately. Your invoice will make more of an impression sent alone rather than with the product or service performed. Furthermore, avoid having your invoice arrive on a Friday. Nobody wants to face bills right before the weekend.

Quality Control

Go after one customer at a time, and do whatever it takes to meet his or her needs. Do not assume that because you've satisfied a customer once, you don't have to do everything you can to satisfy that person again. Constant quality control should never be ignored. Quality control means digging deep to show your customers that you appreciate them. Treasure your customers by paying attention to their underlying needs, acknowledge your flaws, and resolve conflicts quickly and positively.

Never be rude to customers. It's better to lose money on a customer from one sale than risk losing future work, which could lead you to even more customers. No matter what, it is best to follow the adage "the customer is always right." Customers have a right to their opinions, even if you know they are wrong. Don't argue with customers. It simply isn't good policy. If you do disagree with a customer, just offer another idea for them to consider. If you can't change their minds, don't worry about it. The customer will be back after they find out you were right.

What if you made a mistake on a customer's order? Do what Crystal Maes, the 15-year-old owner of Crystal's Party Supplies in Cleveland, New Mexico, did. When Crystal mistakenly delivered the wrong custom-designed card to a client, she made it right by giving her the right card, plus a couple of free ones. Today, that lady is still a regular customer of Crystal's.[138] Crystal found out early in her career to treat customers like they own her, because they do.

Good Customer Service

Every business owner knows how important good customer service is to the success of their business. Why not take it up a notch and add to your website click-to-call technology? The feature, thanks to VoIP (information about VoIP can be found on the previous floor), gives customers real-time support, differentiates your site from the competition, and can boost sales, too.

For a customer to connect directly with a sales or customer service representative, they simply click on an icon on your site and input their phone number. Within seconds, they receive a call from a representative who can assist and guide them. While click-to-call is not for every business, if your average transaction totals at least $50, customers tend to abandon their shopping carts, or you sell globally, you're a good candidate.

Click-to-call providers include eStara (www.estara.com), LiveOffice (www.liveoffice.com), and LivePerson (www.liveperson.com). The smart thing about the click-to-call connection is that you can see what page and what product a customer is looking at. You even know where the customer is located, which helps the customer service representatives establish a personal connection with customers. Having a click-to-call system will eliminate the need for voice mail, improving productivity.

Keep in Touch with Customers

Keeping in touch with customers throughout the year makes great business sense. "Don't give your customers a chance to get bogged down with their busy schedules and forget about you after the [last job]," says business writer Angi Semler. "Communicate with them several times throughout the year, whether it's by sending a newsletter (or e-mail), mailing a letter announcing something newsworthy about your company, sending holiday cards, holding an open house, or throwing a customer appreciation event. Look for ways to further establish in their minds that you are the only choice, and take steps to further solidify that customer relationship."[139]

Blogging

Maintaining a blog helps business owners — especially home-based business owners — develop strong relationships with their customers. What is a blog? It's an online web log or journal that is becoming the chosen web format over conventional sites. This is because the site architecture of a blog is such that search engine robots from Google and Yahoo can find it and index it easily and faster. And because blogs live in a closely networked world where other bloggers send visitors back and forth, it's the perfect way to buzz market your business, as visitors chat about each other. You can create rich media through your blog. To learn more about blogging, visit www.typepad.com (a paid "do it yourself" blogging platform that's easy to use); www.wordpress.com (a free blogging platform that's more complex but ultimately more flexible. You'll need a professional to assist you in establishing your blog.); www.goblogwild.com (home of the blogging guide, *Go Blog Wild* by Andy Wibbels). Practice blogging by creating a blog site on Vox (www.vox.com), a free, easy-to-use service created by the blog software company Six Apart. This blog site posts go only to the groups you specify. According to an *Entrepreneur* survey, consumers are 50% more likely to be influenced by blogs than by TV or radio.[140] Blog along!

Hiring Employees

If your business really takes off, hire family and friends to work for you. If you get multiple jobs for the same day, hire a sibling or friend to fill in the jobs you can't service. If you have, for example, a hot dog cart, minimum wage is what you might consider paying your workers. If you operate a lawn care service, paying them half of what the job takes in will benefit both you and your employee. Write down your agreed-upon pay in advance, so that there is no misunderstanding after the job is done. Only hire responsible, trustworthy people. Your reputation hangs on their work ethic.

While it is fine to hire family and friends for occasional jobs, if you have more work than you can handle by yourself, or intend to open a storefront, plan to hire employees. Before putting out the "Help Wanted" sign, there are several requirements that you should know. Below is a list of organizations that you need to contact in order to be a successful employer.

- **U.S. Department of Labor** (www.dol.gov/esa/welcome.htm) The Fair Labor Standards Act is a federal law that sets guidelines for hourly wages, including information addressing tips, overtime wages, and restrictions on child labor.
- **U.S. Equal Employment Opportunity Commission** (www.eeoc.gov) The Federal Anti-Discrimination Laws prohibit discrimination in the workplace on the basis of race, gender, pregnancy, national origin, religion, disability, or age.
- **Internal Revenue Service (IRS)** (www.irs.gov) The Federal and State Income Tax Laws outline requirements for withholding income tax from employees' paychecks.

- **U.S. Social Security Administration** (www.ssa.gov) The Federal Insurance Contributions Act requires employers to withhold and deposit social security and Medicare taxes from employees' paychecks, and make matching contributions.
- **The Federal Unemployment Tax Act (FUTA)** (www.irs.gov) This act outlines employers' responsibilities regarding a federal and state program that pays unemployment compensation to workers who lose jobs.
- **The 1970 Occupational Safety and Health Act** (www.osha.gov) This act requires employers to provide a safe and healthy workplace.
- **Legal Information Institute** (www.law.cornell.edu/topics/employment.html) Worker's Compensation Laws in most states require employers to purchase worker's compensation insurance, so that benefits can be paid to employees who become ill or injured on the job.

Before You Hire Your First Employee

Running your own business is intimidating enough, but hiring your first employee can be nerve-racking. Do you know who you should hire? What should you ask—and what you can legally ask—when interviewing potential employees? How do you find the most competent employees? Tools, developed by employee litigation lawyer, consultant, and speaker Don Phin, are available to aid you in hiring the best employees. These tools can be found at www.inc.com/keyword/hiringtools. You can find do-it-yourself legal advice on www.nolo.com, a publisher of self-help legal fare that counsels you on many areas, including hiring and firing employees.

An Employer Begins the Right Way

When Jen Keller, 17, from Somerville, New Jersey, decided to open Strung Out Beads and Wiring, a make-your-own-jewelry store in downtown Somerville, she had a lot to learn before opening her store on Main Street. Right away Jen knew she would need several employees, not only after the store opened, but also before to build displays, unpack boxes, and help to set up.

To become educated about fair hiring practices, Jen read the book *Starting and Managing Your Own Business in New Jersey*, published by the Service Corps of Retired Executives (SCORE). From this manual, Jen learned about the legal responsibilities of an employer to follow fair hiring practices, avoid discrimination of any kind, provide a safe work environment, and how to handle

178

payroll correctly. She also learned how to use a standard job application form for applicants, set up beginning wages for all employees, and how to install security cameras in several key locations. Jen also created a handout outlining operating procedures for the store, and required employees to read it and sign a statement saying they would abide by the terms. Finally, Jen hired a company to handle her payroll.[141]

Keep Track of Business

No matter how busy you are with your business, whether you operate from your home or from a storefront, it's best to keep track of your progress. To keep it simple, you could have two jars, one for money in and the other for money out. Or you can make deposits into your bank account. At the end of the month, after you have paid all of your expenses and there is money left over, this is your profit. Repeat this every month and, after several years, you could be one wealthy Generation Y-er. If you are short on income one month, look at your business plan and figure out ways you could drum up more business or cut some expenses.

Business owners benefit from having a separate bank account for their business. A business checking account can aid business owners when they prepare their business taxes.

Accounting

Record keeping is extremely important for anyone operating a business. When 12-year-old Happy Hats owner Christine Keck sells her products to various stores, she needs to know where her inventory is located at all times. "I number all of my products and put price tags on them," notes Christine. Then she makes two lists, one for herself and one for each store selling her products. This helps keep an inventory of incoming and outgoing hats, the amount they sell for, and when more should be ordered.[142] Good record keeping can make it much easier to be prepared for paying your business taxes.

Paying Taxes

Keeping good records allows a business owner to determine whether he owes taxes, and if so, how much. All businesses, including teen businesses, have to satisfy their tax responsibilities. To learn more about paying your business taxes, contact your local office of the Internal Revenue Service (IRS) to get information about your income tax responsibilities. You can also see an accountant who specializes in taxes for small businesses. TurboTax® and Quicken® are two tax software programs that can guide you through the entire process of filing if you choose to file your own taxes.

Many people are under the impression that if you barter goods or services, you need not pay taxes. This is simply not true. Your business is taxed in the same way as for cash income when bartering for goods or services that directly benefit your business. The IRS does look upon barter as income that must be reported on form 1099B. Keep a record of your barter and expenditures for tax purposes.

Try, Try Again

Inspirational writer Denis Waitley has said, "Failure should be our teacher, not our undertaker." Failure is a delay, a temporary detour, but *not* defeat. Thomas Edison's father called him a "dunce," and even his headmaster at school told him that he would never amount to anything. When the head coach of the Penn State University football team was asked by the media how he felt when his team lost a game, he replied, "Losing was probably good for the team, since it was how the players learned what they were doing wrong."[143]

When the company of Lunden De'Leon, 30, failed in 1999, she was forced to close her business doors. Then she took time to go back to school, attend classes on how to break into the music industry, and that's when she realized that she had an interest in wanting to start her own record label. But then fear kicked in, fear that the failure of her PR business would translate to failure in a recording business. Lunden was smart enough, however, to realize that, while losing isn't fun, it was essential to winning. When her PR business didn't work out as planned, she analyzed her decision-making process to figure out what went wrong. Overcoming her fear and reflecting on the positive business skills that she had, Lunden started her record label Dirrty Records, in Beverly Hills, California in 2002. Learning from her past failed business experience helped Lunden grow her record label with 15 employees to nearly $4 million in annual sales. [144]

Michael Frederickson did not let failure of his first business stop him on the entrepreneurial track. At the age of 11, Michael invented and sold a magnetic tie tack. When it didn't work out for him, the self-taught computer whiz created Micah Tech, a business designing websites, which he runs out of his bedroom, working about 30 minutes a day—after he completes his homework. Michael's projected earnings for this year are about $13,000.[145] "Failure is a step to success," says Laima Tazmin, 15, president of LAVT LLC, a web consulting company and winner of the "Young Entrepreneur" contest sponsored by Fleet Bank.[146]

It's also true that you learn a lot more from a mistake than an early success. When Betty Boop made her cartoon debut in 1930, she appeared as a dog! Unsuccessful, Betty Boop "reinvented" herself, looking similar, but wearing earrings instead of floppy ears and a bob instead of poodle fur.

Your business is up and running, and you're making money. If you haven't already been doing so, the next floor, Develop a Savings Habit, is the right place to be if you need ideas and encouragement to save for a strong financial future.

10th *Floor*

Develop a Savings Habit

"If you can count your money, you don't have a billion dollars."
~J. Paul Getty (1892–1976)

Americans are simply not saving enough for their retirement. Many adults have let the savings rate slip down in favor plasma televisions, new cars, and houses bigger than they need. This teaches children that it is OK to spend now, that it is not necessary to delay gratification. Getting into loads of debt does not prepare children for their futures in a smart financial way. Teaching children that the wrong kind of debt is OK is not the message they should learn from their parents.

There is a Chinese proverb that says, "A great fortune depends on luck, a small one on diligence." If you are a diligent saver, you won't need to win the lottery. You will be capable of creating a small fortune for yourself, on your own. The way our world economy is set up, you can depend only on yourself to see you through your life time of financial needs. No one else will be there with a financial safety net. James Koutoulas, a 17-year-old high school senior in Cooper City, Florida, is diligent about saving and investing toward his financial future. "I can't count on Social Security," says James, who spends about three hours a day researching stock investments.[147]

Choosing to Save

You really can build wealth on any income. If you save now, you'll be better able to keep debt at bay when you are older. The American Savings Education Council has a website at www.choosetosave.org that has more than 130 calculators that people can use to determine everything from what their savings will earn over time to how to pay down debt and how to plan for retirement. "It's a big step from saying 'I need to save' to actually starting to save," says Cheri Meyer, director of the Choose to Save Program. "Sometimes small steps can help get people over that hump." The sooner people start, the better, she added. "People shouldn't underestimate what saving even $10 or $20 a week will get them over time."[148] Everyone's goal should be to get the most from his or her money.

Small Change Does Add Up

It's OK to think small, especially when so many people think that, to save, you have to have a lot of money. Just a few pennies saved now can grow into a substantial amount later. Putting just 50 cents a day into your jar adds up to $15 a month, or $180 a year. Anyone can build wealth, and putting some coins into a jar is a great way to start. The website at www.americasaves.org suggests a dozen ways to nickel and dime yourself to a sizeable savings account, along with strategies to achieve your goal.

Saving Early Makes a Difference

Saving money when you are young is very important because you have the longest time horizon, allowing the compounding of interest a long time to increase your net worth. According to Lynn

O'Shaughnessy's financial column in *The San Diego Union-Tribune,* in an article titled "Retirement? Sock It Away Early and Be a Millionaire," she points out that Americans typically don't start thinking seriously about saving for retirement until they near their own mid-century mark. These "savings slackers may ultimately find themselves pulling the equivalent of a college all-nighter for the rest of their working lives in an attempt to prepare financially for the day when the paychecks stop."

If you're still young, there is a simple way to avoid this pitfall. Save early, save regularly, and get it over with. In fact, if you invest early and then stop saving altogether, chances are great that you'll be financially better off than people who begin saving a dozen years later and continue to save for a longer time.

Lynn shows the early-bird approach to saving and how it can work for you:

> Suppose a 25-year-old decides to save $5,000 a year for retirement for 10 years. After saving nearly $100 a week for a decade for a total of $50,000, our investor calls is quits. She doesn't dump any more cash into the account, but she does not withdraw any, either. Left alone, the portfolio, if it generates an annual 10% return, will mushroom to $1.4 million by the time she hits 65 years of age. Not bad for just 10 years of sacrifice.

Lynn continues in her article,

> Now let's examine the fiscal fate of someone who doesn't roll out of bed until the age of 35. Our Gen X-er starts saving $5,000 a year, but, admirably, this guy stays committed longer. Instead of feeding the retirement kitty for 10 years and bailing, he maintains the routine for 30 years. After three decades, our earnest saver will have chipped in $150,000. At this point, you're probably thinking that this guy started later, but certainly finished stronger than the 25-year-old. Actually, the portfolio of our more energetic saver, assuming the same rate of return, would ultimately grow to $820,000. That ending balance is

40% less than the portfolio of the woman who bailed early.[149]

When Should You Start Saving?

It doesn't matter how young (or old) you are. Any time is a good time to start saving—but the younger, the better. "I start the money lessons at age 3, when the kids begin saying 'I want, I want,'" said Neale S. Godfrey, author of books on finances and children. "You want to teach them the natural consequences of money."[150] Some people in the financial industry believe children's spending and saving habits are shaped as young as between 5 and 9 years old. This period will determine whether children are savers or spenders. Others believe that, once you learn good savings habits, an older person can lose the spending habit and develop the saving habit. An old dog *can* learn new tricks. It's just that the younger the dog, the more tricks she will have in her bag!

And it doesn't matter how much (or little) you make. Craig Mahan, 21, saves $600 a month on an annual salary of $13,000—money he earns working at his local grocery store in Excelsior Springs, MT. Although Craig recently paid cash for a 2000 Monte Carlo, he still contributes $4,000 a year to a Roth IRA.[151] At this pace Craig could be a millionaire when he's 60.

Develop a Savings Plan

To help you spend less than you earn, you need a savings plan. A savings plan is necessary if you want to accumulate wealth. To be motivated to save money, you will need something specific to save for. Write down your goals and visualize them, whether they're a relaxing retirement, a mortgage-free home, or a big-screen television. In one study of American workers, 83% said setting a savings goal helped them toward their dream retirement.[152] People who regularly keep a written record of their goals are more likely to reach them.

Make Savings Automatic

"You actually can start investing with as little as $50 a month if you choose a monthly automatic savings option," says financial adviser Allyson Lewis, author of *The Million Dollar Car and $250,000 Pizza*.[153] If savings can be automatic, people are more likely to save. If you are an employee, have your employer set up an automatic payment to your savings or mutual fund account for every paycheck period. What money you don't see you won't miss. If you are self-employed, have an automatic monthly payment drafted from your savings account to your mutual fund. To get this easy process started, visit your bank.

It Doesn't Take Much

Do you need a lot of cash to retire rich? No, you don't. Just $100 a month—about $3 a day—earning 8% compound interest, can get you $140,855 thirty years from the time you start. Fidelity Investments ran some numbers that show you how much of a boost you can get from investing early and with a small amount: Save $3,000 every year from the time you are 20 until you are 70, earn 8% compound interest a year on your money, and you could end up with more than $2 million. If you wait one year and don't start saving until you are 21, you'll end up with almost $150,000 less. Wait 10 years, and start when you are 30, and you'll have $839,343 when you're 70. Imagine what Generation Y-ers can do if they start saving $3,000 a year at the age of 14 or 15!

James Trippon, a Houston money manager, certified public accountant, and author of *How Millionaires Stay Rich Forever*, says that many of the nation's 7 million millionaires saved their way to wealth. Furthermore, "Millionaires always save," says Trippon. "But the key to their success is starting early." The most successful people know that every dollar you save today will be worth ten dollars in the future when invested properly.[154]

186

The Invisible Rich

When editor in chief of *Kiplinger's* magazine Knight Kiplinger lead a personal-finance seminar at a high school, he posed this question to teens: "When you see a man cruise by in his $65,000 BMW 550i, what do you assume about him?" The teens collectively replied, "He's rich." Then they were asked, "And a man who drives by in a ten-year-old Chevy Impala?" They responded, "He's struggling."

The answers were exactly the launching pad that Mr. Kiplinger was looking for, to have a discussion of deceptive appearances and realities. Mr. Kiplinger points out that the BMW is probably leased, so he can infer only that the driver earns enough to manage an $1,100 monthly payment. While Mr. Kiplinger knows nothing of his net worth, which may be great, he also pointed out that it could be non-existent.

As for the man driving the old Chevy Impala, maybe he is struggling financially. But Mr. Kiplinger also points out another possibility: He is making as much, or more, than the BMW guy, but he's not saddled with lease payments. And quite possibly, he is investing his money instead of making leasing payments, in mutual funds that are growing at 10% a year. The message Mr. Kiplinger makes is, "The biggest barrier to becoming rich is living like you're rich before you are."[155]

Keep Track of Daily Expenses

Can't find money to save? Keep track of your daily expenses for one month to see where the money goes. Then look for a way to spend $3 less each day. Once you have $100 (in five weeks, since $3 a day adds up to $21 a week), consider investing in a mutual fund at TIAA-CREF, which allows small, regular investments. At 4 % interest, in 20 years your $3-a-day will grow to nearly $33,000. If a 12-year-old found $1.50 a day to save, money that would otherwise be spent on daily junk food, at the age of 42, she would have amassed $31,118 — after 4% compound interest is factored in. What 42-year-old couldn't use $31,000 toward a down-payment on a home? If you want to save big, you have to sweat the small stuff.

The 90/10 Saving and Spending Rule

Americans have been taught to save 10%, and spend 90% of their income. Why not reverse it when you're a kid? This might seem a bit extreme. But, after all, you are a kid. You probably don't have significant bills to pay, like rent, nor do you have a wife or husband and kids to support, so you don't have to worry about putting food on the table. Turn your youth into a financial golden egg. Instead of spending that $10 you just earned washing a car, tell yourself, "I'll spend this $10 when I earn $100." Then save 90%, or $90, for future goals. "You'll respect the $10 that you can spend even more, and spend it wisely," says Turner. "If saving 90% is too difficult, start with 50%, then inch your way up to the highest possible percentage that you can save."

Oddly enough, a 16 year old might have more discretionary income than they do at 23 when they might have college loans and car loans to pay off. So this is the time that Generation Y-ers really need to establish a savings and investing habits.

If you're a mid-20s Generation Y-er (or older) and have many financial responsibilities, a goal of saving 90% probably won't happen. You should, nonetheless, make every effort to save as much as you can. It's your responsibility to save enough for your future, and it's up to you to determine how much you can give up today for your tomorrow.

Buying and Holding Real Estate

Count your real estate purchases as part of your retirement savings plan. As with any market, real estate is cyclical, so when the market is down or you don't want to bother with a leaky faucet anymore, resist the temptation to run out and post a "For Sale" sign. "There's a great saying that if you sell real estate quickly, you get rich," notes Turner. "But if you hold it, you get wealthy." Real estate can make you wealthy. Buy carefully and hold indefinitely.

Finding Your Savings Rate

To find out what your savings rate is, start by listing all your sources of income: salary, rental income, interest, and anything else to arrive at your "disposable income," then subtract the taxes you pay. Disposable income is the income you can spend after taxes have been taken out.

Let's say, for example, your income last month was $2,000, of which $400 went for taxes, leaving you with disposable income of $1,600. You then spent $200 on your credit card, $600 on rent, $100 in utilities, and $200 on food (a true example of an economical person). After your expenses of $1,100 were subtracted from $1,600, you are left with $500 to save. As a percentage of disposable income, your savings rate was $500 divided by $1,600, or 31.3% — better than the current *minus* 0.5% personal savings that Americans saved in 2005.[156]

Saving for Your Own Retirement

Most Americans rely on three forms of retirement: a company pension, Social Security, and personal savings. It appears that all three of these options are in trouble, and Generation Y-ers know it. They also know that savings rates of all generations of Americans are among the lowest in the industrialized world. In 2004, that average rate stood at 1%; in 2005, less than 0% — which means Americans spent more than they earned![157] In *Forbe's* 2005 Retirement Guide, 40% of workers say they are saving nothing for retirement.[158] Furthermore, about 70% of Americans expect to work into retirement in order to make up the shortfall in their savings, according to a survey by Prudential Financial Inc.[159] It's up to the next generation—Generation Y—to set a positive example of personal savings rate, not the negative one currently held by Baby Boomers and Generation X.

We cannot control the pension or Social Security plans, but we can control our savings plan. According to the Financial Planning Association, tomorrow's retirees will need to depend more on their own savings to fund retirement because comfortable company pensions will become fewer and retirees won't be able to depend on Social Security.[160] The more you save now, the more likely that you'll be able to afford a globetrotting retirement. "Dick started planning our retirement three years after we got married," Corinne Kostukovich says. The Kostukoviches are in an enviable position, visiting places like the California redwoods, Australia, New Zealand, and Fiji. They have 10 more years of robust health and plan to take full advantage of traveling.[161] If you don't start planning for your retirement early in your working life, you might find yourself facing what could be your worst option: being forced to work forever. You are never too young to begin planning for your retirement. To get retirement-planning tips and tools online, visit www.SmartMoney.com/retirement. For a close estimate of how much money you will need for retirement, fill out the retirement-savings calculator at choosetosave.org or dinkytown.net. The new online calculator from A.G. Edwards (www.nesteggscore.com) lets you figure out how well you are building wealth vs. the rest of the U.S. public.

The sooner you start to save for retirement, the less you will need to save. If you push aside the thought that you can start saving for retirement later in your life — that the small amount you can save won't make a difference, or, worse, are hoping for a miracle to fund your retirement, you're simply planning to be poor. Lynn O'Shaughnessy's *Retirement Bible* is an excellent guide to help Generation Y-ers plan for a successful retirement.

Periodic Investment Calculators

The MSN Money Savings Calculator on the Internet is an excellent financial tool that can help you see how your money can grow by calculating different compound interest rates. You can find this calculator on the Internet by Googling MSN Money Savings Calculator. To find a host of other calculators to guide you on your financial path, Google "Periodic Investment Calculators" on the Internet.

Tithing

There are many books that teach kids to save money by using the three-jar method. One jar is for long-term savings, the second jar is for immediate spending, and the third jar is for tithing, giving to charity. It is a beautiful thing for children to learn to be giving. However, if children start to give away *large* amounts so soon (and 33% is a large amount when you follow the three-jar method of savings), how can they save a reasonable amount to invest for the strength of their own financial future? Children will not turn into mean, money-grabbers by not starting out giving to charity from the moment income is earned. When all financial building blocks are in place, these individuals will be in a strong financial position to help charities the rest of their lives, from the interest, and not principal, of their investments. If you do wish to start tithing, 10% of your income is very reasonable. In the meantime, give your time before giving a dime. Volunteer.

▶◀

Are you ready to make a big financial splash? On the next floor, Income Streams Lead to an Ocean of Money, you can do just that. Jump in!

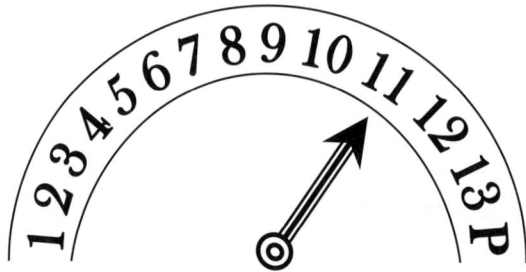

11th *Floor*

Income Streams
Lead to an Ocean of Money

"If you wish to get rich, save what you get. A fool can earn money; but it takes a wise man to save and dispose of it to his advantage."
~Brigham Young (1801–1877)

We have all heard the Chinese proverb, "Give a man a fish and he eats for a day, teach a man to fish and he eats for a lifetime." If parents hand out money to their children at every whim, even into adulthood, they are feeding their temporary needs. Parents are doing nothing to educate their children for a successful financial future. What if the parents soon die? They won't be around to "feed" their children's needs, and their children risk ending up living a very uncomfortable life. No parent should want their children to be eaten alive by money sharks!

Income Streams

Money that is deposited on a regular basis, from a variety of sources, is known as income streams. Multiple streams of income mean you have more than one way to make money. Income streams can stem from loose change, allowances, extra jobs, lunch money, found money, garage sales, birthday cash, slush fund, recycling, clothing budget money, business money, windfalls, royalties, rental income, and compound interest. These income streams flow into a river. The river flows into an ocean, deep enough to float your financial boat.

A variety of income streams, listed below, can pool together to create a wealthy financial ocean. Employ any combination of streams simultaneously, on a regular basis, and watch your streams gush into a fantastic ocean of money.

Allowances

For every parent who agrees that a child should get an allowance is one who disagrees. Those who do agree fall into two camps: parents who don't want to hand money over to their children without getting elbow grease in return and those who think that chores shouldn't be tied to allowances. Allowances shouldn't depend on doing chores or getting good grades—stuff that kids should try to do anyway.

Are you receiving an allowance and haven't seen an increase in a few years? Make a list of reasons why you deserve a raise, figure out how much more you think you need, and present this information to your parents. Allowances not coming your way? "You have to tell your parents, if you don't have any money to manage, anyway to make mistakes on a small scale, then you'll never learn and may end up making big mistakes," says Perla Camarillo, a San Diego parent who believes in giving children allowances so they can learn money management.[162] To learn more about saving, spending, and getting the most out of your allowance, visit www.orangekids.com. There is also an allowance calculator at www.statefarm.com/jscript/allow.htm that you can use to see how saving your money can really pay off. Never underestimate the power of an allowance income stream.

Extra Jobs

Look for extra ways to earn money regularly around your home or neighborhood. If it's not already a chore, ask your parents if you can mow the lawn once a week for pay. Offer to vacuum window screens twice a month. Ask a neighbor if you can regularly drop off and pick up their weekly dry cleaning for a fee. If you continually find extra work, this income can stream right into your bank account.

Lunch Money

Every Friday I give Turner (and Mia) $5 to purchase lunch at the school cafeteria. He has the option to buy lunch or save it and bring a sandwich, cookies and fruit to school, which costs me an additional dollar per child. For the past eight years, Turner has saved $20 a month from this income stream. For ten school months, that comes to $200. Multiply that by 8 years and you get $1,600. Turner was able to save $1,600 by not eating cafeteria lunches, and that doesn't even include the compound interest that he earned on this money. Remember, this amount equals just one lunch a week.

In our town, parents often give middle and high school children $50 a week, on a debit card, solely for lunch. That's $50 per week, times four weeks, equals $200 per month. Ten school months later, that adds up to $2,000. At 4% interest, and a four-year investment of $8,000, you would have $8,771.12; at 6% interest, it adds up to $9,075.93; at 8% interest you'll have $9,394.40. Upon high school graduation any graduate could walk away from high school with "cafeteria money," nearly $10,000 richer!

Found Money

David Bach, author of *Start Late, Finish Rich: A No-fail Plan for Achieving Financial Freedom at Any Age*, says spending $5 less a day will grow to $948,612 over 40 years at a 10% annual rate of return when the magic of compound interest goes to work. If a child, at the age of 10, saves $15 a week for 40 years, earning a 10% annual rate of return, at the age of 50 he will have amassed over $385,000. Your actual investment totals $28,800. The rest is purely interest earned. Imagine if you doubled, tripled, even quadrupled the amounts you invest as you get older. It really doesn't take much effort to become a millionaire.

Where to find the money to save $5 a week? Author David Bach talks about finding your "latte factor," a metaphor for where you're spending money on little things you could cut back on without changing your lifestyle.[163] For example, if you go to a movie once a week and spend $5 on popcorn and a soda, just giving up the popcorn and soda will be your latte factor. This money is "found money," and is considered an income stream when you regularly deposit it.

Garage Sales

If you have enough stuff that you can hold a garage sale three or four (or more) times a year, consider garage sales as another income stream trickling toward your financial goal. Garage sales have always been an American favorite. If you feel you don't have quite enough stuff to sell on your own, ask friends to join in your efforts. If you purchase a classified ad to advertise your garage sale, be sure to mention that it is sponsored by kids. For example, "Kids' stuff for sale. Sold by kids." This encourages other kids to shop at your sale, as well as adults who like to support neighborhood kids. Make sure your classified ad is somewhat longer than the other ads. Purchasing a longer classified ad can result in more sales. People will think that it's going to be worth their trip when they see you have a lot of items to sell. Although a longer ad costs more, people will be drawn to your ad because it is longer.

Birthday Cash

Birthday cash can become an income stream if you save it annually. Six-year-old Bradley Robeson and his 8-year-old brother, Andrew, from Fort Lauderdale, Florida, save their birthday money every year and invest in mutual funds.[164] It's amazing how much money kids can accumulate if they save their birthday cash every year.

While some parents and grandparents like to give things rather than money, others like giving cash because it frees them from shopping. Ask your parents and grandparents to give monetary gifts instead of things for your birthday (and other holidays). This allows you extra income, tax free, to add to your savings investments. Things wear out, but money is your future if you invest it wisely. Gift givers never have to worry if the present is the right size or the right color. Cash always fits! (And the return factor is low.)

Include in your birthday income stream money received from returning duplicate gifts. If you receive a duplicate gift, or a gift you don't need, return it for cash. If you don't have a receipt and can only receive a store gift card, opt for the card. Gift cards can be exchanged for cash. A secondary gift card market, SwapAGift.com and eBay Inc., let gift card recipients exchange their cards for cash, usually less than the face value of the card. eBay had a $20 Starbucks Corporation gift card up for auction with a high bid of $17.50. For $4, www.swapagift.com lets you sell unused cards. Or trade it for cash at www.giftcardbuyback.com. On several occasions Turner has received Target gift cards as gifts. As his mother, I was able to purchase the cards from him, full value, to buy household supplies. Turner saved the money in his bank account.

Slush Fund

When you subtract a check from your checking account ledger, round up the amount to the next dollar. Doing so repeatedly creates a slush fund, one that can be included as an income stream if transferred at the end of each month into your savings account. This also applies to the coins you have at the day's end. Every evening place the coins into a "slush fund" jar. At the end of each month, deposit the coins into your savings account at the same time you transfer your checking account "slush fund."

To add to your slush fund, "Start by setting up an automatic investment plan so you pay yourself first," says Rob Bennett, author of the blog www.PassionSaving.com. "But, pay yourself last, too, by adding up any cash you saved that day and stashing it in your bank account."[165]

Some banks, such as Bank of America, have a Keep the Change™ program. When you enroll in their Keep the Change™ savings service, they round up the amount of any Visa® Check Card purchase that you make of your checking account to the next whole dollar amount, and transfer the amount in excess of the purchase price from your checking account to your savings account. A savings program like Keep the Change™ is certainly worth investigating.

Turn an old debt into a slush fund. After you pay off a credit card debt or car loan, keep making that monthly payment—only now to your savings account. Like left-over change, you won't miss it because it was never in your budget to spend.

Recycling

If you have recyclables, take the time to make a bi-monthly or monthly trip to cash them in. This income steam not only puts money into your savings plan, but also helps keep the environment clean. Ambitious kids in our neighborhood have been known to make $30 or more on weekends recycling.

Clothing Budget

Many parents can encourage their children to save money on clothing. Every year Turner and Mia receive a clothing allowance of $300 each for the entire school year. With the prices of name-brand shoes and clothing what they are, $300 doesn't go far.

That's where these kids have to be financially savvy to come up with their clothing solution. They have the option to save their clothing budget money, spend it all, or save part and spend part.

It may be hard to get kids to forego cool clothes in favor of thrift store clothing, or even department store sale clothing. If kids understand that they will benefit financially, in the long run, by buying used or on sale clothes, they might warm up to last season's styles in favor of saving money in the bank. For more tips on kids learning about money management, visit www.practicalmoneyskills.com.

Your Business Money

If you have regular money coming in from your business or employer, this money is an excellent income stream. If you are constant with saving your business (or employment) earnings, you can become financially independent from this income stream alone. Retiring early won't just be a possibility; it will be a reality.

Most businesses have a variety of income stream opportunities within their business. A magician might sell instructional CDs (his own or another's) on magic tricks, create products that sells at shows, sell products from other companies within the business, write a how-to book about magic, and give private magic lessons—in addition to entertaining. An author not only writes a book, he or she can sell seminars on the topic, sell excerpts from the book, turn excerpts into magazine articles, sell excerpts to business groups as reprints, create products to accompany the book, even investigate if a chapter within the book can be expanded into a book of its own. Business owners should investigate all income opportunities within their business, to maximize on all possible income streams.

Windfalls

We are all inclined to spend money we weren't expecting—a gift, a bonus, a tax refund—more freely than we would regular income. It is easy to mentally categorize unexpected money "free money," and start spending it. Don't blow a holiday bonus on anything you wouldn't buy otherwise. Instead, put the "found money" into a savings account for just one month and consider how to spend it later. By the time the month is up, the money will likely feel more like savings than a windfall, and you'll be less likely to use it on a shopping spree. One-time income streams could be a bonus check from an employer, an income tax refund, an inheritance, even an insurance settlement. Melanie Watson, 33, of Vancouver, British Columbia, Canada, received a $9,000 insurance settlement, and, within four months, she spent it all. Melanie admits that she would be financially better off now had she saved the money.[166] Don't let a windfall blow away!

While some windfalls don't come with a tax bill, others do. Generally there isn't a tax on an inheritance, and child support isn't taxable. But if you win the lottery or win in Las Vegas, that's considered taxable income. If tax money isn't withheld from a taxable windfall, be sure to put aside 25% to pay the IRS. It's better to pay your tax liability up front. "You never see the money, so you don't spend it," says Daniel Silvershein, a tax attorney in New York.[167]

Royalties

Royalties are payments made to the creator of intellectual property. The owner creates the work once, then gets paid for it on a continuing basis. For example, software giant Microsoft invented the Windows operating system for personal computers. Computer manufacturers such as IBM pay a royalty to Microsoft in exchange for being allowed to use the Windows operating system in their computers. In the fashion industry, designers such as Liz Claiborne and Ralph Lauren license the right to use their names on clothing in exchange for royalties. For example, they may sign a contract with a company that makes pants that allows the company to place the designer's name on the pants. In the book publishing industry, authors are paid both a fee for their services and a royalty rate that entitles them to a percentage of their books' profits. In the music industry, royalties are paid to music copyright holders and to songwriters by anyone who derives a commercial benefit from the copyrighted material. In the television industry, popular satellite TV services such as Direct TV and cable television services pay network stations a royalty rate so that they can broadcast those channels over their systems. In the oil and gas industry, companies pay landowners a royalty rate for the right to extract natural resources, such as natural gas, from the landowner's property.

Look at royalties as being paid over and over again for work performed once. You wrote a book, and it went into several reprints; you paid for your land, and can derive benefits from it for as long as you own it; your namesake is used for design; you wrote a song, and it continues to sell in the form of CDs, downloadable music on the Internet, on the radio, and incorporated in a television show that goes into reruns; you continually sell lithographs from an original painting; you created a popular board game that brings in royalties. These are just a few of the types of intellectual property than can earn the creator royalties.

Rental Income

A positive cash flow from rental income is the ultimate lifelong royalty income stream. Now imagine owning multiple rental units, in the form of residential homes, apartment complexes, even office buildings. Once rental property is purchased and it's in turn-key condition (clean and ready to rent), you won't have much to do except collect rent. Using an example from Turner's rental, say the rent you receive on your rental property is $845 a month. Your monthly mortgage, which amounts to $450, and monthly property taxes and insurance, which amounts to $180, total $630. Your monthly rental income of $845, less your mortgage, monthly property taxes, and insurance of $630, equals a positive cash flow — or net operating income (NOI) — of $215 a month. If your mortgage is a 15-year note, as Turner's is, the NOI of $215 (which represents an Annualized Total Return — ATR — of 14.41% from his property investment), is *then* invested into mutual funds and CDs month after month earning compound interest — yielding yet another income stream.

How Rent Royalties Grow

For simplicity's sake, let's say that Turner earns an average ATR of 10% for the next 15 years, derived from the rental income royalties. Over the 15 years, this adds up to $56,419. This comes from 15 years of rental income totaling $24,300, and $32,119 generated by the magic of compound interest. At the end of the 15-year mortgage, the home is paid for, in full, with the funds from renting the property (by renters), and the NOI and ATR increase (example provided under "Calculating Your Investment Property Annualized Total Return" below).

Calculating Your Investment Property Annualized Total Return

Turner's quarterly investment statement for his USAA Growth & Income Fund Custodial Roth IRA account, dated July 1 to September 30, 2005, reads that his mutual fund's ATR (interest earned) is 15.05%. (The statement further reads that the account's ATR for the previous 3 years stood at 17.14%.) Turner's Wells Fargo CD is currently paying him 4% interest for the next 10 months. But exactly what percent is he making on his rental investment?

To come up with the Cash Flow Percentage (a measure of actual cash generated from property), take the monthly rental income and subtract the mortgage, property taxes, and insurance. The result is the monthly Net Operating Income (NOI) — income from a property after operating costs have been paid. Multiply the monthly NOI by twelve to get the yearly NOI:

$845 (monthly rental income)
–450 (monthly mortgage)
<u>–180 (monthly property taxes and insurance)</u>
$215
<u>x 12 (months)</u>
= $2,580/ yearly NOI

Next, take the yearly NOI of $2,580 and divide that by your investment, in Turner's case, his down payment of $17,900. This translates to a 14.41% ATR:

$$\$2,580 \div \$17,900 = 14.41\% \text{ ATR}$$

This ATR will fluctuate when Turner needs to spend money to maintain his property, if his property taxes and insurance go up, if he has vacancies, if he charges higher rent, or when his mortgage is paid off. Furthermore, since Turner purchased his home, the equity in his home — the difference between the home's appraised value and the balance of the mortgage loan — has risen over $20,000, at least on paper. (A paper gain is an increase in the market value of an investment. This increased valued doesn't become realized until the investment is sold.) This paper gain of over 100%, added to the 14.41% ATR, is a total gain of over 114% on a two-year investment. Since this represents a "paper gain," Turner only looks at the ATR of 14.41% that is generated from the down payment of his rental property, realizing that the market could just as easily go the other direction. Finally, the tenants are paying his mortgage, property taxes, and insurance every month by paying Turner rent. When his 15-year mortgage is paid off, Turner will reap an even higher ATR on his initial investment:

$845 (monthly rental income)
–$180 (monthly property taxes & insurance)
$665
  x 12 (months)
= $7,980/yearly NOI

Divide the yearly NOI of $7,980 by the down payment investment of $17,900 to come up with a 44.58% ATR. (This information is based on rents, property taxes, and insurance remaining the same a dozen years from now for calculating simplicity.) Talk about an awesome monthly royalty check!

Set Aside Maintenance Budget

Turner continues to set aside a budget for maintenance (money that would be used for things like replacement of water heater, plumbing, roof, etc.), in the event items need replacing. Replacement money will come from his property income stream, but not until these items need to be addressed. In the meantime the rental royalties income stream is automatically invested to earn compound interest, stuffing Turner's financial pillow for an even softer fall when he needs capital replacements. After all, it gets hot during summer months in Texas, and Turner expects the new air conditioning unit that came with his home will only last so many years.

Up Stream Income

Pay an extra $25 on your home mortgage and build equity in your home even faster. By adding an extra $25 a month on a $62,000, 15-year mortgage, Turner will shave 13 months off his loan. The loan will be paid off more than one year early, saving him $5,787.96 in interest. Paying extra money every month on a mortgage is what Turner calls an "up stream income," since you won't realize the savings until your loan is paid off. Furthermore, you will realize another "up stream income"—the equity that builds up in your home—after owning your home several years and refinancing or selling it. Finally, the ultimate "up stream income" a rental property owner realizes is when the rental income pays off his mortgage.

Property Appreciation

Real estate typically appreciates in value the longer you own it, unlike a car, which depreciates in value. Say you purchase a home for $79,900. Ten years from the time you purchase the home, adding 7% year after year of appreciation, your home would be worth $160,572—double what you paid for. If it only appreciates 5% year after year, at the end of the 10-year period your home would be worth $131,596—still a respectable investment gain!

203

Even if the property doesn't appreciate at all, when the mortgage is paid for by rental income, you are still ahead of the game since your renters paid for your home!

Compound Interest

Compound interest means you earn interest on the interest a bank pays you for letting it keep your money in a savings account. "The process is so amazing that your savings can more than double if you just give compounding enough time," says Curt Rohrman, a manager in the USAA First Start Program®, which is geared for kids interested in savings, investing, and managing their money.

Compound interest is a powerful financial tool. You can save more for retirement in your 20s and 30s than you can during the rest of your working life. A 20-year-old opening an individual retirement account gives them decades and decades for their money to compound.

By saving earlier in life, your money is working harder for you. Your money is working hard by earning compound interest. The compound interest now attaches itself to the principal, making the principal larger than it was originally. This amount goes through the process of being compounded, and more interest is earned. The new interest is added to the original principal plus the compounded interest, and the process starts all over again.

Curt Rohrman offers this example of short-term compound interest. "Imagine you have $50 in a savings account. It's time for the bank to pay you interest. You've earned 12 cents to your $50. Your new balance is $50.12. Next month you'll earn interest on $50.12 instead of just $50." Be prepared to move your money from your bank to another when you spot a better interest rate. Before you open a savings account at the local bank or credit union or when you are switching banks or credit unions, make sure your money will be insured; check bank listings at www.fdic.gov or www.ncua.gov for credit unions.

What are Dividends?

Dividend is another term for interest. You can find a listing of the companies that have raised their dividends every year for 25 years or more by buying *Mergent's Dividend Achievers*, a paperback published every three months; it costs $45. If it's free information you want, Mergent posts a list of stocks that have raised their dividends at least 10 years in a row at www.dividend achievers.com. Click on "Constituents" under "Dividend Achievers Indices."

Rule of 72

Have you ever heard of the Rule of 72? The rule says that to find the number of years it takes to double your money at a given interest rate, you just divide the interest rate into 72. For example, if you want to know how long it will take to double your money at 8% interest, divide 8 into 72, and you get 9 years. The higher the interest rate, the quicker your money will double. The Rule of 72 assumes your investments are tax-deferred and earning compound interest. As long as the interest rate is less than about 20%, the rule is surprisingly accurate. You can also run it backwards. If you want to double your money in six years, just divide 6 into 72 to find that an interest rate of about 12% is what you would need for this to happen.

You are now swimming in an ocean of money, and if you are thinking about purchasing an investment property to include in your financial portfolio, the next floor, Buy Your First Home or Rental Property, is where you need to land. The process Turner went through to purchase his rental property is featured on this floor.

12th Floor

Buy Your First Home or Rental Property

"Without savings, it's hard to even think about buying a home."
~Eileen Alt Powell, *Associated Press*

Real estate is an important element in gaining financial freedom. Owning income-producing properties (be it apartments, warehouses, commercial buildings, or single family homes and condominiums for rent), a growing number of people are taking advantage of such investments. According to one survey, there are more than 37 million investment units in the United States, and the number is constantly rising.[168]

When people found out that Turner, at the age of 13, purchased his first rental property in Flour Bluff, Texas, they were dumbfounded. After all, we live in California, where home prices are the most expensive in real estate history. People wanted to know, "How did he think of buying a home as an investment? How did he save up enough to buy the home? Why buy a home in the Corpus Christi area? Where is Corpus Christi? How much did the home cost? How did he find the property? How did he buy a property at the age of 13? How will he manage an out-of-town property? How did he get renters?" The questions still continue.

Admittedly, I didn't think that Turner would have the money for the down payment and closing costs until after he turned 18. Looking back on the seven years it took him to save, from several income streams, it now makes sense. While property prices have skyrocketed in California and other parts of the United States, real estate remained reasonably priced in Texas. Two months before his 14th birthday, Turner purchased a 3-bedroom, 2-bath, 2-car garage home in an excellent school district in a town called Flour Bluff. Turner is very proud that he was in a position to ride a historic real estate wave that many of his contemporaries may miss, unless they, too, buckle down early in their lives and make their homeownership dream happen.

Turner's Real Estate Transaction

Turner was always fascinated with investments. At the age of 7, he asked many questions about business and finance. He even wrote to Personal Finance Editor Kenneth Hooker of *The San Diego Union-Tribune*. Turner wanted to know how he could become a millionaire by the time he turned 40. Mr. Hooker printed Turner's letter and information about the magic of compound interest working for you when you're young. Fascinated beyond words after reading his letter and Mr. Hooker's reply in the business section of the Sunday newspaper, Turner was bent on speeding up his savings plan. That's when he wanted to establish a business that he could operate right away. Not certain what that would be, he headed to the local library and looked up books on kid businesses. He wanted a business that he would love to do, manage for a long time, and make money. So he ruled out the lemonade stand. What caught his interest was a pet care business. After doing the research and writing up a business plan, Turner was ready for the dogs!

Turner didn't want his parents to invest a dime in his business, nor did he want to spend any of his own money. He wanted to get the word out about his business for free, so he started with the local newspaper. Together, Turner and I came up with his first press release. Since Turner didn't have any clients' pets that he could pose with, he posed with his goldfish. That picture, along with the press release, made it into the local newspaper.

Turner's First Client

A week later Turner received a call to care for a caged rat and guinea pig for two weeks. As the client was paying in advance for Turner's services, she asked him a few questions.

"What are you going to do with your money?"

"Buy a house," responded Turner.

"What about college?" she asked. "Don't you need to first save for college?"

"No," responded Turner. "A house is what I'm saving for."

"But you'll need a car before you need a house," came her reply.

"I need a house with a garage," stated Turner. "Then I'll have a place to put the car. Then I can drive myself to college!"

I am telling this story to show you that you are never too young to learn about the correct order of things. In the financial world, it makes sense to make wise investments before spending lavishly. While a car can be a boon for business, if you live in a town where it makes sense to bike, choose that over purchasing a car. Or take public transportation. Generation Y-ers are young enough to be creative in their means of transportation. I'm amazed at how many Generation Y-ers, teens in particular, feel they need a car simply to get to school. And many of these teens don't even work! Why not learn how to work and save first, then spend and enjoy later — which could include buying a car?

Did you know that the average car payment in America is $378 a month, over 55 months? According to financial writer Dave Ramsey, "If, at the age of 25, the average person invested that money in a decent growth-stock mutual fund over 40 years, he'd have \$4.4 million."[169] And just imagine how much more you'll save if you don't have to shell out \$300 *or more* every month for car insurance. If you'll be *driving* the car, as does Shadi Salehpour, 19, from Del Mar, California, you, too, could be spending about \$420 a month for gas.[170] In all, a car can cost a teenager more than \$1,100 per month—and this doesn't include the cost of car repairs. Ride a bike, pay a parent (for gas) to drive you, or get a bus pass, and, at least throughout your teen years, invest the money you would spend on owning a car.

Saving to Purchase Rental Property

Turner created many income streams to reach his goal. His \$4 weekly allowance started the stream. Next came his Friday lunch money, which he opted to save by brown-bagging it on Fridays. He saved birthday money, Christmas money, recycling money, and odd-job money. Combined with money from his pet service, Turner saved an average of \$200 a month the first year. As he got older, he became more ambitious. Many gifts Turner received for his birthday and Christmas, he chose to return for cash. His pet care jobs tripled. In all, Turner increased his savings to an average of \$400 a month—more during the holidays. Several months shy of his 14th birthday, he had saved 20% of the down payment for a home in Flour Bluff, Texas. He would need a loan, in the form of a mortgage, for the additional 80% due to the seller.

Choosing an Area to Purchase Real Estate

Turner read a real estate book that listed 15 of the most affordable places to purchase homes in the United States. Corpus Christi, Texas, was on the list. Turner's grandparents also live in Corpus Christi. Turner knew that he wanted to buy a home in Nueces County, particularly in the Flour Bluff district near Padre Island, Texas.

Prior to purchasing his home, he searched the Internet for properties on www.realestate.com, and typed in the area he was interested in buying in. He also located realtors on the Internet by

Googling "Corpus Christi, Texas, Realtors," and found one on Padre Island, near the area where he was interested in investing. Turner contacted the realtor and told her about his goal to purchase a home. He also told her that he couldn't afford a home for more than $70,000, with a 20% down payment. Furthermore, the home had to be constructed of brick, have 3 bedrooms, 2 baths, a 2-car garage, be located in a great neighborhood in an excellent school district. Why? Resale value was important, in the event he could not afford his goal and had to sell quickly. Turner did his homework and had the realtor keep her eye out for a property that fit his needs. Turner figured that, in the Flour Bluff area, he could receive rent above the mortgage payment, property taxes, and insurance due to the excellent school district.

Don't Give Up

For the first six months Turner could not find a property that fit his criteria. Not only did he look in Flour Bluff, but he also looked in several other areas around Corpus Christi that had excellent schools. (Several Corpus Christi, Texas, realtor websites featured school ratings.) As for Flour Bluff, homes that met his criteria seemed to be priced about $10,000 more than Turner could afford when he started his search. In the meantime, he continued operating his pet care business, continued keeping income streams pooling together, and most importantly, kept his grades up. He was on a mission, and not finding a property wasn't going to dampen his spirits.

The Home Finally Surfaced

A year later, Turner was in a better financial position. He had worked even harder, continued wearing "Holy" clothes to school (his clothes wore thin, the holes got bigger), but his prayer was answered. Turner's realtor called and said she had found the perfect house in Flour Bluff. It was $79,900. It wasn't $70,000, but it was under $80,000. And that was good because by that time, a year later, the quality of homes he was interested in had increased in price to more than $90,000.

Another Bidder Surfaced

When Turner submitted his offer, he found that another person had just put a bid on the home. I told Turner that many people offer less, that I was confident that the other bidder's offer was $2,000 less than asking price. But neither of us actually knew what the other bidder's offer was. When I suggested that Turner offer $1,000 less than the asking price, he disagreed. He wanted to offer full price, not risking the chance of losing the property to the other bidder. At the airport, on the way back to California after viewing the home, Turner asked that his realtor write up a full-price offer, with a three-month closing.

Why a three-month closing? Turner, by then, had the 20% down payment, so he was able to avoid paying PMI (Private Mortgage Insurance), an extra monthly insurance payment added to your monthly mortgage payment if your down payment is less than 20%. "You don't want to pay for something that you can't write off," says Pierre Dunagan, president of Chicago-based mortgage company The Dunagan Group.[171] So it was important to Turner to save up the 20% needed for the down payment to avoid this non-tax deductible expense. But what he didn't have was money for the closing costs, which amounted to nearly $2,300. The contract was drawn. Turner knew how hard it was to find something in his price range, and that it could be a year or longer before another great deal would surface, so a full-price offer was his only hope. Ironically, it was one year later before another excellent deal came up (more on that later).

The Offers Were In

The next day Turner's realtor called to inform him that both offers were in, that it would be later that day before he would find out anything. That evening, the realtor called. First, the bad news came. The other bidder offered $4,000 above the asking price.

Turner's heart sank. Then the good news came. Turner won the bid! How? Because Turner offered a conventional loan, and the other bidder offered an FHA loan. (Google these types of loans on the Internet to find out their differences.) In an effort to get the owner to pay the closing costs of approximately $2,000, the other bidder offered $4,000 above the asking price—approximately $2,000 of which the owner could pocket. He also wanted to have title to the home by the end of the month. The sellers, by Turner's sheer luck, wanted to stay in the home another three months, in time for their new home to be built. Turner won the contract.

He was beside himself. It was now November, time for people to go on Thanksgiving vacation. Turner's business phone rang. Then came December, time for people to go on Christmas vacation. Turner's business phone rang. New Year's came, more pet care. By January 15th, Turner was ready to close on the home.

Qualifying for a Loan

The three things that lenders consider when you apply for a loan are your credit score, your debt-to-income ratio, and the down payment. "If you've got two of the three elements working for you, you're in good shape to buy," says Jim McMillan, a senior loan officer with JP Mortgage/JP Morgan Chase.[172] The adults in the family could qualify for a loan, but could Turner—at the age of 13?

We contacted USAA, a company our family has been doing business with throughout my husband's military career. Even the USAA representative wasn't sure if Turner would be able to obtain the loan (to cover the additional 80% of the home's cost due to the seller) on his own, because he'd never been asked this question before. Turner had the 20% down payment banked with USAA and had been a client of theirs for over seven years. His diligent savings track record proved that he would be an excellent risk. As it turned out, unless he was married at the age of 13 in the state of Texas, he could not get the loan in his name. He could, however, have the title of the home converted to him on his 18th birthday. So, the loan was drawn up in the names of his father and I. (Turner opted for the 15-year, fixed rate note. While the

212

payments on the 15-year note were slightly higher than on the 30-year note, the loan percent, at 5.25%, was cheaper.) The monthly mortgage payment was deducted from Turner's Wells Fargo account automatically.

Visiting Texas After Closing

The next week, not wanting Turner to miss school, I took a trip to Corpus Christi to visit my parents and see Turner's house. I hired painters to paint the inside of the home, had the carpet steam cleaned, and advertised the home for rent in *The Corpus Christi Caller & Times*, all paid for by Turner. By the end of the week, nearly 20 showings later, I selected the perfect couple to rent the home after running a credit check on them. It is really worth the effort to be extremely selective about who you choose to rent to. If you're not totally comfortable to whom you're going to rent, don't rent to them. One person who wanted to rent the home said, in his deep Texas drawl, "My rifles will fit great in this here closet!" I'm not saying that I would not rent to someone who owns guns; in the end, we rented the home to a Texas trooper and his fiancée, who had all the proper permits and training for gun handling.

Rental Property Manager

A rental property manager is responsible for the care and upkeep of a property. Property managers generally handle the financial and operational needs of the property, ensuring that rent is collected and that mortgages, taxes, insurance premiums, and maintenance bills are paid on time. In a nutshell, a property manager advertises vacancies; screens and places tenants; collects security deposits, rents, and late fees; facilitates standard upkeep, such as trash collection and lawn maintenance; facilitates repairs, such as backed-up toilets; prepares units for rental after a tenant moves out; renews leases; handles complaints about tenants (noise, unsupervised children, etc.); files appropriate paperwork for evictions; prepares reports on income and expenses for the owner; maintains the condition and therefore, the value of a property; and stays apprised of all aspects of the ever-changing federal and state laws, local codes, regulations, and license requirements. In other words, the job of a property manager is to advertise your property for rent, run a credit check to find a tenant likely to pay rent, provide rental applications and leases, collect a rental deposit, collect the rent on time, hire a plumber if your kitchen faucet is leaking, and see that your mortgage/insurance/taxes are paid on time. In return you pay a percentage of the rent, usually 8% to 10% of your income, to a property manager.

Property Manager and Self-Manage Combo

Another option available to a landlord is having a property manager do a one-time rent-out. For a higher percent of the first month's rent, usually 25% to 50%, a rental manager will advertise the property for rent, run a credit check to find a tenant likely to pay rent, have a lease filled out and ready to be signed, collect the rental deposit and first month's rent, and return the signed lease and rent check to the landlord, less his/her fee. At this point the landlord becomes the rental manager, and the rent checks will come directly to him or, if specified, the bank in which an automatic mortgage payment is set up.

Out-of-state property owners truly benefit from a one-time rent-out through a professional property manager in the area in which they own the rental property. They have the benefit of a professional manager who knows about all that is involved in the rental industry and has access to rental applications, leases, credit check, not to mention good salesmanship. It really is worth 50% of the first month's rent to have a professional property manager carefully screen prospective tenants and find you an outstanding one.

Self-Manage Property—Long Distance

Since owning the property, Turner has been an absentee landlord, managing his property himself. There really hasn't been much for him to do physically except deposit his rent check. His bank account is set up for automatic mortgage withdrawal on the 5th of each month, so, when the rent check arrives on or before the first of the month, he has time to deposit it. Wells Fargo wires the funds to his mortgage company free of charge.

The current month's rent check is not the check Turner counts on to pay the mortgage. He has buffered his account so that, in the event the rental check arrives late to his account or takes time to clear the bank, he still can pay his bills on time through his automatic draft account.

As for insurance premiums and property taxes, these are incorporated into Turner's mortgage payment (set up through USAA in an escrow account). Every month when the mortgage payment is due, 1/12th of the yearly insurance premiums and 1/12th of the yearly property taxes are incorporated into the mortgage payment. When the mortgage payment is wired to the mortgage company every month, the taxes and insurance premiums attached to the payment are set aside in an escrow account. When the property taxes and insurance premiums come due, the mortgage company will pay them.

Yellow Pages

Purchase a Yellow Pages directory from the city in which you buy rental property. This telephone book will be invaluable for operating your real estate business. If your tenant calls you and says your tub faucet is dripping continuously, look up a plumber, and call him to meet with your tenant to take care of the leak.

Plumbers work on an hourly pay scale, which means that when they fix that leak and it takes them 10 minutes to do so, you'll still be billed for an hour's time. Why not have your plumber do some preventative plumbing work for you that will fit in the hour that you will be paying for? For example, have the plumber snake your drains in the kitchen and bath. This snaking process will unclog hair in the bathroom tub, shower, and sink drains, and clear food debris from your kitchen sink. Having clear pipes helps keep you from making emergency calls to your plumber, which will save money in the long run. Next time your tenant has a noisy toilet tank drip, remember to include the snaking of all drains, including your garage sink drain, in the work order.

Hiring a Property Manager

There may come a time when Turner will need to hire a property manager on a monthly basis. That's when he'll look for a licensed real estate broker, preferably someone who has properties of his own and knows what it's like to be an owner. If you're using a real estate agency, ask if they have a property management department instead of a realtor who is just managing property on the side.

Review their tenant applications, their leases, their owner's reports, their screening processes, and their repair policies. Find out what the limit is on how much the property manager can spend on repairs without your approval. You will also need to know about their marketing plan, their vacancy rates, and their procedure for dealing with tenants who haven't paid the rent.

Running a Credit Check

A credit check is the process of evaluating an applicant's request to rent your property. A credit report is a confidential report on a consumer's payment habits as reported by their creditors to a consumer credit agency. This report helps the landlord or property manager determine the likelihood that the applicant will be responsible about paying the rent. A credit report tracks personal credit worthiness through a score. This score, known as a FICO score, was developed by Fair Isaac & Co. to evaluate the likelihood that consumers will pay their bills. FICO scores range from a low of 300 points (highest risk) to a high of 850 (lowest risk). Credit checks on potential tenants will also allow you to see if they have any outstanding judgments in the local courts for unpaid rent. Three major credit agencies include Equifax, (888) 766-0008, www.equifax.com; Experian (formerly TRW), (888) 397-

3742, www.experian.com; and TransUnion, (800) 888-4213, www.tuc.com.

By the end of 2006 the nation's largest consumer credit bureaus will unveil a new credit scoring system, VantageScore, which will give lenders a better measure of borrowers' credit-worthiness and make the process easier to understand. VantageScore's new credit scoring scale is:

Score	Grade	Credit Outlook
901–990	A	Excellent rating; low interest rate
801–900	B	Good rating but short of excellent
701–800	C	Fair; moderate risk
601–700	D	Higher risk means higher interest rate
501–600	F	Highest risk; may not qualify for loan[173]

FICO scores will continue to range from 300 to 850. VantageScore will have scores ranging from 501 to 990. "There could be confusion among consumers unless they make it clear that there are two systems," said Linda Sherry, a spokeswoman for Consumer Action. "People have gotten used to thinking a certain number like 700 is a good score. That might be true if it's a FICO, but might not be under the new system."[174]

Get a Good Software Program

Property management software is very helpful when you manage rental property. It can help you save time by preparing tenant billing, remind you when leases are nearing their ending dates, and help you create and print important notices. When you own a single rental property, it isn't necessary to have a software program. If you own multiple units, a software program is probably a good idea.

There are many programs to choose from, including Tenant Pro, Rent Roll, and Yardi Systems. They are available online and some offer a free trial download. Tenant Pro is user friendly and is priced at $600. When you purchase one of these programs, don't forget to add tech support. It's good to have this support available until you become familiar with the software.

Tenants as Your Employees

Turner treats his tenants as his employees. "If you show them you care, and that you listen to what they're saying, you'll get quality residents who pay the rent on time and not cause problems," says Turner. "Tenants who feel respected treat you with respect." To accomplish this goal, Turner takes care of issues relating to his rental home in a timely manner. He even allows quality tenants to break a lease, if, for example, they have found a home to purchase in the middle of their lease. Rewarding outstanding tenants shows that you have appreciated their efforts in paying rent on time, reporting problems before they become major issues, and giving you little trouble—all qualities of outstanding tenants. Someday the newly-minted homeowners may rent their home in the same manner of attitude.

One landlord who owns several rentals and treats his tenants as employees is Mike Butler, author of *Landlording on Auto-Pilot*. Mike, a retired police officer, developed management methods to minimize inconveniences often caused by tenants while still delivering superior service. Not only does he treat his tenants with respect, he holds an annual Christmas party for his independent contractor suppliers, such as electrician, plumber, maintenance people, handymen, roofer, tree trimmer, and other vendors. Although his annual costs for such a party are less than $1,000, when his properties need fast service his vendors usually put him at the top of the list.[175]

Where to Advertise Rental Property

Many people use the free website Craigslist to find tenants for their rental property. If you live near a military base, you can also list your property, for free, on the Automated Housing Referral Network (AHRN) at www.ahrn.com. The city newspaper rental classified ad section is another place to list your rental. When you purchase an ad, ask if they can link your listing to their website's classifieds. Many newspapers will include this added service, for free, when you purchase a regular newspaper listing. (Have digital photos handy in the event you can include them on the website listing.) And remember to post a "For Rent" sign (purchased at a hardware store) in front of your rental. Properties displaying a sign often rent before a classified ad appears in the paper!

Rental Property Near Military Installations

If you have rental property located near any U.S. military installation, log onto the Automated Housing Referral Network (AHRN) to list your property for rent. Military families transferring to your area will be able to find your property for rent before they move to the area. This is when a digital camera comes in handy. AHRN will allow you to post digital photos with your listing. It may seem odd to you, however, many military families rent properties simply by looking at photos. To list your property for rent with AHRN, visit their website at www.ahrn.com. The service is free, and you can list your property for as long as it takes to rent.

Become a Real Estate Angel Investor

Just recently Turner loaned his younger sister, Mia, $7,000 so that she could purchase a rental home in Flour Bluff. Mia, who owns Affordable Pet Care, is now a landlord like her brother. With Turner's loan, Mia was able to purchase a home in a subdivision across the street from Turner's rental. A year after Turner purchased his home for $79,900, Mia paid $85,600 for a home similar to his. Mia, like her brother, was in a dual-bid situation. Mia offered $100 *over* the asking price. The other bidder came in at $2,000 less than the asking price. Mia won the bid. She collects rent and has automatic payment of the mortgage, property taxes, and insurance. Like her brother, Mia manages her own property by telephone. If there is an ant problem, Mia calls the bug people (exterminators) and sends them over to get rid of the critters.

Only the Good Buy Young

Afraid to take the real estate leap because you are young? According to the most recent data from the National Association of Realtors, home buyers between the ages of 18 and 34 made up 39% of the market last year. And Generation Y-ers younger than 25 made up 12% of first-time home buyers.[176] One of these young people, John W. Schaub, now 32, a very successful real estate investor, wrote a book on how to create wealth purchasing real estate. In his book *Building Wealth One House at a Time*, John reveals why investing in local houses is the safest long-term realty investment, how he buys without obtaining bank mortgages, and how to select profitable houses that will attract quality tenants. Melody Jiggetts, 25, could not stomach paying rent any longer to live in an apartment. When rent for her one-bedroom Whittier, California apartment increased nearly 30% in a two-year period, she decided she'd rather pay her own mortgage than someone else's. So she entered the inaugural *Black Enterprise* (www.blackenterprise.com) Own Your First Home Contest, hoping for a chance to win $10,000 toward the down payment on a home of her own. Although she didn't win the contest, she learned so much about investing in real estate from *Black Enterprise* that, in September of 2005, Melody bought and moved into a home of her own.[177]

Helpful House-Hunting Sites

Go to www.domania.com or www.GetMyHomeValue.com and enter an address in the area you want to research to see recent sales in the neighborhood. Add to this effort by visiting www.realtor.com, using their search-by-Zip-code feature to find the asking prices for nearby homes for sale. Or, visit the Multiple Listing Service (www.mls.com), which includes homes being listed by numerous real estate and mortgage firms and insurance companies.

On the website www.realtytimes.com, real estate agents from around the country weigh in on their local housing conditions. They often talk about whether it is a buyer's or seller's market, and whether prices are rising or falling. The site also offers news and advice. On the website www.housing.com, you can find information on various kinds of mortgages, learn how your credit rating affects your ability to buy a house, calculate the value of your salary in different cities (adjusted for cost-of-living expenses) and more. Visit BusinessWeeks' online site http://bwnt.businessweek.com/housing_boom/index.asp to find an interactive table that lets you study how more than 30 major metro areas stack up on nine different housing-related measures. You can judge how vulnerable your own market is to a steep price decline using indicators based on prices, construction, jobs, incomes, rental rates, etc. On PropertyShark (www.propertyshark.com) you can search for foreclosure bargains or map out environmental hazards not typically disclosed until escrow. The service is free, and is available at most East Coast communities, however, a national distribution of the service is to come. These helpful websites can aid you in your home search.

Find the Next Housing Hot Spot

You may have heard about "the real estate boom." If only you could get the inside scoop on where the next hot housing market will be! Home Depot thinks it knows just where the next—and the next—hot spot will be. Home Depot invests as much in researching demographic, employment, and wage trends as do real estate investors. The qualities that make for housing hot spots (rising prices, rising sales, lots of construction) are the same ones Home Depot seeks when scouting locations for new stores. Where can you find Home Depot's coveted list of upcoming store openings? At http://www.careers.homedepot.com/grandopenings. If you're looking for an area to purchase a home for around $100,000, read *The Perfect $100,000 House* by Karrie Jacobs. Her book chronicles a 14,000-mile road trip in the summer of 2003—after her post-*Dwell* career as a freelance writer—in search of her affordable dream home. If you just want to find

areas   that   sell   houses   under $50,000,   visit
www.HousesUnderFiftyThousand.com.

How Much Mortgage Can You Afford?

There are several websites that offer online calculators with a variety of features designed to assist prospective home buyers in figuring out what monthly mortgage payments they can afford. These websites can help you determine the loan amount you can qualify for by income, savings, and down payments. Bankrate.com features calculators for determining a mortgage payment and finding out how much you can afford (www.bankrate.com/brm/calculators/morgages.asp); HSH Associates, Financial Publishers' simple calculator provides quick affordability estimate results (www.hsh.com/calc-how much.html); LoanSaver.org calculates monthly payments based on home price, down payment, length of loan, and annual interest rate (www.loansaver.org/calculate.php); Realtor.com can help you determine the loan amount you can qualify for by income, savings, and debt payments (www.homefair.com/homefair/ usr/qualcalcform.html); and Mortgage Calculators contains calculators on more than two dozen mortgage-related topics (www.mortgage-calculators.org).

▶◀

You now have a general idea about purchasing rental property. If you happen to live in an affordable area, purchase a rental property near your home. If you do your research and stay true to your goal, you, too, can be the owner of a rental property as part of your investment plan. The next floor, Fine-Tune Your Lifestyle, will help you see that you can create your own wealth.

13th Floor

Fine-Tune Your Lifestyle

"With a few modest behavioral changes,
becoming wealthy is fairly easy for most Americans."
~Richard B. McKenzie, co-author of *Getting Rich in America*

It's not difficult to get wealthy in this country. It's really all about lifestyle and mind-set. If you learn early in life to live beneath your means, becoming wealthy is fairly easy. Horace Madison and Solomon Smallwood, financial planners for the firm MadisonSmallwood Financial Group, provide wealth management for some of the biggest stars in the entertainment business. They have developed a practice helping young musicians, athletes, and actors make—and keep—more money. They explain to their clients that it's easy to be rich. Being wealthy is the difficult part, because it means keeping more of the money you make, and making it work for you. Several of their clients, including music moguls Outkast and Usher, are not only rich, they are also wealthy! For people who become rich at a young age, money can be both a "gift and a curse," says the financial duo.[178] Learning to handle it, by saving and investing, will make a difference in your future.

Money is a tool, and you can learn how to use it so it can make more money. If you don't learn how to make your money work for you, and you are always working for your money, you will never obtain financial freedom. Rather than concentrating on getting rich, have the knowledge to retain wealth and make it work for you. What if a 16-year-old begins saving $365 *a month* (earned from a part-time job), and continue to save the same amount each month for 44 years, earning a 6% rate of return? When this teen turns 60, he will have a net worth of $1,000,000! You will find that a simple, repetitive savings plan is all it takes for a young person to become a millionaire. You don't even need a million-dollar idea!

Becoming Wealthy is a Choice

You have the choice to become wealthy, and the opportunity has never been better. Young people today are more aware of savings and investment than the previous generation, and they are planning for the future. "Generation Y-ers are fortunate because they have time on their side," says Turner. "They can afford to be aggressive in their investments because they will have a long time before they will need the money."

The Older You Writing to the Younger You

Imagine that you are 20 years older. If you could write yourself a note of advice to the person you were back then (which is actually now), what would you say? Author Naomi Wolf was asked this question by Ellyn Spragins, author of *What I Know Now*, in a recent *O* article. Naomi, now 43, wrote in her Dear Younger Self letter, "Invest $50 in the stock market every month, girl. You don't need to eat out so much. Think of all that compound interest—you could start a nonprofit when you are in your 40s!"[179] It was the first of 7 entries she wrote to her younger self! What will you be writing to your younger self when you are 20 years older? Will you be telling yourself to invest in the stock market because the younger you never bothered to look into investing in the stock market? I'll bet not because you, a financially savvy Generation Y-er, took advantage of the automatic DRIP stock-purchasing program (information about DRIPs can be found on the next floor) 20 years ago! Will the older you write to the younger you, telling you to purchase a home with a 15-year mortgage? I'll bet not because you, a financially knowledgeable (and now mortgage-free) Generation Y-er, knew to secure a 15-year mortgage when you purchased your home 20 years ago! Instead, you'll be writing a letter to the younger you that kindness is everything, as was Naomi's last entry.

Learn to Control Your Money

"Don't be controlled by money," says Turner. "Learn to control it. By being honest with yourself about your wants and needs, you'll be in control of your money and feel smarter." If you can't spend less than you earn, stay away from stores. Life is more manageable when your money is managed well. You won't be considered greedy when you are building your financial wealth. "The very act of saving alone gives you a greater sense of control over your money," says Walter Updegrave, personal finance writer for *Money* and author of *How to Retire Rich in a Totally Changed World*, who first became interested in money when he realized he didn't have any.[180]

Live Within Your Means

Children who are given their every whim—special toys, dance lessons, fashionable clothes and shoes, even a car, have a hard time living within their means as adults. One such person, Jenn Andrlick, a 23-year-old editorial assistant in New York, is the first to describe herself as a recovering "spoiled brat." As a child in Omaha, she says, she regularly manipulated her parents into buying her lots of things, including a car. She even admitted that she was the envy of all her friends because, "I always had more than anyone." Now, as a young adult, she is finding it hard to budget and live within her means and still relies on handouts from her parents. These days she envies her roommates, who know how to balance a budget. The roommates learned early in their lives the balance between spending and saving, something Jenn wish she had done.[181] "Parents should use their money to help their kids become independent," says Jon Gallo, co-author of *Silver Spoon Kids: How Successful Parents Raise Responsible Children*, "not to maintain their independence."[182]

Pay Yourself Before You Pay Uncle Sam

You can bypass paying the government on money you earned by investing in your company's 401(k), since your contributions are made in pretax dollars. Over a 20-year period, you'll save over $40,000! More information about investing in a 401(k) can be found on the next floor.

Spend Less Than You Earn

The secret of millionaires is that they learned early in their working lives to live on less than they earn, so they always have enough to invest in something that pays back. It is hard to spend less than we earn when there is so much media telling us that in order to be cool, we must buy, buy, buy. Saving money instead of spending it is always a trade-off. If you can do this one simple step, you will be ahead of most people. If you need a reminder to spend less, keep a picture of your goal in your wallet. Reading the book *The Millionaire Next Door*, by Thomas J. Stanley (no relation) and William D. Danko, might inspire you to "act like a real millionaire instead of spending like a fake one," advises financial writer Lynn O'Shaughnessy.[183]

Live a Simple Life

Living a simple life is one of surest ways to becoming financially wealthy. If you learn to live simply early in life, you will have more money to do things later in life and have more free time to do it. Living simply means that you won't be too focused on buying and consuming things now.

There are many fun things to do that don't cost money. Visiting public libraries, attending free concerts in the park, volunteering, going to the beach, hanging with family and friends, visiting museums on free day, becoming a journal writer, maybe even discovering new bike paths—are just a few things to keep you in good spirits and your mind and body active, not to mention how it adds money in your bank account (by not spending). If you like to stay home and need a few free laughs, log onto www.jokes.com. If you Google "Freebies" on the Internet, you can find free things like visiting Ben & Jerry's on their free cone day.

Lots of businesses offer freebies on your birthday, so check the store's website (or call their customer-service department) for deals like a free scoop of ice cream at Cold Stone Creamery, free dessert at Borders cafés, or a $5 coupon at Red Lobster. Want some free educational fun? You can tour a candy-making factory, ice cream factory or movie studio—often for free. Find one near you by visiting www.factorytoursusa.com.

There are unlimited online opportunities and courses you can take for free. You can learn to speak a new language, choosing from more than 100 at www.word2word.com. Click on "free online courses" and select French, German, Spanish, even Punjabi! (Many of these courses include audio, to aid in correct pronunciation.) Or take up photography. If you want to become a better photographer, or master it, you'll find tutorials at sites like www.photo.net. Click on "learn," and you'll find lessons on subjects ranging from portraits to underwater photography. Want to learn how to play an instrument—for free? The site www.berkleeshares.com offers lessons perfected at the Berklee College of Music, which can be downloaded for free. Get free computer software—like Sudoku puzzles—at www.jumbo.com.

Control Spending Leaks

"Many Generation Y-ers are in so much debt because they dribble their money away in small, barely noticeable amounts," says Turner. "If you want to accumulate wealth, you must control your spending leaks." If you're a better spender than a saver, it's time to make the change. If you're saving 10% and spending 90% of your money, look at where all your leaks are. Are you spending $3 on sodas and donuts at school or work every day? Do you spend $5 on a comic book and candy bar every weekend? That weekly $20 leak in your financial faucet adds up to $960 in one year, not including compound interest. Is it worth it to you to spend nearly $1,000 a year on sodas, donuts, comic books, and candy bars? Say that between the ages of 13 and 18 you take the $960 each year and invest it in a mutual fund that pays you 3% compound interest. In five years, at the age of 18, this account would amass to $5,101.

A spendthrift can turn into a financially responsible person. If going "cold turkey" is too hard, try saving half of your money to begin with. You can always increase the amount you save when you are ready. This *can* be done when you are young and without responsibilities. As you become older and have more responsibilities, for example, paying for car insurance, gas, and car repairs, then you can loosen the financial reins so that you can pay for your responsibilities. Hip-hop mogul Russell Simmons says financial planning should be a priority for Generation Y, rather than spending their money on material things. "They don't need to pay attention to the bling," he says. "Rappers spending countless money are on television. But in real life, these artists are very responsible with their money."[184] Even rapper LL Cool J urges his fans to be financially responsible. "The biggest misconception probably comes from the hip-hop community itself—that the money lasts forever," says LL Cool J. "You have to do the right thing with it."[185] It is important that Generation Y learn about financial responsibility, and the sooner the better.

The $108,000 Louis Vuitton Handbag

My daughter, Mia, wants to purchase a $613 Louis Vuitton handbag—well, that's what she calls the barely-bigger-than-a-wallet handbag. Let's say that Mia instead chooses to invest the $613 Louis Vuitton handbag money. To find out what the value of this one-time, single deposit can be worth over a period of time,

Mia visits the website www.MsFinancialSavvy.com. She clicks on "Calculator" under "Daily Tools." She then clicks on "Savings Calculator," and selects "Single Deposit Calculator." She enters $613 in the single deposit slot, 8% interest she expects to earn, and 8 years for the time she plans to invest the money. By the time Mia turns 21, her Louis Vuitton handbag money will be worth $1,160. The interest earned from the $613 deposit is $547, nearly the cost of the original purchase. At this time the money is in the bank. The purse, which, according the salesman, needs replaceable $50 leather straps every six months due to natural cracking of leather, is nowhere in sight.

Let's take this one step further, to Mia's possible retirement at the age of 65. She plugs in 52 for the years she plans to invest, at an 8% return. At the age of 65, Mia's Louis Vuitton handbag money will be worth $38,737; at 9%, $64,919; at 10%, $108,138! Add in a one-time Play Station portable (PSP), half-dozen PSP games, and an iPod money and you could retire a quarter-of-a-million dollars richer!

Being Popular is Pricey

In his book, *Is There Life After High School?*, author Ralph Keyes believes that the very characteristics that make a person popular in high school are detriments to success in life. So what makes a kid popular? Brains? No. Creativity? No. Independence? No. What it does take, according to Ralph Keyes, is a certain look, a certain walk, and a certain talk.[186]

The "certain look" part costs money. Teenage Research Unlimited estimates that teen girls, alone, spend over $21 billion a year on clothes and accessories.[187] The boys were not far behind in their clothes spending. Furthermore, it is easy for teens to have that "certain walk" to accompany that "certain look" with iPods and cell phones attached to their ears. These kids always seem to have money to do fun things, like going to see popular movies and eating pizza out with friends.

Being popular *is* expensive. You're saying, "But I need to be the typical teen and spend $4,000 a year on things to be cool—an iPod, cell phones, the latest clothes…" As the proverb goes, "A fool and his money are soon parted…" Advertisers are trying to separate these fools from their money, and many are doing an excellent job succeeding at it. Being "cool" is for financial fools. To be popular now and broke later—or to be average now and wealthy later—which is your choice?

Don't Keep Up with the Jones' Kids

It's hard to not keep up with the Jones' kids when kids' marketers try—and succeed—at making children their best consumers. Advertisers spend over $15 billion a year telling kids what's hot. Kids are a big business to these advertisers. According to Susan Linn, a Harvard psychologist and author of the book *Consuming Kids: The Hostile Takeover of Childhood*, "The marketers call it 'cradle-to-grave brand loyalty.' They want to get kids from the moment they're born."[188]

When you see the coolest of things, walk away. If you want those cool things now, those marketers have succeeded in trapping you with their bait. Often kids don't even like the latest style of clothes, but want them to "fit in with the crowd." Actor Will Smith said it best when he referred to Generations X and Y going into financial debt just to impress unimportant people: "Too many people spend money they haven't earned, to buy things they don't want, to impress people they don't like."[189] Don't let the Jones' kids lead you down Consumer Way. This street will most certainly lead you to thrift stores when you're older, because you won't have money to shop anywhere else.

Don't Be Your Friend's "Best Friend"

If friends expect you to pay for their fun because you're making money, get new friends. You're not making money to treat friends or to be popular with them because you have money. You are making money to save for a financially secure future. Billionaire Richard Branson knows how to pinch pennies. As a millionaire for nearly 30 years, his thriftiness is legendary. If you go out to dinner with Richard Branson, expect to pay for your own meal. Richard

Branson never carries money around and even borrows money from his friends. Furthermore, any luxury items he buys for himself must also pay their own way, and so his island, Necker, is available to rent if you can spare a few grand.[190]

Don't Hang Out with Big Spenders

Hanging out with big spenders will drain your savings. If your friends want to blow $15 on a movie and popcorn *every* weekend, don't hang out with them. Find friends who will play basketball with you at a nearby court, ride bikes, go to the park, or rent movies from the library. You have the power to control financial leaks.

Avoid Impulse Buys

When you're swooning over a potential purchase, Sandy Shields, director of TheFrugalShopper.com, suggests that you imagine owning the item in the future. Picture having to clean it, take care of it, and store it. How many after-tax hours do you need to work to pay for it? If you are buying on credit, imagine all the hours you'll have to work to pay for it (and don't forget the interest!). Then ask yourself if you still want it. If you see something that you truly want to buy, wait a day or two or even a month. Then, after having slept on it, if you still need the item, go back and buy it. But remember The Frugal Shopper's advice! People who learn about delayed gratification and goal setting early in life reap huge rewards later in life.

Be Interested, Not Interesting

The nature of the beast is that popular kids are interesting, loaded with interesting interests to share. When you are interesting, you are taking others' time; when you are interested, you are giving others time, that is, allowing them an opportunity to educate you. When you're busy being interesting, you miss the opportunity to be interested. Being interested means you are listening to what people have to say, learning from others because everyone has a story to tell. If you invest more time being interested, and less time being interesting, you will have an open mind to learn great things around you. If you come to the dinner table interested and curious, life becomes more interesting for everyone at the table. Jim Collins, author of *Built to Last: Successful Habits of Visionary Companies*, says, "By practicing the art of being interested, the majority of people can become fascinating teachers."[191] Come to the table with a curious mind and your dessert will be served to you in many flavors, including new friendships, contacts, business leads, and knowledge—not to mention your becoming a more interesting person!

Become a Planned Spender

Become a smart shopper by learning to use coupons, keeping an eye out for sales, and by comparing unit pricing. Soon enough you'll be living on your own and making your own purchases. Becoming a "planned spender" results in savings of 20% to 30%, money that can be invested in your future. Take the time to cut out coupons from the Sunday newspaper and store circulars. Carry a pocket calculator with you so you'll be prepared to compare unit pricing. Sometimes you'll find a competitor's product cheaper than a similar one purchased with a coupon. Don't feel like cooking and want pizza or a sandwich? Chances are your favorite pizza parlor or sandwich shop runs regular coupon sales on these items. If your favorite pizza parlor and pizza coupon don't match, call the manager to see if they will honor the competitor's coupon. Many businesses have a practice of accepting competitors' coupons just to keep the sale under their roof!

Don't Make Loans

The old saying by Polonius (a counsel for the royal family), "Neither a borrower nor a lender be," should be your motto. You can better help your friends in financial need by helping them figure out smart spending practices or ways to earn money.

Don't Ask for Bailouts

When you've spent all of your month's allowance in two weeks, and there isn't any money left to go out for a pizza, don't borrow from friends or ask your parents to bail you out with a loan or advance on your next allowance. When you ask for bailouts, it's like living off a credit card when someone tides you over with additional money. In a survey commissioned by The Charles Schwab Foundation, about a third of today's teens owe money to a person or to a company—and 14% of them owe more than $1,000. "If teenagers are already accumulating debt," says Carrie Schwab Pomerantz, Chief Strategist of Consumer Education for Charles Schwab & Co., "it's going to be that much harder for them to accumulate wealth for retirement."[192]

If you run out of money before you run out of days before your next paycheck or allowance, do something creative to keep busy. Read library books, run around your block, visit friends. "If you have debt, I'm willing to bet that general clutter is a problem for you, too," says Suze Orman, author of *The Money Book for the Young, Fabulous & Broke*.[193] If you run out of money before your next paycheck, clean your room and/or organize your workspace. You might just clear a path to making more money as you become neater and more organized.

If you want to earn money, ask around the neighborhood if there is any work you can be hired for. My editor, Joan McColly, tells a story about when her own son, who, while in college, spent his entire monthly allotment on skis. For the remainder month he ate Bisquick. In the end her son made a wise investment purchasing the skis because, now, he's the Director of Marketing for a major ski resort. Even college kids need to know the importance of budgeting. It's important to know that eating fast food at the beginning of the month can impact your ability to buy gas for your car at the end of the month.

Don't Use Credit

The world doesn't owe you a thing. You owe it to yourself to work hard, save smart, and never go into debt. Credit—when it's misused—can be a dreaded monster. You don't want credit to be in charge of you; you want to be in charge of it. Spending money you don't have, either through credit cards or loans from family or friends, is the fastest way to run into money trouble. Many Generation Y-ers ages 18 to 24 are doing just that. People in this age bracket spend about 25% of their monthly income just on debt repayment, according to Demos, a New York nonprofit organization that found that credit card debt for people in this age bracket climbed 104% between 1992 and 2001.[194] What's even more shocking is that, according to a JA Worldwide study of 1,065 teens, 6% of kids ages 13 and 14 use credit cards.[195] We can only hope that parents have instructed these kids how to use credit cards properly. Obviously there is nothing wrong with a credit card if the balance is paid off every month. If you must use a credit card, use a charge card that must be paid in its entirety every month, such as American Express. To make sure that you are ready for the financial responsibility of owning a credit card, read about the consequences of consumer credit at www.careprogram.us. You can also become Credit-Ed Certified at www.citi.com/us/cards/cm/student/index.htm. This site includes a free online course in money management for teens!

John C. Ninfo, II, a U.S. Bankruptcy Court judge and founder of the Credit Abuse Resistance Education (CARE) Program—which teaches students the fundamentals of finances—offers college students tips on intelligent use of credit cards. His tips, featured in *The Next Step Magazine*, can help Generation Y-ers to learn the fundamentals of using credit cards wisely:

- One credit card is all that you need for convenience or an emergency.
- Use cash, a check, or a debit card as often as possible. If you can eat it or drink it, pay cash for it.
- Having more than one credit card will not improve your credit rating. Don't listen to anyone who tells you otherwise.
- Having one credit card, staying within your credit limit and paying off the balance on time every month will prevent you from having to deal with late fees and over-limit fees.
- Got a balance? Put the card away!
- Don't use your one credit card to pay for anything that costs less than $20.

- Students often end up with several credit cards and find themselves getting into debt with them because they want to continue to live the lifestyle they had at home or that wealthier friends enjoy. But on their budget, they can't afford those lifestyles.
- Never put anything on your one credit card that you can't pay for at the end of the month when the bill comes. If you do charge something, pay the bill in full and on time every month.
- Stay away from store charge cards. By doing so, you will spend less in the store. Store charges generally accrue interest on unpaid balances at higher rates than a major credit card would, such as Visa or MasterCard.[196]

Eliminate Student Debt

There is a solution for new graduates who want to begin work by eliminating student debt. Such programs repay student loans in return for work in underserved areas. When Brian McDonald, now 24, graduated from college, he followed a traditional career path in corporate finance. Several months later he was laid off, and that's when he made a radical switch and became an American Corps volunteer (www.americorps.gov) in Albuquerque. Brian worked for a nonprofit organization that made micro loans to low-income entrepreneurs. During his year of service, Brian earned a stipend of nearly $10,000. In addition, AmeriCorps' loan-repayment education awards paid off 25% of his $19,000 in student loans. After his time with American Corps, Brian began a career in community-development finance with the federal government.[197]

Another service program to consider is the National Health Services Corps (NHSC) because it offers two-year loan repayment contracts to clinicians working with the nation's underserved. Currently, the maximum loan repayment with NHSC is $25,000 per year. When deciding whether to work for these types of programs, you would need to weigh the benefits of loan repayment versus working in the field with higher pay, that is, if jobs are available.

Don't Spend Your Tomorrows Today

Say you have credit card debt with a balance of $4,000, with 18% interest. Do you realize that it would take 45 years to pay it off with the minimum payment? Spending your tomorrows today is what you'll be doing if you use a credit card and don't pay off the balance each month. Making minimum payments on your credit cards will keep you from saving for your future. You'll lock yourself up and lose your freedom when your credit card controls you. Credit use is fine if it is part of a thought-out plan, however try not to own a credit card if you don't need it. The later you start using credit cards, the more you'll respect them. According to Dave Ramsey, 80% of graduating college seniors have credit-card debt—before they even have a job![198] If you have credit card debt, First Command Bank's (www.firstcommandbank.com) online "Credit Card Repayment Calculator" can help you climb out of it. Type in your account balance, interest rate, and planned monthly payment; the calculator will tell you how long it will take you to pay off your debt. It will even give you a payment schedule. After logging on the site, click on "Calculators." Then select "Loans" and click on "How Long Will It Take To Pay Off My Credit Cards?" If you must have a credit card, compare the rates of hundreds of credit cards by logging onto www.cardratings.com or www.creditcards.com.

Debit Card

Better yet, get a debit card from your bank. A debit card is not a credit card, although acts like one. A debit card is a plastic card issued by a bank and used for making purchases. This payment card is linked directly to a customer's bank account; this allows purchases to be made with currently available funds that are instantly deducted from the account.

Make sure you keep track of the amounts deducted so that you don't overdraw the account, just as you would if you wrote a check. Don't assume that a debit card will be denied if your account lacks sufficient funds. Most banks will cover your shortfall, then charge you a fee—stacked in the bank's favor! When *Good Housekeeping* writer Monica Gagnier was saving for a house, she and her husband used debit cards instead of credit cards for their daily expenses. Within one year, the couple ended up paying almost $2,000 in overdraft fees! "Say you make three $5 purchases in one day with your card," says Monica. "Last stop is the grocery store, where you spend $99. Unfortunately, there was only $90 in your account that day, so an overdraft fee is in your future—but presumably only one, since the three smaller purchases went through first," says Monica. But that's not what happened. "Some banks reorder your charges so the $99 purchase would appear first. The bank then clears all four debits, in order, and you incur four overdrafts instead of one."[199] If your overdraft protection fee per transaction is $25, instead you'll have to pay $100 for four overdrafts due to the bank "reordering" your drafts.

More and more banks are charging a fee (up to $1.50) for each transaction made on a debit card. Even if you're charged only 50 cents for each transaction, it really adds up—not to mention that it's annoying to be charged to use your own money. The reason why banks have begun charging a fee on debit card transactions is that banks receive a very small fee from retailers for every debit transaction—unlike with a credit card, which they receive a percentage of the total purchase. To recover their losses from debit card transactions, banks are now instituting transaction fees.

When Credit Does Make Sense

Borrow only to invest in such things as a home, business, or even an education. Good debt pays for items that will improve your financial standing, like borrowing money to buy a home or borrowing for education. Borrow money only on items that boost your earning power. Borrowing to purchase a basic car to get you to work falls into the category of good credit. Borrowing to purchase a high-end car is not good use of credit.

If Your Credit is Tarnished

If you have credit card accounts, log on to www.annualcreditreport.com to get a free credit report. If your record is somewhat tarnished, don't panic. Begin fixing it today. Pay off your debt, and, above all, make sure your payments aren't late. Keep your credit card accounts open but stop using them.

This allows you to show you are a good credit risk, that you don't run away from your financial obligations. Once your accounts are paid up, pay with cash or a debit card instead.

Live Cheaply As Long As You Can

Newly-minted adults tend to overestimate how far their paychecks will go and spend too much on apartments, cars, eating out, etc. One way to approach living cheap is to keep living like a broke college student for a few more years—even when you're earning bigger paychecks. This gives you a better handle on what you can really afford and be able to free up more money for goals like buying a home and retirement.

Allow Yourself Occasional Splurges

Don't always refuse yourself occasional splurges on the path to your saving goal. If you want a new pair of shoes or a day out to a movie with popcorn, occasionally treating yourself can be viewed as a small reward along the way to your goal. If you don't give in to these occasional splurges, you might be discouraged from the whole idea of saving. If you make some foolish purchases, live with your mistakes. You'll learn from them to make better choices.

Personal Finance Programs

Many schools are starting to offer entrepreneurial and personal finance training programs to children to ready them for the realities of life after school. This will help equip them with the money management skills they need to succeed personally and in the business world. "Financial education needs to become part of our curriculum so that it's not just the rich kids who learn about money, it's all of us," says David Bach, author of *Start Late, Finish Rich*.[200] Caitlin Petre, a recent Ivy League graduate who lives in New York City, applied for a cocktail waitress job at an upscale bowling alley in Manhattan. When she won the job position, she was handed a W-4 form to fill out. Having had various summer jobs and been exempted from taxes because she was a full-time student, she didn't even know how many allowances to claim—or what an allowance was—and guessed throughout the application. Later Caitlin asked her other Ivy League graduate friends to shed light on the matter, but none knew any more about finances than she did. She and her friends were graduates from Wesleyan, Barnard, Stanford and Yale, yet none of them knew what a Roth IRA was or how to master a basic tax form. "Heaven help us when April comes and we have to file tax returns," says Caitlin.[201]

If your school offers a program like JA Worldwide, look forward to a great learning experience—a place where teachers stress long-term results over short-term gains. Wykeham Collegiate, a private girls' school in Maritzburg, South Africa, starts teaching money management skills to girls before they become teenagers. Girls, Inc. (www.girlsinc.org) runs a 10 to 12-week economic literacy program that teaches finance to girls ages 6 to 18. All high school students in Utah are required to take a semester course on personal finance prior to graduation. Students at Coronado High School in Coronado, California, are required to take one semester of Economics, personal finance, and management. Wall Street Wizards (www.wallstreetwizards.org) offers monthly sessions for high school students from the San Francisco Bay area to learn about investments and finance. Here students are assigned mentors, participate on investment teams, and take field trips to shareholder meetings and stock exchanges in San Francisco and New York.

In a recent study, Stanford University economics professor Douglas Bernheim found that people who received a course in financial education in high school were better than average savers by the time they reached middle age.[202] Students at Chicago's Ariel Capital Academy get at least one lesson a week in managing money, starting in kindergarten. "I save 40% of the money I get," says Mario Gage, 14, a recent graduate of the academy. "My friends from other schools spend everything. They come to me to borrow."[203]

If your school doesn't offer personal finance programs, you can bring it to your home, thanks to Youth Resources For Teen Programs (www.daveramsey.com). *No Matter What*, a 7-week video course taught by author Dave Ramsey, covers everything from how to save for an emergency fund to figuring out what it will cost you to live on your own. Teens will learn to form their own values and ideals as they are challenged to create a list of "No Matter What"s to keep with them forever (for example, "No matter what, I will never go into debt.").

Ice Yourself

While this isn't financial information, your health and safety should be a concern along your financial path as you fine-tune your lifestyle. Place emergency telephone numbers in all family members cell phones using the ICE method. The acronym ICE (In Case of Emergency), developed by the National Association of Emergency Medical Technicians, can aid paramedics if you or a family member are hurt and they need to call someone. Simply type ICE into the cell phone's directory and include a name and number under the heading. Typing ICEMom, ICEDad, ICEAunt, and ICEUncle designates the next of kin. Inform all ICE contacts that they are listed, and give them basic medical information.

Don't Smoke

You'll miss an income stream opportunity, a huge one, if you smoke. A new study shows that people who don't smoke have a net worth that's double that of people who smoke more than a pack a day. The money smokers spend on cigarettes comes out of income that they would otherwise save and invest. And let's not forget that smoking inflates your insurance bills. If you pay for your own health insurance, and you're a smoker, expect your premium to be raised more than 20%. Furthermore, according to one study, smokers are 70% more likely, on average, to need root canals than those who never smoked.[204]

Let's assume that cigarettes cost $2.50 per pack. If you smoke one pack a day, your monthly cost is $75; your annual cost is $900. Assuming your cost with a 10% annual interest rate, your 20-year loss of income is $56,952; your 30-year loss of income is $254,304; your 50-year loss of income is $1,299.329. If you smoke two packs a day, your 50-year loss of income is $2,598,658. These numbers show what would happen if you did not smoke and invested the money you would have spent on cigarettes at 10% compound interest for 20, 30, or 50 years. Recent statistics show that the average smoker spends $3,391 per year on the habit[205] — nearly four times the amount in the above example! Talk about your retirement going up in smoke!

In Idaho, the average cost for a pack of cigarettes is $3.71. In Oregon, a pack of cigarettes cost $4.14. If you live in Washington State, the average price for a pack of cigarettes is just over $5. Imagine the loss of income over 50 years if you smoked two packs of cigarettes a day in Washington! That is, of course, if you live 50 years after you started smoking as a teenager…

The sad statistics are that each day, more than 3,000 teenagers start smoking regularly. At least 4.5 million teenagers are smokers.[206] Smoking is not just hazardous to your health; it is truly hazardous to your wealth! To help you stop smoking, professional counseling is available, for free, at 800-QUITNOW.

The next floor, Bank On Your Financial Future, will educate you on various financial vehicles so that you can make the most of your investments. My goal in writing this section is to help you learn financial strategies that will help you create wealth, hang on to it, and keep you from ever declaring personal bankruptcy.

Penthouse

Bank on Your Financial Future

"Never invest money that you can't afford to lose!"
~Bob Barker, The Price Is Right™

Turner's motto is, "Play now and pay later. Or pay now and play later." By this he means you can play now, satisfy temporary fleeting pleasures and spend, spend, spend. Or you can work hard now, save and invest your money now, and have a better chance at securing an enjoyable, lasting financial future. Money is like a vote. "You can vote for immediate gratification and spend your money now," says Turner. "Or you can vote for a better future and save, save, save. Money you earn (and save) today will give you self-respect and freedom tomorrow." The choice is yours.

On this floor you will find information on various types of investment accounts, including IRAs, money market accounts, certificates of deposit, mutual funds, savings bonds, as well as information about purchasing stocks. The information is a basic guide to give you direction. In-depth information about any of these investments can be found at your local library or by Googling them on the Internet.

Avoid Magical Thinking

Many times people go into an investment with high expectations that they will make a fortune on an investment—often without doing research on their choice of investment. These expectations often blurr the decisions they make with what to do with their money. When *Money* Managing Editor Eric Schurenberg had his first $5,000 to invest, he acted on a tip. Eric dreamed that his stock investment would multiply so much that he would be able to, at least, afford a sports car. Instead, all that was left of his investment, three years later, was $500. Had he known what he knows now about investing, Eric wouldn't have invested it all on the stock of an insurance company he knew nothing about. "While it's obviously important what you do with that first $5,000, it also matters *why* you do it—because the expectations you bring to investing will color the decisions you make with your next five grand and the one after that," says Eric. Losing $4,500 was a painful financial lesson for him, but what Eric did learn from his experience was: Avoid magical thinking; don't believe in crystal balls; and live below your means.[207]

Keep an Open Mind

Don't be myopic and think you know everything. Managing your money wisely is always a work in progress. If you think you know it all, you won't be open to new possibilities and might miss other financial opportunities. Take time to learn everything you can in classes at school, from books and magazines, or even talk to your parents or other adults for guidance. If your school offers business and financial literacy courses, take them.

Uniform Transfer to Minors Act (UTMA)

A custodial account is an account created for the benefit of a minor someone under the age of 18 or 21, depending on state and legislation, usually at a bank, mutual fund, or brokerage company, with an adult — usually a parent or guardian, as the custodian. In order to invest, according to TeenAnalyst.com, you'll need one of these accounts if you're under 18.[208]

The adult who acts as the custodian for the account will fill out the application as custodian. The account is then registered under the minor's name and social security number. This allows the tax liability for any earnings on the account to be applied to the owner of the account, the minor. The custodian of your account could be any adult — a parent, grandparent, guardian, or even a friend. Once the minor reaches the required age (different in some states, but usually 18), he or she can own the account outright.

Open a Bank Savings Account

When you've gained some experience in handling money, it is time for you to open a savings account. Saving in a bank account is a great way to accumulate money so that you can buy something you really want in the future. After all, we all save for a reason: to spend! Saving and spending are linked and require balance. Taking little steps, like skipping popcorn and a soda at the movies, can add up to significant amounts that can be added to your account. Even just filling out a deposit slip for $5 will make you significantly more successful. (To make depositing even easier, fill out a dozen deposit slips in advance, including all information asked on the deposit slips. Then, when you are ready to deposit money into your account, simply fill in the amount and deposit.)

Ordinary savings accounts usually are not a great deal for Generation Y-ers under the age of 18. The average bank requires a balance over $200 to avoid monthly fees of around $3, which pay only .5% in interest. If your account balance is under $200 throughout the year, you would pay $36 in fees and only earn 50 cents in interest. Although they don't advertise it, most banks offer a no-fee, no-minimum option for minors. Ask bank managers at various banks about savings accounts for minors, then compare terms to find the best deal. To make sure that your money is safe from Internet fraud, counterfeit checks, and

244

embezzlement, choose a bank with a "blanket bond" that protects you in those cases.

Traditional IRA

The acronym "IRA" means Individual Retirement Account. An IRA is a government-sponsored personal retirement program that allows individuals with earned income to save money for their retirement in a tax-advantaged program. There is no minimum age for contributing to an IRA. Any person, any age, who earns money from an after-school or summer job or any type of job (investment income does not count) can put as much as $4,000 a year into an IRA account as of this writing. Taxes on traditional IRA contributions and earnings are deferred until distribution begins. According to investment writer George Mannes, "A young worker who contributes $4,000 a year from ages 14 to 18 and lets it ride at 8% for the next 50 years will amass a nest egg of more than $1.1 million, even if she never saves another dime." The teen's total outlay is $20,000, and the retirement kitty will be worth $1,100,612.[209] If outlaying $20,000 over a five-year period proves impossible, invest a one-time $4,000 into an IRA. If a teen, at the age of 18, invests $4,000 in an IRA where it can grow at 10% a year untouched by the IRS and in 49 years—when this teen can apply for social security—the account will be worth $425,000.[210]

IRAs for kids are not illegal. Some IRA sponsors do have reservations about opening retirement accounts for kids because minors can't legally enter into binding contracts. A growing number of mutual fund families and many big brokerage firms are, however, willing to open IRAs for kids—although many require an adult to co-sign the paperwork. Put as much as you can into an IRA. In 50 years, the older you will be thrilled with the result. Charles Schwab (www.schwab.com), T. Rowe Price (www.troweprice.com), Vanguard Investments (www.vanguard.com), and Etrade (www.etrade.com) are some companies that allow minors to open IRAs.

Benjamin O'Shaughnessy-Bigelow, an 8th grader at High Tech Middle Media Arts in San Diego, CA, knows how delighted he'll be as a wealthy retiree. Ben was quick to open an IRA account with his earnings as a soccer referee. Having learned how to use online financial calculators at an early age, Benjamin likes to project how much money he'll have when he's 65, and how long it will take him to become a millionaire.[211] Working with online financial calculators can really motivate Generation Y-ers to get on the right financial track early in their working lives. It certainly works for Ben!

You may be able to take money from your IRA early without paying the 10% penalty for making an IRA withdrawal before retirement age. Under the little-known IRS provision code 72(t), you can take penalty-free distribution for a variety of purposes, including higher education expenses. First-time home buyers are allowed to borrow $10,000 apiece — $20,000 per couple — to pay for a down payment or closing costs.

Roth IRA

The Roth IRA was created in 1997 and named for the late Republican Senator William Roth, Jr. The Roth IRA functions a little differently than the traditional IRA. Contributions are never tax deductible since the Roth IRA is funded with after-tax contributions. However, retired individuals do not have to pay taxes when they take distributions once they reach the age of 59 ½. Unlike traditional IRAs, there is no mandatory withdrawal age. Single filers who make more than $110,000 and couples with a taxable income above $160,000 are not eligible for Roth IRAs. To calculate IRA minimum withdrawals, plan to visit the Retirement Resource Center (www.Fidelity.com) when you near retirement age.

As of this writing the limit you can save per year is $4,000 (in traditional or Roth IRAs), providing you don't earn more than $110,000 a year ($160,000 for couples). Beginning in 2008, your maximum IRA contribution allowed will be $5,000. Finally, you can make contributions to an IRA up until April 15th for the previous year. Google "Roth vs. Tradition IRA Calculator" on the Internet to find a variety of calculators that tell you how much you can contribute to a Roth or Traditional IRA, which will provide the most retirement income, and more.

How to Open an IRA

In order to open an IRA, a person must first establish an account with a bank, mutual fund company, or a brokerage firm. These firms then act as a fiduciary, a person or organization that holds something in trust for another. The fiduciary is responsible for establishing the IRA and helping you select the plan investments. Once the IRA account has been established, the individual can contribute up to a predetermined maximum per year.

Autopilot Your IRA Savings

To trick himself into saving, Robert Goldberg, 30, from Philadelphia, PA, has set up an automatic transfer of $200 a month to his Roth IRA. At 12% interest, over a 30-year period of tax-free gains, he will receive $610,403; at 13% interest, $744,681; at 14% interest, $909,934. [212] Not a bad return stemming from a monthly salary of $3,140, of which 6% goes toward a 401(k) plan, $750 toward rent, $220 toward a car payment, and $172 toward auto insurance.

Lucky Breaks for Teen IRA Owners

If you are an ambitious teen who has worked to save a sizeable amount of money to invest in your IRA before starting college, you're in luck. Few colleges factor tax-advantaged retirement accounts into the federal formula when applying for college financial aid, no matter how large your account is. "Very few people know or understand that," says college planner Troy Onink in Russell, Pennsylvania.[213] According to investment writer Ashlea Ebeling, private schools expect students to contribute 25% of any assets in their names to college bills each year when calculating financial aid.[214] Furthermore, the federal formula requires a 35% contribution. But keeping your money invested in a tax-advantaged retirement account won't be factored in when applying for financial aid. Why work hard all your teen years just to have to spend down any accounts you've built just to qualify for financial aid? Owning and investing in an IRA is like having financial armor.

SEP IRA

SEP (Simplified Employee Pension) IRAs are funded with tax-deductible employer contributions; employees are not permitted to contribute. Contributions can vary from year to year, giving a business owner plenty of flexibility, and there are no filing requirements with the IRS. Accountants often recommend SEP IRAs to small-business owners. SEP IRAs allow business owners to contribute up to 25% of self-employment net profit a year, up to $41,000 per year. It is worth it to aside the full amount.

The downside of SEP IRAs is that you must contribute to your employees' accounts at the same rate that you contribute to your own. On the other hand, a SEP IRA can be a strong incentive to attract and retain quality workers. If your goal is to provide an even stronger incentive, offer a SIMPLE IRA (Savings Incentive Match Plan for Employees). Companies with fewer than 100 employees can set up a SIMPLE IRA for them. In doing so, the company can automatically deduct contributions directly from employees' paychecks; in addition, the employer makes contributions. The drawback to simple IRAs is that the plan limits your own ability to save to just $9,000 a year.

401(k)

A 401(k) is an employer-provided retirement savings plan. The 401(k) contributions are pretax and the money grows tax-deferred; that is, earnings are not taxed until they are withdrawn by the investor. It allows you to invest pretax dollars in a range of mutual funds, stocks, and bonds. (Pretax dollars is money that exists before any federal, state or local taxes are taken out.) Contributions to your 401(k) are taken directly out of your paycheck before taxes, so your actual take-home pay is less and therefore you pay less in taxes. Investing pretax dollars allows you to have more money working for you and earning interest.

The downside is that your investment choices are limited to what your company offers. And, as with the Roth and traditional IRAs, early withdrawal may bring both taxes and penalties.

Even cautious investors can strike it rich investing in a 401(k) plan. A recent study by Putnam Investments found that how much you contribute—not how well you pick stocks—is the most important factor in getting your 401(k) plan to grow.[215] Your goal should be to contribute 10% of your annual income to a 401(k) plan, or enough to receive matching funds from the company that employs you. According to Vanguard Group (known for managing mutual funds and administering 401(k)s), a worker who invests the $13,000 maximum (the new limit is $14,000) can invest tax-free into a 401(k) each year—and have a nest egg of $1.166 million after 30 years, provided the portfolio returns 8% and costs 1.38% a year.[216]

Consider this example of a 401(k) investment provided by Fidelity Investments, which is based on an 8% annual rate of return compounded monthly. If you save $23 a week in a 401(k) for 30 years, you'll end up with $150,030. In addition, your company may match your contributions—some go as high as $1 for every $1 you invest.[217] If you are or become employed, it would be wise to look into your employer's 401(k) plan and contribute the maximum allowed.

Why should you try hard to save the maximum amount possible? Let's say you have a $60,000 starting salary with a 3% annual raise. Factor in a 50% match over a 30-year time span (earning 8% interest). If you save 3% of your income, you'll end up with $429,000 in 30 years; save 6% of your income, you'll end up with $858,000 in 30 years (note: employer match ends at 6%); save 9% of your income, you'll end up with $1.1 million dollars.[218] Saving 9% of your income in a 401(k) can provide you with a retirement nest egg of more than $1 million!

To see if you are paying a reasonable amount in expenses for your 401(k), first check with your benefits department to explain the expense ratio and any other fees for your plan, as required by law, then compare the total to the average cost of a similar-size plan listed below.

Plan Size	Average Cost*
50 participants	1.40%
100 participants	1.31
200 participants	1.26
500 participants	1.20
1,000 participants	1.17
5,000 participants	1.12

*These costs assume an average per participant balance of $40,000. Data: *401(k) Averages Book*[219]

It's unfortunate that few young people sign up for the 401(k)s. Instead they're paying off college and credit card debt. They are too bogged down with debt to think about retirement. According to a Vanguard survey, only 26% of people under 25 participated in 401(k)s last year.[220] For young Generation Y-ers just getting started, investing for retirement may seem like a chore for a goal too distant to consider. But saving for the future doesn't have to be painful, and starting now will give you a nest egg that can see you through your retirement years. If you don't have a 401(k) investment started, *BusinessWeek* Online's *Smart Steps for Young Investors* offers five alternatives for getting a head start on retirement. For a simple approach to savings, target-date life-cycle funds allow new investors to pick a retirement time, helping them see how much they would need to save in order to reach their goal. Visit www.businessweek.com/go/younginvestor to find the investing survival guide and click on "Life Without a 401(k)."

Solo 401(k)

More than ever before people are becoming self-employed. One of the advantages of being self-employed is the unique retirement savings plan that it affords—the Solo 401(k), which boasts many of the same features as its corporate counterpart. Relatively new, this self retirement plan has some attractive benefits.

There are significant differences between the Solo 401(k) and the traditional 401(k) plan. First, you are allowed to put away a portion of your income annually, up to $44,000, tax-deferred. (You can only put $14,000 in a traditional employer-sponsored 401(k) plan.) Contributions grow tax-deferred. The opportunity to set aside more tax-sheltered retirement money, more than any other retirement plan out there, is the biggest advantage of the Solo 401(k) plan. Anyone who has their own business should consider setting up a Solo 401(k) plan. If you earn money from a side business, like landscaping, auto detailing, or computer programming, you might be eligible to set up a Solo 401(k) plan.

There are limitations when considering the Solo 401(k). Businesses that have no other employees beyond an owner and a spouse are eligible to contribute, such as a mom and pop store. The pair can contribute each of their income separately for a maximum of $88,000 annually. Businesses that have full-time employees, however, need to open a different kind of plan that covers all their staff, such as a SEP IRA.

Roth 401(k)

The new Roth 401(k) offers all the tax-free advantages of a Roth IRA but with higher contribution limits. Most workers can contribute up to $15,000 per year and $20,000 for people 50 and older. Unlike the Roth IRA, which allows only people who earn less than a certain amount to contribute, there are no income limits on the Roth 401(k).

Money Market Accounts

A money market account is similar to a bank savings account, except that money market funds aren't government insured. Also, as with some savings accounts, you are usually required to make a minimum deposit. Money market accounts usually bring higher interest rates than bank savings accounts. Where you put you savings will depend on when you will need to access your money. For short-term goals, a money market fund account, through a bank, savings and loan, or credit union is often best. It gives you a higher interest rate than a regular savings account.

Money Market Account Virtual Bank (877-998-2265) is a money market account that requires only a $100 minimum deposit. ING DIRECT (877-469-0232) requires just a $1.00 minimum deposit. Internet banks are usually the most generous with interest rates. Mybankingdirect.com (866-285-1856), which has been known to pay competitive interest rates, is one Internet bank to check out. For money market fund rates, visit www.bankrate.com/brm/rate/mmmf_home.asp.

Certificates of Deposit

Certificates of Deposit (CDs) are a good way to start investing if you want to avoid the ups and downs of the stock market. You could put half of your money in the stock market and half into a CD, then track them to see which one does better. CDs can be purchased at most financial institutions.

With a certificate of deposit, you're required to make a minimum deposit. You will be expected to commit your money for a specific term, usually no less than three months. During this time, your money earns a fixed rate of interest. The longer you commit your money, the higher the interest rate. If you break the agreement, you'll lose all the interest you've gain—and be penalized. You can search for top CD yields at www.kiplinger.com/personalfinance/money/credit.

Mutual Funds

The best long-range investments for beginners are mutual funds. They can be purchased without sales commissions and low annual fees (so that more of your money goes to work for you). Mutual funds are a great choice to include in your investment plan. Mutual funds spread your money over a wide range of the stock market—and maybe the bond market too (because diversification equals safety).

The easiest measure of a mutual fund's performance is its net asset value (NAV), which reveals how much an individual share is worth. If the NAV increases with each statement, it is winning at the stock market. On the other hand, a consistent decrease in NAV over a 12-month period signals a poorly performing fund.[221]

Certified financial planner Nathan Mesereau suggests that you pick a mutual fund by its 10-year track record. Most companies publicize their 3- or 5-year average returns for mutual funds. Ask the brokerage house to show you the 10-year performance record so that you can be sure to select a fund that has performed well over the long term.[222] For a better understanding of mutual funds, read Lynn O'Shaughnessy's *The Investing Bible*. If you plan to open a mutual fund account, research it for free at www.mfea.com, where you can find lists of top-performing funds or search for fund information by name or category. For additional information on mutual funds, and to access a cost calculator, visit the U.S. Securities and Exchange Commission's website at www.sec.gov/investor/tools/mfcc/mfcc-intsec.htm.

Stock Market

A study by the NASDAQ (an acronym for National Association of Securities Dealers Automated Quotations) stock market reports that 19% of all investors are people between the ages of 18 and 34.[223] According to a 2005 survey by JA Worldwide, about a quarter of young teens own stocks. Ambitious young people seek out financial advice more than most expect. Vince Coyner, president of YoungBiz.com (www.youngbiz.com), a Virginia-based website for teen investors, says that "believe it or not, the e-mails I get are largely from enterprising youth seeking investment advice, rather than parents looking for ways to force their teen-ager to invest their allowance."[224]

By law minors are not allowed to invest in the stock market, but their parents or guardians can invest on their behalf. Parents should encourage minors to take a portion of what they've saved and invest it. While it's typically up to parents to teach their children how the stock market works, many middle and high schools are introducing the stock market to students. Furthermore, parents and children can visit their local library or bookstore to find appropriate literature on the subject. *The Little Book That Beats the Market*, by Joel Greenblatt, written in a language that even a sixth-grader can comprehend, is designed to help young audiences understand the stock market. Joel, a founder of the successful investment firm Gotham Capital, provides excellent investment advice and makes it easy to act on. Subjects like valuation and cost of capital are disguised in a parable about expanding a schoolyard gum-peddling business into a chain of storefronts and helps teach Generation Y-ers about the stock market. A cover-to-cover read of this book takes less than two hours.

Bethany Murphy, 11, from Mt. Laurel, New Jersey, has become very knowledgeable about the stock market by way of a school project. Bethany became interested in the market from a fourth-grade school project when she entered the local newspaper's stock contest. Bethany opened an account with Stein Roe Young Investor Fund. As well as her initial investment, Bethany won an essay contest sponsored by Stein Roe, which added another $5,000 to her portfolio. Bethany plans on using her stock investment to help pay for college.[225] You can do your own stock research by logging onto www.jumpstart.org. The website www.wannalearn.com has a free tutorial on almost any subject you can imagine, including how to choose a stock. For a list of high dividend stocks, go to www.dogsofthedow.com.

How the Stock Market Works

You become part owner of a company when you purchase a share of its stock. The more shares you purchase, the more ownership you have. Say you have $1,000 to invest. Shares are selling for $10 each, so you can buy 100 shares in the company. If the company's share price goes up by $1 the next day to $11 per share, your gain is $100 — a 10% return in one day. But you have no *real* money until you sell the stock.

How to Purchase Stocks

The most common way to purchase stocks is to use a brokerage. There are two types of brokerages: full-service and discount. Full-service brokerages offer expert advice and manage your account. They are expensive. Discount brokerages offer little personal attention, but they are much cheaper. To dig up a great deal of information on purchasing stocks, Google "How to Purchase Stocks" on the Internet.

DRIPs

If you're keen on building wealth, you can become wealthy drip by drip. Dividend Reinvestment Plans, also known as DRIPs, allow shareholders to invest cash directly through a company (or its agent) to buy more shares of the company's stock. They allow you to use the quarterly payments to acquire more shares in a company, and odd amounts are no problem, since the plans buy fractional shares.

DRIPs are a great way to invest small amounts of money at regular intervals and build wealth. According to Vita Nelson, editor of *Moneypaper*, a newsletter devoted to DRIPs, DRIPs are the "best-kept secret on Wall Street."[226] Why haven't you heard about DRIPs? Because companies can't advertise their DRIPs. Why? Because the Securities and Exchange Commission rules won't let them say much about this fantastic way of saving and building wealth. Because brokers can't make commission off DRIPs purchased directly from the companies, they won't tell you about this great stock-investment method. When you purchase through DRIPs, you eliminate the middleman. More money goes into your pocket for your wealthier financial future.

There are more than 1,000 companies that offer DRIPs, including Coca-Cola (KO) and Home Depot (HD). The minimum investment typically range from $250 to $500, however, Sharebuilder.com allows investors to invest as little as $4 a month, has no account minimums, and no minimum investment is required to start. Some plans, like that of Exxon, have an IRA option, including a Roth IRA.

To get started, you need to own at least 1 share of stock, because DRIP programs are generally available only to existing investors. DRIPinvestor.com, Sharebuilder.com, and *Moneypaper Inc.'s* Directinvesting.com can show you how to buy that first share.

Matching Deposits

If you are employed by a company, many offer matching contributions to various savings funds. For example, for every dollar you deposit, your employer might match half a dollar. This free money is valuable to your overall savings retirement goal. Take advantage of it as soon as it is made available to you, and max out what you contribute. If you are self-employed, you don't get this matching deposit benefit. You might, however, enlist your parents or grandparents to match your deposits. Parents can contribute a matching amount to encourage kids to really get in gear to save. Although we never offered this match, we did give Turner a 10% investment return of $100 when his bank account first reached $1,000.

U.S. Savings Bonds

U.S. savings bonds, a safe and easy way to save money, are debt securities issued by the U.S. Department of the Treasury. Savings bonds are considered one of the safest investments because they are backed by the full faith and credit of the United States. Savings bonds are registered, so the Treasury can replace them if they are lost or stolen. How much can $100 per month in savings bonds grow? At 4% per annum, compounded semi-annually, after 5 years, your investment would grow to $6,630; after 15 years, $24,609; and after 30 years, $69,405. Series EE, HH, and I savings bonds can be purchased where you work, bank, or online at www.savingsbonds.gov. You can check the value of your bonds anytime by visiting the same site. There are several types of U.S. savings bonds you can purchase:

- **Series EE Bonds** These savings bonds replaced the Series E bonds on July 1, 1980. They are purchased at a discount of half their face value in denominations of $50, $75, $100, $200, $500, $1,000, $5,000, and $10,000. You are limited to buying $30,000 (face value) during any calendar year. EE bonds increase in value as the interest accumulates and pay interest for 30 years.

You can delay the tax consequences by exchanging them for Series HH savings bonds for up to 20 more years. When EE bonds mature, or come due, you are paid your original investment plus the interest the bond has earned.

- **Series HH Bonds** You can purchase Series HH bonds, but only in exchange for Series EE or E bonds and Savings Notes (also known as "Freedom Shares," which were only available between May of 1967 and October 1970), or with the proceeds from a matured Series HH bond. Unlike EE savings bonds, Series HH savings bonds are purchased at their face value in denominations of $500 to $10,000. The nice thing about these bonds is that there is no limit on the amount you can purchase. Series HH savings bonds don't increase in value and have a maturity of 20 years.

- **Series I Bonds** Series I savings bonds are sold at face value and offer a real rate of return over and above inflation for up to 30 years. You can purchase Series I savings bonds in $50 to $10,000 denominations, up to $30,000 in any calendar year. New rates are announced each May 1st and November 1st. The Series I savings bonds can be redeemed anytime after 12 months of ownership.

A Helpful Website

TeenAnalyst.com is an easy-to-navigate website geared to young investors who are searching for investment information made easy. Every month the site receives hundreds of questions from young readers. These questions cover a number of different topics, and TeenAnalyst.com makes an attempt to respond to as many as possible. Here you can learn foreign exchange market basics, how trading currencies work and some of the possible risks and rewards associated with it. You can also learn about low-cost stock investing, general investing in stocks, bonds, and mutual funds. If you want information on starting a business, you'll find helpful information on creating a business plan, structuring a business, getting financed, and marketing. If you're looking for information on preparing for college, entrance tests, choosing a college, financial aid, and scholarships, TeenAnalyst.com can help. Finally, career information relating to internships, résumés, salary tables, and interviewing can give you that competitive edge when you get onto your career track.

Imagine what power you could have if you were more interested in creating a strong financial foundation for your tomorrows than gratifying yourself today. You can learn that, if you make wise spending and saving choices today, your future can be funded by the interest from your investments alone. Your financial future, more than ever before, depends on making good financial choices. No one is born financially smart, so, learning to make good financial choices early in your life will allow you to have good control over your financial future. Whether you "make a job" or "take a job," take the time (and learn) to do the right thing with your money. If Generation Y can learn the dangers of financial negligence at an early age, it is more likely to be a wealthy generation in the future. Only you can pave a golden path to your financial future.

Success. They say it can be lonely at the top. Note that this elevator has unlimited capacity. Now that you are in the penthouse of financial success, send down this elevator to siblings and friends so that they, too, can join you. Now you won't be lonely at the top. Generation Y, going up!

Bibliography

Abbe, Elfreida. *Writer's Handbook, The.* Waukesha: Kalmbach Publishing Co., 2004.

Bach, David. *Start Late, Finish Rich: A No-fail Plan for Achieving Financial Freedom at Any Age.* New York: Broadway Books, 2005.

Berry, Jon and Ed Keller. *The Influentials: One American in Ten Tells The Other Nine How to Vote, Where to Eat, and What to Buy.* New York: The Free Press, 2003.

Brown, Damon. *The Pocket Idiot's Guide to the iPod.* New York: Alpha, 2005.

Butler, Mike. *Landlording On Auto-Pilot.* Hoboken: John Wiley and Sons, 2006.

Card, Orson Scott. *Characters and Viewpoint.* Cincinnati: Writer's Digest Books, 1999.

Collins, Jim. *Built to Last: Successful Habits of Visionary Companies.* New York: HarperCollins, 2002.

Gallo, Jon, Eileen Gallo and Kevin J. Gallo. *Silver Spoon Kids: How Successful Parents Raise Responsible Children.* New York: McGraw Hill, 2001.

Greenblatt, Joel. *The Little Book That Beats the Market.* Indianapolis: Wiley, 2005.

Harrow, Susan. *The Ultimate Guide to Getting Booked on Oprah: Ten Steps to Becoming a Guest on the World's Top Talk Show.* Oakland: Harrow Communications, 2004.

Hess, Kenneth L. *Bootstrap: Lessons Learned Building a Successful Company from Scratch.* Carmel: S-Curve Press, 2001.

Huff, Priscilla Y. *Build a Successful Small Home-Based Enterprise.* Hoboken: John Wiley & Sons, Inc., 2006.

Jacobs, Karrie. *The Perfect $100,000 House: A Trip Across America and Back in Pursuit of a Place to Call Home.* New York: Viking, 2006.

Jordan, Jacquie. *Get on TV: The Insider's Guide to Pitching the Producers and Promoting Yourself.* Naperville: Sourcebooks, Inc., 2006.

Keyes, Ralph. *Is There Life After High School?* New York: Little, Brown & Co., 1976.

Kiyosaki, Robert T. with Sharon L. Lechter C.P.A. *Rich Kid Smart Kid: Giving Your Child a Financial Head Start.* New York: Warner Business Books, 2001.

Kiyosaki, Robert T. with Sharon L. Lechter C.P.A. *Rich Dad Poor Dad: What the Rich Teach Their Kids About Money – That the Poor and Middle Class Do Not!* New York: Warner Business Books, 2000.

Kobak, James. *How to Start a Magazine and Publish It Profitably.* New York: M. Evans & Co., 2002.

Kobliner, Beth. *Get A Financial Life: Personal Finance In Your Twenties and Thirties*. New York: Fireside, 2000.

Lamott, Anne. *Bird by Bird*. New York: Anchor Publishing, 1995.

Lee, Dwight R. and Richard McKenzie. *Getting Rich in America: Eight Simple Rules For Building A Fortune – And a Satisfying Life*. New York: HarperPerennial, 2000.

Levine, Gail Carson. *Writing Magic: Creating Stories That Fly*. New York: HarperCollins, 2006.

Levy, Richard C. and Ronald O. Weingartner. *The Toy and Game Inventor's Handbook*. Indiana: Alpha Books, 2003.

Lewis, Allyson. *The Million Dollar Car and $250,000 Pizza*. Chicago: Dearborn, 2000.

Linn, Susan. *Consumer Kids: The Hostile Takeover of Childhood*. New York: New Press, 2004.

Lynn, Mary. *Every Page Perfect*. Silver City: Lynnx Ink, 2001.

McAuley, Jordan. *Celebrity Black Book*. Atlanta: Mega Niche Media, 2006.

McKee, Robert. *Story*. New York: HarperCollins, 1997.

O'Shaughnessey, Lynn. *The Investing Bible*. New York: Hungry Minds, Inc., 2001.

O'Shaughnessey, Lynn. *The Retirement Bible*. New York: Hungry Minds, Inc., 2001.

Orman, Suze. *The Money Book for the Young, Fabulous & Broke*. New York: Riverhead Hardcover, 2005.

Pieter, Ryan. *Obtaining a #1 Ranking in the Search Engines*. (ebook).

Ross, Tom and Marilyn Ross. *eZines: A Complete Guide to Publishing for Profit*. Cincinnati: Writer's Digest Books, 2002.

Ross, Tom and Marilyn. *The Complete Guide to Self-Publishing*. 4th ed. Cincinnati: Writer's Digest Books, 2002.

Schaub, John W. *Building Wealth One House at a Time: Making it Big on Little Deals*. New York: McGraw-Hill, 2005.

Shaw, Eva. *The Successful Writer's Guide to Publishing Magazine Articles*. 2nd ed. Loveland: Rodgers & Nelsen Publishing Company, 2000.

Spragins, Ellyn. *What I Know Now: Letters to My Younger Self*. New York: Broadway Books, 2006.

Stanley, Thomas J. and William D. Danko. *The Millionaire Next Door*. New York: Pocket Books, 1996.

Trippon, James. *How Millionaires Stay Rich Forever: Retirement Planning Secrets of Millionaires and How They Can Work for You*. Bellaire: Bretton Woods Press, LLC, 2004.

Truss, Lynn. *Eats, Shoots and Leaves*. New York: Gotham Books, 2004.

Updegrave, Walter. *How to Retire Rich in a Totally Changed World: Why You're Not in Kansas Anymore*. New York: Three Rivers Press, 2005.

Weltman, Barbara. *The Complete Idiot's Guide to Starting an eBay Business*. New York: Alpha, 2005.

Wibbles, Andy. *Blog Wild*. New York: Portfolio, 2006.

Woodward, Cheryl. *Starting and Running a Successful Newsletter or Magazine*. Berkeley: Nolo, 2005.

About the Author

Anna Stanley has been an entrepreneur nearly all of her "military brat" and "military wife" life. At the age of 9, while living in Rota, Spain, Anna began a babysitting business serving both Spanish and American families. At the age of 14, she resumed her babysitting business when she moved to the United States, which lasted until she turned 18. In addition to babysitting, Anna simultaneously worked as a clerk at a convenience store, at a movie theater, and at a snow cone stand after school, on weekends, and during the summer. At the age of 19, while attending a community college, Anna took her entire savings and purchased three rental properties in Corpus Christi, Texas, becoming a real estate investor and landlord. Two years later, she moved to California and began teaching an exercise program at various gyms while attending college. Two years later Anna began directing beauty pageants, both in California and Texas, preliminaries for the Miss America and Miss U.S.A. pageant systems. During her dozen years as a pageant director, she wrote and published *Producing Beauty Pageants: A Director's Guide* and *The Crowning Touch: Preparing for Beauty Pageant Competition*. *Producing Beauty Pageants* was incorporated into The Learning Channel's *The Secret World of…* series, while *The Crowning Touch* was featured in *Muskrat Lovely*, a film by Amy Nicholson, a Myrtle & Olive Production. Anna's entrepreneurial spirit was also passed along to her two children, Turner, 16, and Mia, 13. Both own their own pet care businesses, and both, too, are also real estate investors and landlords. Their stories are featured in this book, the first of the *Going Up?*™ series of books written by Anna Stanley.

Recommended Websites

www.abcsmallbiz.com (dedicated to all small businesses and those seeking to start their own business)

www.adcomparator.com (simultaneously tests up to 15 varying aspects of any ad, website, or e-mail campaign)

www.allbusiness.com (files available on topics ranging from writing a business plan to preparing a budget)

www.bankrate.com (compare rates, from mortgages to CDs)

www.Biz4Kids.com (teaches kids about entrepreneurship)

www.business.gov (guides you into launching a business, managing it, growing it, and getting out of it)

www.businessmag.com (for hosting solutions)

www.catalogrep.com (you will find 14 criteria to judge whether your product has potential to be a catalog winner)

www.choosetosave.org (has more than 100 calculators that consumers can use to determine everything from what their savings will earn over time to how to pay down debt and plan for retirement)

www.circlelending.com (to obtain their free guide, "Financing Your Small Business: How to Borrow From People You Know"; acts as an intermediary between business owner and their family or friends)

www.CNNMoney.com (educates about markets, jobs, economy, personal finance, small business, etc.)

www.copyright.gov (for general information about copyright)

www.creativebusiness.com (to obtain free forms, including a "Work for Hire" agreement)

www.dinkytown.net (all sorts of calculators, including an auto loan vs. buy calculator)

www.dividendachievers.com (identifies companies that have increased their annual dividend payments for 10 or more consecutive years)

www.dogsofthedow.com (a stock-picking strategy devoted to selecting high-dividend stocks; for a list of high dividend stocks)

www.domania.com and www.GetMyHomeValue.com (to research recent home sales in a given neighborhood)

www.Dripinvestor.com (a source for commission-free stock investing)

www.edit.com (offers do-it-yourself website editing)

www.emigrantdirect.com (high-yielding bank money market account)

www.entrepreneur.com/calculators (helps you calculate your start-up costs before you start your new business)

www.entrepreneur.com/tools/pricingcalculator (an interactive calculator to help you with pricing your products)

www.Entreprenuer.com (educates on every aspect of business; provides information to help you write your business plan)

www.european-patent-office.org/ (European Patent Office)

www.eventuring.org (geared to those who are building companies that innovate and create jobs and wealth)

www.freepatentsonline.com (allows you to print the full text of U.S. patents to aid in your patent search)

www.FromPatentToProfit.com (educating inventors and small businesses about the methods of inventing and patenting)

www.GilsonGraphics.net (high quality graphics and website design)

www.girlsinc.org (runs a 10 to 12-week literacy program that introduces finances to girls ages 6 to 18)

www.geocities.com (designer that can help business owners with their design needs)

www.GoDaddy.com (learn how to register a domain name)

www.goinstitute.org (to find information on overseas outsourcing)

www.Groovejob.com (lists cool jobs by ZIP codes)

www.housing.com (provides information on various kinds of mortgages, calculates the value of your salary in different cities, even more)

www.hsbcdirect.com (high-yielding bank money market account)

www.hsn.com (provides an application and details on becoming a HSN vendor)

www.ja.org (educates America's youth about American free enterprise)

www.jpo.go.jp/ (Japanese Patent Office)

www.jumpstart.org (provides information for stock research)

www.kauffman.org (the largest organization solely focused on entrepreneurial success at all levels)

www.licensing.org (has listings of licensing agents and general licensing information)

www.linkexchange.com (helps create cross-links with sites like yours)

www.linktree.info (provides a free link analyzer that helps increase your website's link popularity)

www.mindyourownbiz.org (supports entrepreneurship among teens)

www.money.cnn.com/tools (includes all sorts of calculators, including a rate of return calculator)

www.moneyinstructor.com (educates on basic money skills)

www.MyTotalMoneyMakeover.com (provides tools to help track your expenses, budget your spending, and eliminate your debt)

www.NetworkSolutions.com (learn how to register a domain name)

www.nolo.com (self-help legal fare that counsels in many areas)

www.orangekids.com (learn about saving, spending, and getting the most out of your allowance)

www.outsourcing.com (information on overseas outsourcing)

www.outsourcingnetwork.net (information on overseas outsourcing)

www.PayPal.com (allows you to set up a free shopping cart and merchant account to accept credit cards)

www.practicalmoneyskills.com (tips for kids on money management)

www.prsecrets.com and www.publicityhound.com (sites for publicity tips)

www.qvcproductsearch.com (to obtain an application and details on becoming a QVC vendor) www.redroller.com (to find the best prices for your shipping needs)

www.register.com (learn how to register a domain name and to search for available domain names; will guide you through the entire process of creating a do-it-yourself website)

www.resumedoctor.com (for helpful tips on writing a successful résumé)

www.rockportinstitute.com (for helpful tips on writing a successful résumé)

www.salary.com (a provider of employee compensation data and software)

www.savingforcollege.com (comparison of the 529 college savings plans)

www.sba.gov (provides a guide to writing business plans)

www.sba.gov/teens (a Small Business Administration teen business link; to obtain "Teen Entrepreneur Guide to Owning a Small Business")

www.schwab.com (to learn about financial planning and retirement)

www.score.org (submit questions for free business advice)

www.SmartMoney.com/retirement (to get retirement-planning tips and tools online)

www.takeittothemarket.com) (a seminar series)

www.teachingkidsbusiness.com (teaches kids about the business world)

www.TeenAnalyst.com (educates teens and young people about investing, college, career, business, credit, and much more)

www.themoneycamp.com (financial literacy program for kids and grownups)

www.thomasnet.com (search for thousands of suppliers by industry, product type or location; to find a comprehensive list of professional prototype developers)

www.tradepub.com (to find free, industry-specific trade publication subscriptions)

www.troweprice.com (a money fund that lets you invest $50 a month)

www.uiausa.com (for sample confidential patent agreements; for sample confidential agreements for novice inventors)

www.uiausa.org (United Investors Association; this organization can help guide you to effectively develop ideas into successful marketed products)

www.ulausa.com (United Inventors Association, a nonprofit inventor's support group)

www.uspto.gov (The U.S. Patent and Trademark Office)

www.vox.com (a free, easy-to-use blog service)

www.wannalearn.com (offers a free tutorial on almost any subject you can imagine, including how to choose a stock)

www.WhichVoIP.com (a free search engine to find a VoIP product plan that best meets your needs)

www.wordtab.com (visit The Big List to find ideas for creating slogans)

www.xe.com (currency conversion website)

www.youngbiz.com (young entrepreneurs can learn about starting their own business, money smarts, careers, etc.)

www.youth2work.gov (the U.S. Department of Labor's website for young workers)

264

Index

271

Endnotes

[1] Look Smart® Find Articles, http://www.findarticles.com/p/articles/mi_mODTI.

[2] *Entrepreneur.* December 2004, 22.

[3] Productsafety.org, http://www.consumer-action.org/press/articles_money wise_survey_shows_americans_are_not_financially_fit/.

[4] Johnson, James. "Enterprise." *Black Enterprise.* May 2006, 45–48.

[5] Bigda, Carolyn. "Boost Your Teen's Take-Home." *Money.* July, 2006, 22.

[6] "Error-Proofing the Job Application Process." *Black Enterprise,* July 2006, 72.

[7] Neilson, Amy Rauch. "Creating a Company Culture: How to Make Your Own Core Values the Core of Your Business." *Entreprenuer.com, TeenStartUps.com,* June 2003, http://www.entrepreneur.com/tsu/articlesba/0,6829,309078,000.html.

[8] Block, Sandra. "In Debt Before You Start." *USA Today.* June 12, 2006, 1–2A.

[9] "Readers Respond." *Y&E – The Magazine for Teen Entrepreneurs,* http://ye.entreworld.org/SF2002/readers-respond.cfm.

[10] Marsh, Rob. Telephone interview, March 17, 2006.

[11] Erickson, Christian. E-mail message to author, March 6, 2006.

[12] Rockwell, Jr., Llewelly H. "Teen Entrepreneur Shut Down for Charging $30 for Installing Wire Mesh." *UnderReported.com,* March 1, 2004.

[13] Ibid.

[14] Grunwald Associates, http://www.grunwald.com/.

[15] Huff, Priscilla Y. "10 Essential Steps for a Successful Home-Based Business Launch." *Home Business,* September/October 2006, 16–22, 104–106.

[16] *Inc. Magazine,* June 2005, 10.

[17] Robinson, Marita Ensio. "Biz Launch: 7 Systems Good to Go!" *Y&E – The Magazine for Teen Entrepreneurs,* November 2005, http://ye.entreworld.org/1-2000/bizlaunch.cfm.

[18] Neilson, Amy Rauch. "Start a Fashion Business." *Entrepreneur.com, TeenStartUps.com,* June 2002, http://www.entrepreneur.com/tsu/article/0,5788,300461,00.html.

[19] "Ask Inc." *Inc. Magazine,* February 2004, 38.

[20] Murray, Lori B. "The Price is Right." *Y&E – The Magazine for Teen Entrepreneurs,* May 2000, http://ye.entreworld.org/5-2000/7day_pricing.cfm.

[21] Manassero, Emily. Telephone interview, November 1, 2005.

[22] Christian, Amy Fennell. "Get Creative with Your Location." *Entrepreneur.com, TeenStartUps.com,* August 2003, http://www.entrepreneur.com/tsu/articles ba/0,6829,310612,00.html.

[23] Greco, Patricia. "Dream Job." *Good Housekeeping,* October 2006, 102.

[24] Debelak, Don. "Mass Appeal." *Entrepreneur,* August 2005, 116–118.

[25] Neal, Molly. "Mail Order Maven." *Small Business Opportunities,* September 2006, 46–48.

[26] Larson, Sandy. "Not Your Typical Mom and Pop Store." *Home Business,* March/April 2006, 55.

[27] Arora, Pankaj. "Secrets of Bootstrapping: Creative Ways to Shave Bucks Off Those Start-Up Costs." *Entrepreneur.com, TeenStartUps.com,* September 2002, http://www.entrepreneur.com/tsu/article/0,5788,302878,00.html.

[28] Robinson, Marita Ensio. "Biz Launch: 7 Systems Good to Go!" *Y&E – The Magazine for Teen Entrepreneurs,* http://ye.entreworld.org/1-2000/bizlaunch.cfm.

[29] Neilson, Amy Rauch. "Should I Borrow My Start-up Cash?" *Entrepreneur.com TeenStartUp.com,* July 2002, http:www.entrepreneur.com/mag/article/0,1539,301239-----,00.html.

[30] Jameson, Marnell. "When Life Hands You Lemons…" *Woman's Day,* August 2, 2005, 96.

[31] Murray, Lori B. "Hatchery of a Business." *Y&E – The Magazine for Teen Entrepreneurs*, January 2001, http://ye.entreworld.org/1-2000/stage4.cfm.

[32] Penttila, Chris. "Making the Trade." *Entrepreneur*, July 2005, 84.

[33] Grossman, Leslie. "The Million-Dollar Divide." *Pink*, August/September 2006, 30–32.

[34] "How to Start a Business for (Almost) Nothing." *Inc. Magazine*, July 2006, 101–107.

[35] Ibid.

[36] Worrell, David. "Bootstrapping Your Startup." *Entrepreneur.com*, October 2002, http://www.entrepreneur.com/bizstartups/bootstrapping.

[37] Johnson, James C. "Finding Cash for Your Business." *Black Enterprise*, September 2006, 50.

[38] Johnson, Raelyn C. "Blackgirl Rules! Publisher Kenya James Wins Our 2003 Teenpreneur of the Year Award—Entrepreneurship." *Black Enterprise*, September 2003.

[39] Worrell, David. "It's in the Cards." *Entrepreneur*, April 2005.

[40] Neilson, Amy Rauch. "Should I Borrow My Start-up Cash?" *Entrepreneur.com, TeenStartUp.com*, July 2002, http://www.entrepreneur.com/mag/article/01539,301239-----,00.html.

[41] Copeland, Michael V. "My Golden Rule." *Business 2.0*, December 2005, 108–130.

[42] Salkever, Alex. "Brother, Can You Spare A Dime? The New Alternative to Banks and VCS: Person-To-Person Lending." *Inc. Magazine*, August 2006.

[43] Christian, Amy Fennell. "Getting a Loan or Grant." *Entrepreneur.com, TeenStartUps.com*, December 2000, http://www.entrepreneur.com/tsu/article/0,5788,304886,00.html.

[44] Tiger, Caroline. "A Custom Blend." *BeE Woman*, Spring 2006, 32–34.

[45] Spaeder, Karen. "Innovation." *Entrepreneur*, October 2006, 70.

[46] Gunderson, Amy. "Grants for Rural Biz." *Inc.*, September 2003, 20.

[47] Neilson, Amy Rauch. "Raising Start-Up Cash." *Entrepreneur.com, TeenStartUp.com*, April 2002. http://www.entrepreneur.com/tsu/article/0,5788,298814,00.html.

[48] O'Connell, Brian and Dianne Tricarico. "Touched by an Angel." *Pink*, April/May 2006, 60–65.

[49] Copeland, Michael V. "How to Find Your Angel Investor." *Business2.0*, March 2006, 47.

[50] Ibid.

[51] Neilson, Amy Rauch. "Send Me an Angel…Investor." *Entrepreneur.com TeenStartUp.com*, October 2002, http://www.entrepreneur.com/tsu/article/0,5788,303741,00.html.

[52] Pennington, April Y. "On a Shoestring." *Entrepreneur*, February 2004, 111.

[53] Hall, Doug. "One, Two, One, Two…Exercising Your Way to Better (Business) Health." *BusinessWeek SmallBiz*, Fall 2006, 22.

[54] "Young Biz 100," http:www.youngbiz.com/yb_mag_news/mag_03top100_76.htm.

[55] *Y&E – The Magazine for Teen Entrepreneurs*, 2002, http://ye.entreworld.org/SF2002/readers-respond.cfm.

[56] Aushenker, Michael. "Teen Titan Devin Lazerine Starts a Time Warner-distributed Rap Magazine." *The Jewish Journal*, January 4, 2002, http://www.jewishjournal.com/home/preview.php?id=7955.

[57] Trebilcock, Bob. "Scams Even Smart Women Fall For." *Ladies' Home Journal*, March 2006, 84–89.

[58] Keegan, Paul. "Meet the Daredevils." *Money*, April 2006, 122–126.

[59] Tovia, Joanna. "Thinking Pink." BusinessOwner.com, October 11, 2005, http://www.thecouriermail.news.com.au/businessowner/story/0,9998,16863792-37639,00.html.

[60] McAuley, Jordan. *Celebrity Black Book*. Atlanta: Mega Niche Media, 2006.

[61] *Entrepreneur*, June 2004, 88.

[62] Childress, Sarah. "The Scissor Sisters." *Newsweek*, October 16, 2006, E12.

[63] Black, Heather. "Olivia's a Famous Artist…at 16!" *Woman's World*, December 27, 2005, 5.

[64] Neilson, Amy Rauch. "Find a Niche…Create a Business." *Entrepreneur.com, TeenStartUps.com*, June 2004, http:www.entrepreneur.com/article/0,4621,315799,00.html.

[65] Teenreads.com. "Author Profile: Christopher Paolini," http://www.teenreads.com/authors/au-paikubu-christopher.asp.

[66] Magee, Maureen. "Scripps Ranch Teenager Realizes Her Novel Dream." *San Diego Union-Tribune*, December 27, 2004, sec. B2.

[67] Heilemann, John. "Freedom of the Press." *Business 2.0*, June 2006, 38–40.

[68] Ross, Marilyn. Telephone interview, 2006.

[69] Mayeux, Patty. "Financial Fitness." *Y&E – The Magazine for Teen Entrepreneurs*, May 2001, http://ye.entreworld.org/5-2001/step6.cfm.

[70] http://www.kidsway.com/

[71] "Young Biz 100," http:www.youngbiz.com/yb_mag_news/mag_03_top100.htm.

[72] Ibid.

[73] Ibid.

[74] Ibid.

[75] Ibid.

[76] Ibid.

[77] "Snapshot: Making Merry." *Entrepreneur*, December 2005, 25.

[78] JA Worldwide Student Center. "Teen Business Stories," http://studentcenter.ja.org/aspx/PlanBusiness/Stories.aspx.

[79] Kwon, Beth. "A Magazine Grows in the Bronx." CNNMoney.com, *Fortune*, http:www.fortune.com/fortune/smallbusiness/smallbiznotes/0,15704,399086,00.html.

[80] Aushenker, Michael. "Teen Titan Devin Lazerine Starts a Time-Warner Distributed Rap Magazine." *The Jewish Journal*, January 4, 2002, http://www.jewishjournal.com/home/preview.php?id=7955.

[81] Cooper, Steve. "Mags to Riches." *Entrepreneur,* June 2006, 108–114.

[82] "2003 Fleet Youth Entrepreneur Day Awards," http://ccnyc.neighborhoodlink.com/ccnyc/genpage.html?n_id=367387533.

[83] Neilson, Amy Rauch. "Raising Start-Up Cash." *Entrepreneur.com TeenStartUps.com*, April 2002, http://www.entrepreneur.com/tsu/article/0,5788,298814,00.html.

[84] American Pet Product Manufacturers Association. "Pet Industry Statistics and Trends." http://www.appma.org/pubs_survey.asp.

[85] "Scoopers are No. 1 for Doggy's No. 2" *The Boston Globe, San Diego Union-Tribune*, Sunday, November 12, 2006, I-2.

[86] Company Information. http://www.scoopandsackit.com/.

[87] Bizymoms. "Tired of Dooing the Dog-doo Two-step?" http://www.bizymoms.com/ideas/pooscoop.html.

[88] USAA® "Go Forth and Multiply." *U Magazine*, Issue 24, Spring 2002, 4–6.

[89] JA Worldwide Student Center. "Teen Business Stories," http://studentcenter.ja.org/aspx/PlanBusiness/Stories.aspx.

[90] "2003 Fleet Youth Entrepreneur Day Awards," http://ccnyc.neighborhoodlink.com/ccnyc/.

[91] *Entrepreneur*, July 2006, 86.

[92] Allis, Ryan Pieter Middleton. "From E-mail to Riches." *BusinessWeek Online*, http://images.businessweek.com/ss/05/10/young_entrepreneur/source/3.htm.

[93] "Young Biz 100," http://www.youngbiz.com/yb_mag_news/mag_03_top100.htm.

[94] Riehle, Jamie. Telephone interview, March 28, 2006.

[95] Edwards, Ellen. "Generation www: Kids Create Web Sites," *WashingtonPost.com*, March 24, 2004, http://www.washingtonpost.com/.

[96] "Young Biz 100," http://www.youngbiz.com/yb_mag_news/2001youngbiz100/html/computergraphics.htm.

[97] Hatty, Michele. "3 Teens Who Mean Business." *USAWeekend.com*, May 2, 1999, http://www.usaweekend.com/99_issues/990502/990502teenentrepreneurs.html.

[98] Sernike, Kate. "The Harvard Guide to Happiness," http://collegenine.ucsc.edu/Harvard.shtml.

99 "Best Place to Get Bright Ideas!" *Woman's World*. July 4, 2006, 26.

100 Baal, Steve. "She Invented a Best-selling Game...at Age Six!" *Woman's World*, August 9, 2005, 5.

101 "Molds Designer Uses SolidWorks Software to Make 8-Year-Old's Dream a Reality." *SolidWorks Express*, February 2002, http://www.solidworks.com/swexpress/jan/200201_feature_04.html.

102 "Inventor of the Week Archive," http://web.mit.edu/invent/iow/stachowski.html.

103 *Small Business Opportunities*. "Online Moneymakers." May 2006, 22–58 and 130.

104 Neilson, Amy Rauch. "Start a Fashion Business." *Entrepreneur.com TeenStartUps.com*, June 2002, http://entrepreneur.com/tsu/article/0,5788,300461,00.html.

105 Weiner, Randi. "Another Generation Y." *The Journal News*, November 28, 2005, http://www.thejournalnews.com.

106 Larson, Sandy. "The Knight's Still Young." *Home Business*, September/October 2005, 70.

107 "Wristies, the Story of the Young Inventor." http://www.wristies.com/about.asp.

108 "Young Biz 100," http://www.youngbiz.com/yb_mag_news/2001youngbiz100html/arts&crafts.htm.

109 Wilson, Amy. "Small Business: Trading an Office for the Sidewalk." *Money*, September 2003, 37.

110 Marino, Jennifer. "From a Doodle to a Dream." *Time For Kids*, April 1, 2005, http://www.timeforkids.com/TFK/news/story/0,6260,1043173,00.html.

111 "Generation Now." Brainevent.com, http://www.brainevent.com/be/GenNow/20010629.

112 "Young Biz 100." http://www.youngbiz.com/yb_mag_news/2001youngbiz100/html/practical.htm.

113 Christian, Amy Fennell. "The Six Ps of Marketing." *Entrepreneur.com TeenStartUps.com*, June 2004, http://www.entrepreneur.com/tsu/article/0,5788,316165,00.html.

114 "Young Biz 100." http://www.youngbiz.com/yb_mag_news/mag_03_top100_76.htm.

115 Ibid.

116 Hagenbaugh, Barbara. "Full Activity, Study Schedules Have Many Teens Just Saying No to Jobs." *USA Today*, April 7, 2005, sec. 1B.

117 Howard, Allen. "Student's Business Honored." *The Enquirer*, March 15, 2002, http://www.enquirer.com/editions/2002/03/15/loc_howard_some_good.html.

118 Torres, Nichole L. "On a Shoestring." *Entrepreneur*. July, 2004, 106.

119 Hise, Phaedra. "Confessions of an Entrepreneur's Wife." *Inc. Magazine*, March 2006, 90–99.

120 "Teen Business Stories." JA Student Center. http://studentcenter.ja.org/aspx/PlanBusiness/stories.aspx.

121 Armour, Stephanie. "Teens Becoming High-Tech Entrepreneurs." *USA Today*. http://www.usatoday.com/careers/resource/colach5.htm.

122 Maxham, Larry. Telephone interview on July 21, 2006.

123 Pope, Alice. "Secure Your Domain Name." *2005 Children's Writer's & Illustrator's Market*, 61.

124 Neilson, Amy Rauch. "Be Smart...Be Legal!" *Y&E – The Magazine for Teen Entrepreneurs*, http://ye.entreworld.org/SF2002/besmart.cfm.

125 Williams, Geoff. "Reality Check." *Entrepreneur*, June 2005, 120–122.

126 Arora, Pankaj. "Secrets of Bootstrapping." *Entrepreneur.com, TeenStartUps.com*, September 2002, http://www.entrepreneur.com/tsu/article/0,5788,302878,00.html.

127 "How to Start a Business for (Almost) Nothing." *Inc. Magazine*, July 2006, 101–107.

128 Frazier, John. "Advertising is a Numbers Game." *Money 'N Profits*, March-April 2006, 38–39.

129 Kolodny, Lora. "The Art of the Press Release." *Inc. Magazine*, March 2005, 36.

130 Kendy, William F. "Letter Perfect." *Selling Power*, March 2006, 34–36.

[131] Mayeux, Patty. "Financial Fitness." *Y&E – The Magazine for Teen Entrepreneurs*, May 2001, http://ye.entreworld.org/5-2001/step6.cfm.

[132] Gschwandtner, Lisa. "Why Buzz Marketing is Buzzing Everywhere." *Selling Power*, July/August 2006, 66–69.

[133] Ibid.

[134] Hyatt, Josh. "Would a Home Office Pay Off? *Money*, October 2006, 59–63.

[135] "Kid Starts Successful Niche Furniture Business." *Business Fastlane Team.com*, March 8, 2006, http://www.businessfastlane.com.

[136] Koeppel, Peter. "Branding for Success." *Start Your Own Business*, Winter 2006, 94.

[137] Hise, Phaedra. "Confessions of an Entrepreneur's Wife." *Inc.*, March 2006, 90–99.

[138] Hispanic Chamber of Commerce Foundation. "Finding Opportunity." *Minding Your Own Business*.

[139] Semler, Angi. "Cranking Up Customer Service: Rules for Wowing Your Customers and Avoiding Pitfalls." *Aftermarket Business*, October 2004.

[140] *Entreprenuer*, August 2006, 82.

[141] Drew, Bonnie and Andrea Falad. "Teen Boss." *Y&E – The Magazine for Teen Entrepreneurs*, http://ye.entreworld.org/SF2002/teen_boss.cfm.

[142] Barbier, Karen. "It All Adds Up." *Y&E – The Magazine for Teen Entrepreneurs*, http://ye.entreworld.org/5-2001/steps8.cfm.

[143] Waitley, Denis. "Let Failure Spur You On." *AdvantEdge Magazine*, March/April 2006, 58.

[144] Torres, Nichole L. "Try Again." *Entrepreneur: Be Your Own Boss*, 101–108.

[145] Hatty, Michele. "3 Teens Who Mean Business." *USA Weekend Magazine*, May 2, 1999, http://www.usaweekend.com/99_issues/990502/990502teenentrepreneurs.html.

[146] Sauer, Patrick J. "Because She's A Lot Like Other Kids — and Then Again…" *Inc.*, April 2004, 133-134.

[147] Warren, Rachel. "Young Investors." *Knight Ridder News Service. San Diego Union-Tribune*, January 10, 1999, sec. I1.

[148] Powell, Eileen Alt. "Think Small." *Associated Press. San Diego Union–Tribune*, August 18, 2002, sec. H3.

[149] O'Shaughnessy, Lynn. "Retirement? Sock it Away Early and Be a Millionaire." *San Diego Union-Tribune*, May 15, 2005, sec. H1.

[150] Loeb, Marshall. "Tying Teen Chores to Allowance Loses Favor." *Marketwatch, San Diego Union-Tribune*, March 26, 2006, sec. H3.

[151] Anderson, Jessica. "What, Me Retire?" *Kiplinger's Success With Your Money*, Winter 2006, 33-34.

[152] "Manulife USA-Commissioned Survey Shows Workers Who Set Goals Feel More Confident About Retirement." November 17, 2003, http://www.manulife.com/corporate/corporate2.nsf/Public/Homepage.

[153] Lewis, Allyson. *The Million Dollar Car and $250,000 Pizza*. Chicago: Dearborn, 2000.

[154] Buggs, Shannon. "Most Millionaires Save, Not Earn, their Way to Riches." *Houston Chronicle*, February 15, 2004, http://search.chron.com/chronicle/search.do.

[155] Kiplinger, Knight. "The Invisible Rich." *Kiplinger's*, October 2006, 54.

[156] Waggoner, John. "Managing Your Money." *USA Today*, March 1, 2006, http://www.usatoday.com/money/perfi/general/2006-03-01-savings-cover-usat_x.htm.

[157] Crutsinger, Martin. "Personal Savings Rate Turns Negative." *Associated Press. San Diego Union-Tribune*, January 31, 2006, sec. A8.

[158] Colvin, Geoffrey. "Living the Golden Years Without the Gold." *Fortune*, July 11, 2005, 89.

[159] Newhouse New Service. Katherine Reynolds Lewis. "Big Purchases are Busting Budgets." *San Diego Union-Tribune*, July 23, 2005, sec. A1.

[160] Coghlan, J. Graydon. "What Employees Need to Know and What Their Employers Aren't Telling Them." *Opportunity World*, March-April 2006, 81–83.

276

[161] Heimer, Matthew and Kristen Bellstrom. "Retire Happy." *Smart Money*, April 2006, 65–80.

[162] Clifford, Jane. "Time Well Spent: Financial Advisers Help Parents—and Kids—Learn to Manage Money." *San Diego Union-Tribune*, March 18, 2006, sec. E1.

[163] Bach, David. *Start Late, Finish Rich: A No-fail Plan for Achieving Financial Freedom at Any Age*. New York: Broadway Books, 2005.

[164] Warren, Rachel. "Young Investors." *Knight Ridder News Service. San Diego Union-Tribune*. January 10, 1999, sec. I-1.

[165] Kay, Alexandra and Marcy Tolkoff. "Save $500,000 for Retirement." *Woman's World*, October 10, 2006, 41.

[166] Webber, Rebecca. "My Major Money Mistake." *Glamour*, November 2006, 150.

[167] Ransom, Diana. "Respecting a Windfall." *The Wall Street Journal Sunday, San Diego Union-Tribune*, November 12, 2006, H-6.

[168] "Owning Income Property." *Success*, September/October 2006, 68.

[169] Ramsey, Dave. "The Best Reasons for Saving." *Quick & Simple*. April 18, 2006, 31–33.

[170] Clifford, Jane. "Plans in the Tank." *San Diego Union-Tribune*. June 3, 2006, E10.

[171] Scott, Matthew S. "Moneywise: Better Choices, Better Mortgages." *Black Enterprise*, March 2006, 37.

[172] Anderson, Jessica. "Buying by the Numbers, or How Much Can You Borrow?" *Kiplinger's Success With Your Money*, Winter 2006, 38–39.

[173] Sources: Equifax; Experian; TransUnion, March 14, 2006.

[174] Powell, Eileen Alt. "Credit-scoring System Retooled." *Associated Press, San Diego Union-Tribune*, March 15, 2006, C1.

[175] Bruss, Robert J. "Auto-pilot Landlording Explained." *San Diego Union-Tribune*, October 8, 2006, I-14.

[176] Mui, Ylan Q., and Michael Rosenwald. "Young Homebuyers." *Washington Post*, October 27, 2005. http://washingtonpost.com.

[177] Parrish, Tory. "Achieve Your Dream of Homeownership: You Could Win $10,000." *Black Enterprise*, August 2006, 110-122.

[178] Worrell, David. "Wealthy and Wise." *Entrepreneur*, June 2005, 63.

[179] Spragins, Ellyn. "Letters to My Younger Self." *O*, April 2006, 181.

[180] "Ask the Expert." *Money*. May 2004, 14.

[181] Tyre, Peg, Julie Scelfo and Barbara Kantrowtz. "The Challenge: Just Say No." *Newsweek*, September 13, 2004.

[182] Gallo, Jon, Eileen Gallo and Kevin J. Gallo. *Silver Spoon Kids: How Successful Parents Raise Responsible Children*. New York: McGraw Hill, 2001.

[183] O'Shaughnessy, Lynn. "Financial Books Are Worth Look to Help You Pare Gift-Giving List." *San Diego Union-Tribune*, December 11, 2005, sec. H3.

[184] Public Eye. *San Diego Union-Tribune*. September 18, 2006, A2.

[185] Public Eye. *San Diego Union-Tribune*. April 24, 2006, A2.

[186] Keyes, Ralph. *Is There Life After High School?* New York: Little, Brown & Co., 1976.

[187] Teenage Research Unlimited, http://www.teenresearch.com/home.cfm.

[188] Linn, Susan. *Consumer Kids: The Hostile Takeover of Childhood*. New York: New Press, 2004.

[189] Smith, Will. *ThinkExist.com*, http://en.thinkexist.com/quotation/.

[190] "Millionaires' Secrets—Richard Branson." *MSN Money*, http://money.msn.co.uk/Bank_Plan/savings/Journals/MillionairesSecrets/branson/Default.asp?MSI....

[191] "My Golden Rule." *Business 2.0*, December 2005, 108-138.

[192] Schwab Pomerantz, Carrie. "Who's Going to Teach Your Kids About Money? *Charles Schwab On Investing*, Summer 2006, 12-13.

[193] Orman, Suze. *The Money Book for the Young, Fabulous & Broke*. New York: Riverhead Hardcover, 2005.

[194] Kinsman, Michael. "Debt-loaded Message: Bankruptcy Judge Warns Teens of Credit Card Dangers." *San Diego Union-Tribune*, May 19, 2005, sec. C1.

[195] Ibid.

[196] Ninfo II, Judge John C. "Debt Can Drain You." *The Next Step*, March/April 2004, 12–13.

[197] Kountze, Elizabeth. "Shrink Your Loans." *Money*, February 2006, 95–96.

[198] Ramsey, Dave. *The Total Money Makeover*. Nashville: Nelson Books, 2003.

[199] Gagnier, Monica. "Watch Out! Debit Card Rip-Off." *Good Housekeeping*, October 2006, 97.

[200] Bach, David. *Start Late, Finish Rich: A No-Fail Plan for Achieving Financial Freedom at Any Age*. New York: Broadway, 2005.

[201] Petre, Caitlin. "The Lessons I Didn't Learn in College." *Newsweek*, November 13, 2006, 20–21.

[202] Gandel, Stephen. "Everything You Know About Kids and Money." *Money*, August 2006, 112–116.

[203] Ibid.

[204] "Health IQ: Get Smart About Your Body with Dr. Roizen and Dr. Oz." *Reader's Digest*, August 2006, 61.

[205] Lundstrom, Meg. "7 Ways to Stop Smoking." *Woman's World*, July 18, 2006, 15.

[206] The Chemical Heritage Foundation. "A Pack a Day: The Costs." *Magic Bullets: Chemistry vs. Cancer*, 2001, http://www.chemheritage.org/EducationalServices/pharm/chemo/activity/pakday.htm.

[207] Schurenberg, Eric. "Investing that First Five Grand." *Money*, May 2006, 16.

[208] TeenAnalyst.com. "Custodial Account—Definition." http://www.teenanalyst.com/glossary/c/custodialaccount.html.

[209] Mannes, George. "How to Make Sure Your Kids Live Better Than You." *CNNMoney.com*, October 1, 2005, http://money.cnn.com/magazines/moneymag/money mag_archive/2005/10/01/8277963/index.htm.

[210] Fitzpatrick, Seamus. "The Perfect Private Account." *Kiplinger's Retirement Planning 2005*, 70.

[211] O'Shaughnessy, Lynn. "Kids Can Really Learn a Lot When Mom's a Columnist." *San Diego Union-Tribune*. June 4, 2006, H3.

[212] Lankford, Kimberly. "Build a Bright Future." *Kiplinger's*, April 2006, 82–83.

[213] Ebeling, Ashlea. "Money & Investing: College Aid Stratagems." *Forbes*, March 13, 2006, 65–70.

[214] Ibid.

[215] McNaughton, Deborah. "Money Know-How." *First*, April 24, 2006, 84.

[216] Tergesen, Anne. "Does Your 401(k) Cost Too Much?" *BusinessWeek*, June 7, 2004, 138–140.

[217] Hoppe, Jennifer. "Are You a Wimp About Money?" *For Me*, April 2006, 60.

[218] Wang, Penelope. "Your 401(k): The Only Five Rules That Matter." *Money*, August 2006, S1–S6.

[219] Tergesen, Anne. "Retirement Plans." *BusinessWeek*, October 25, 2004, 121.

[220] Pressman, Aaron. "401(k)s Spring a Leak." *BusinessWeek*, June 13, 2005, 78–80.

[221] Hunt, Mary. "Money Know-How." *First*, July 25, 2005, 84.

[222] McNaughton, Deborah. "Money Know-How." *First*, April 3, 2006, 84.

[223] Warren, Rachel. "Young Investors." *Knight Ridder News Service; San Diego Union-Tribune*, January 10, 1999, I1.

[224] Ibid.

[225] Keeler, Doris. "A Good Investment: Teaching Kids How to Invest in the Stock Market." *Children Today*, http://childrentoday.com/resources/articles/goodinvestment.htm.

[226] Nelson, Vita. *The Money Paper, Inc.* http://www.directinvesting.com/moneypaper/media.cfm.